LONDON BOROUGH OF ENFIELD

LIBRARY SERVICES

This item should be RETURNED on or before the latest date stamped. You may obtain a renewal by personal call, telephone or post. You should quote the date due for return, the bar code number and your personal library number. Overdue items will incur charges.

The Last Paragraph

The Last Paragraph

THE JOURNALISM
OF DAVID BLUNDY

Edited and
introduced by
ANTHONY HOLDEN

HEINEMANN · LONDON

William Heinemann Ltd
Michelin House, 81 Fulham Road, London SW 3 6 RB

LONDON   MELBOURNE   AUCKLAND

First published in 1990
Articles copyright © The Estate of David Blundy 1990
Introduction copyright © Anthony Holden Ltd 1990
Epilogue copyright © Harold Evans 1990

The Editor asserts his moral rights
in the Introduction

A CIP catalogue record for this book
is available from the British Library
ISBN 0 434 34435 4

Photoset by Rowland Phototypesetting Ltd
Bury St Edmunds, Suffolk
Printed and bound in Great Britain
by Clays Ltd, St Ives plc

The publishers are grateful to the
editors of the *Sunday Times*, the
Sunday Telegraph, the *Sunday
Correspondent*, the *Spectator*, the
Radio Times, the Burnley *Evening
Star* and the *Condé Nast Traveler*
for permission to reuse the articles in
this collection.
The editor would like to thank Anna
Blundy, Ruth Chatto, Samira Osman,
William Scammell, Ben Macintyre of
the *Sunday Correspondent*, Parin
Janmohammed of the *Sunday Times*
and F. J. ('Stan') Cummins-Stanley in
the *Sunday Times* archives for help in
gathering material; thanks also to
Lewis Chester for sharing his
research notes for his profile of David
Blundy in the *Sunday Correspondent*
magazine, and to Harold Evans for
permission to reproduce his address at
David Blundy's memorial service.

When you have read, you carry away with you
a memory of the man himself. It is as though
you had touched a loyal hand, looked into
brave eyes, and made a noble friend.

Robert Louis Stevenson

Contents

Introduction by Anthony Holden   1

Beginnings

A journey into the jaws of Hell   25
The power that saved crops and a marriage?   28
Just another week in Belfast   35
One man's week   43

USA 1979–1981

Picnic among the ruins   49
How Liz got her unlikely new role   53
Jordan's high life turns sour   59
Benny the Squint, Big Nose and pals   63
Reagan laughs off 'heart attack'
     but gives palpitations to friends   67
Cash from ash   70
Jimmy the Weasel 'sings' Sinatra   76
Lovely Rita's acts of congress give
     Washington the shudders   82
The city where children fear to play   85
The 'Valium of America' backs old formula
     to hook Britain   89
Darwin in the dock   93
Ah well, it's back to the HP sauce   99

Central America and the Caribbean

The Jonestown Tape   105
Gunfire takes over from reggae music
     as Jamaica's new sound   118
Victims of the massacre that the world ignored   123

The innocents caught in Lempa River massacre   131
Crusaders in the crossfire   137
Haiti's unholy war   146
The snake-charmer   150
Noriega's sex trap shackles United States   154

Middle East

Inside Sinai: settlers head for last stand   161
Iraq rallies after the desert fiasco   165
Battle of Manger Square   169
What Reagan's envoy ought to know
   about the Assad family   173
Prince in the firing line   179
'A shell blows out the taxi window'   188
'Israel has never faced an enemy like this'   192
Palestinians face more carnage in fight to the finish 199
The pursuit of happiness in a city of grief   203
Egypt on the brink   213

Africa

Zimbabwe bleeds again   225
How Operation Moses became a human tragedy   232
Charity unlimited – but it doesn't reach the victims 237
110 deg: Geldof fumes as the protocol rises   244
Cover-up   249
Playing the heavy father   256

USA 1986–1989

Where there's life there's soap   269
A town divided by the devil of dance   280
Yawning gap between Bible and Scorsese   286
Frightening world of North the hero   289
TV's unquenchable thirst for sleaze   293
Not much glasnost at Pioneer Point   297
Bush telegraph tells all   303

Epilogue by Harold Evans   307

INTRODUCTION
BY
ANTHONY HOLDEN

In the early hours of 16 November 1989 six Jesuit priests were murdered on the campus of the Central American University in San Salvador. Thirty uniformed men entered the complex at 3 a.m., dragged them from their beds, shot all six in the head and left them out in the yard to die, along with two civilian women who had attempted to come to their rescue. All distinguished academics, including the university's rector, Father Ignacio Ellacuria, the priests had been open supporters of the guerrillas of the Farabundo Marti National Liberation Front, the anti-government FMLN. They were assassinated, in the words of the Jesuit Provincial for Central America, Father Jose Maria Tojeira, 'with lavish brutality'.

As dawn broke over the carnage, those with the courage to say so attributed the killings to the notorious right-wing 'death squads', the paramilitary thugs at the bidding of El Salvador's army intelligence units. A world hardened to news from this god-forsaken land, after a decade of civil war which had already seen 70,000 violent deaths, reacted with revulsion. There had been no slaughter quite so outrageous since the shooting in 1980 of Archbishop Oscar Romero at the altar of his Metropolitan Cathedral, while he was giving communion. In Washington a White House statement condemned the murders as 'barbarous', even as the Pentagon announced that it would be increasing its shipments of weapons to the Salvadoran army at the request of the government.

3

The following morning saw a clutch of foreign journalists huddled on a crossroads in Mejicanos, a seedy *barrio* of northern San Salvador, observing crossfire between government troops and guerrillas. It was the sixth day of the biggest offensive mounted by the rebel forces since the war began; that week alone had seen 800 killed and 1600 injured. Thousands of civilians had fled the capital's north-eastern outskirts, braving the indiscriminate spray of gunfire from government helicopters as rebel forces seized the area. Now thousands more stayed trapped in their homes as government troops regained control.

The journalists held handkerchieves to their noses, so foul was the stench of the unburied dead. All Salvador veterans, the half-dozen reporters and photographers had been talking to some nervous young soldiers – 'trying,' as one of them put it, 'to break the ice' – when a single shot broke the silence, and one of them fell. 'One moment he was standing there, the next he was on the ground,' said *Newsweek*'s photographer, William Gentile. Another burst of crossfire followed, and they all hit the deck. 'Only then did I notice,' said Gentile, 'that he was bleeding. All I heard him say was, "Get me out of here."' With the aid of a white flag and a taxi, three of them managed to ferry him to the Rosales Hospital – where four hours later, without regaining consciousness, he died.

We will never know who killed David Blundy. The bullet which entered his right shoulder, passing through both lungs and severing his spine, was utterly random. It could have come from the US-backed, right-wing government forces or from the leftist guerrillas – from the baddies or the goodies, depending on your point of view, though its victim would most likely have pronounced a plague on both their houses. It might even, according to one of those present, have been that most capricious of bullets, a ricochet.

David's death, at the age of 44, was quite arbitrary. Any journalist drawn, like him, to scenes of conflict, to the chronicling of violent death, lives with the permanent knowledge that he could be next. The job, as he would have been the first to agree, does not involve some macho brand of courage – in Beirut as in Belfast, he confessed to being 'shit-scared' – so

4

much as a willingness to sublimate fear in pursuit of adventure or a good story, preferably both. In the field, the most experienced war reporters tend to be the canniest about the dangers involved, displaying far more caution than the *arriviste* out to make his name. But the experienced ones, those veterans hooked on conflict for reasons even they usually cannot explain, are by definition those who choose to put their lives at risk most *often*. David was killed, in effect, by the law of averages.

In his case, this compulsion to seek out the action was the flip-side of becoming a newspaper institution, a prized and highly paid reporter with the grand title of Chief American correspondent for his third successive Sunday newspaper. For most reporters embarking on middle age, and reluctant to accept promotion to an executive desk in London, Washington Correspondent is a by-line devoutly to be wished. David's feelings were more ambiguous. He loved America, but Washington bored him rigid.

Most Washington correspondents would have been content to file authoritative copy on Salvador's futile civil war from the safety of a State Department briefing room. They had, after all, won their spurs in fields of conflict here and there. Their cuttings books boasted yellowing datelines from danger zones braved in their twenties and thirties. Now they were growing older; they had children (if not always spouses) to make them think twice about returning to the front line. Besides, they were due at the British Embassy that evening for off-the-record cocktails with a passing Cabinet minister. These days, they would tell themselves, they were paid for their brains, not their guts.

Not David. He was chronically reluctant to write about anything he hadn't seen for himself. In his first few weeks as US Editor of a proud new Sunday paper he had displayed his habitual style and wit in the reporting of the Bush presidency, his versatility in tackling anything from a profile of a TV star to revelations about the Lockerbie bombers. Re-reading his weekly output now, as then, however, anyone who knew him can sniff the mounting frustration, the ache to get out on the road, the desperate need for a real story about real people.

When the FMLN rebels launched their big November offensive, he was on the next flight.

As he changed planes at Miami David telephoned London, whence his two-year-old daughter Charlotte sang him a song. Nothing too unusual about that. He was a compulsive caller, who would fend off boredom or loneliness by checking in with buddies and loved ones all over the world, heedless of time zones and the importance others might attach to sleep. That day, as he listened to Charlotte, he was on a high. Salvador had been the scene of some of his best work. The events now unfolding there offered the promise of copy not merely colourful and dramatic, but of international significance.

The priests' massacre happened within hours of his arrival; like all western correspondents worth their salt, he went straight to the scene the following morning. He also visited the British chargé d'affaires, Ian Murray, who urged him to be cautious; the streets of the capital were unusually dangerous, even by Salvador's anarchic standards, as government forces struggled to counter the rebel advance. David promised that he would 'play it safe'. After curfew that evening, his last alive, he apparently told colleagues in the hotel bar that he thought he might be 'getting a little too old for this business'. But none of them, any more than his countless other friends then having similar conversations in similar bars all over the world, could have ever imagined him doing anything else – let alone growing old.

At 5 a.m. the following morning, 11 a.m. London time, David was already up and at work when he received a call from his foreign editor at the *Sunday Correspondent*, Jon Connell. Connell's priority was getting Blundy's copy as soon as possible, but David protested that he was still not quite satisfied. The balance of power in the northern suburbs was changing by the hour. He would file very soon, but first he wanted to go back out and 'see what's happening'. As Connell later put it: 'Most other journalists would have been more than happy with the material he had already accumulated. But David needed to go out for one last look.'

One last look for one last paragraph cost David Blundy his life. It was also very much the measure of his life. David's perennially dishevelled appearance, his unpredictability, his apparently chaotic working methods – he would often need to borrow pencil and paper from interviewees – all concealed one of the most conscientious and dedicated reporters of his time. He of all journalists was the one who would tease and worry his copy through his typewriter, pouring an excess of agony into the eternal problem – never as simple as it might seem – of getting the right words in the right order.

First, however, there was the unenviable business of accumulating those words, at which he was unparalleled. Other reporters might accept second-hand accounts of a massacre, even rest content with watching events unfold on television; others might follow the pack around town, pooling information and sharing interviews. Some even believed they had a right to stop work every so often for the purposes of sleep, food or drink. While David was far from indifferent to all three, especially the latter, he would let nothing get in the way of the chase.

Throughout his adult life, including his storm-tossed career as an *homme fatal*, the business of reporting came first. If Blundy's rangy figure was not in the hotel bar as the pack foregathered in the evenings, it was a troubling sign to rivals that he was out following some scent. If he had disappeared to 'compose', as he would put it, things must be *really* desperate. Like most journalists, David was physically incapable of sitting down to write until the very last minute; in his case, this was also because he was reluctant to do so until satisfied that he had established every viewpoint on the matter-in-hand, weighed them all up, and reached the clearest and fairest way of presenting them. The last paragraph, in other words, had to come first.

He was my best friend for ten teeming years, through the 1970s and beyond, from Thomson traineeships in Hemel Hempstead via a shared desk at the *Sunday Times* to joint by-lines from Ulster and rival ones from the United States. Whether or not I was *his* is rather less certain. His impersonation of me, I am told, was as hilarious as any in his extensive repertoire. I became a better journalist, a better person – more

7

honest, more sceptical – for having known him; yet I cannot think of a single characteristic, let alone a quality, he derived from me or from anyone else. David's trademark was a straightforward, at times ruthless candour. He was never more nor less than himself; what you saw was what you got. A tortured introvert masquerading as an extrovert, his rank insecurity would have him pouring out his innermost feelings to strangers on planes, in bars, in waiting rooms throughout the world. He had a thousand friends, and he had none. Anyone who met him came away thinking they had made a friend for life. And so they had; but when they looked again, he had moved restlessly on.

We were both members of a *Sunday Times* generation which has shown a remarkable, almost tribal sense of kinship since the post-Rupert Murdoch diaspora. For a decade it met three or four times a year for leaving parties; now it will continue to do so for funerals and memorial services. For most of its members, those 'Harold Evans years' will always remain their spiritual home, making subsequent lives and friendships seem curiously out of synch.

Hence, in David's case, the disparity of detail in the newspaper tributes, otherwise united in their affection and admiration. Having shared three vacations with him, for instance, one in Crete and two in Martha's Vineyard, I found myself reading time and again that he had never taken one. Having always called him Dave, I read that everyone called him simply Blundy, and that anyone who referred to him by his Christian name hadn't really known him at all.

'Like approximately a million other people,' proclaimed Simon Hoggart in the *Observer*, 'I was a friend of David Blundy.' In the *Sunday Correspondent*, meanwhile, Jon Connell mused: 'His friendship was rationed. No one had an exclusive hold on it.' Both, in their different ways, were right. It was an unspoken tribute to David's qualities that amid the drama of his death comparative strangers rushed to claim his friendship, while many of his older chums hung back, measuring the degree to which they had been spectators at a movable feast. David's best friend, if truth be told, was probably his daughter Anna, a 19-year-old Oxford undergraduate at the time of his death. Her father, as she told me in the most moving of letters, was certainly hers.

A reluctantly absentee parent, David took a characteristically unorthodox approach to fatherhood. For a man who never shared a home with his offspring, and lived most of his adult life in hotels, he was remarkably assiduous in his attentions to Anna – as he would certainly have continued to be to Charlotte, the daughter borne him in 1987 by Samira Osman, with whom he had lived for five years in London and Washington. They were the still point of his turning world. An eternally rootless figure, wracked by doubt, he thrived on the peripatetic, almost random lifestyle which went with his job. The impermanence of journalism took his mind off the greater imponderables which were forever denying him peace. Week by week some passing professional obsession would consume him, then leave him · collapsed in a bar, or edgily TV-channel-hopping, too much alone with his own thoughts.

In the company he constantly sought these anxieties were masked by a scorching wit, as unsparing of himself as anyone else to hand, which made any random meeting, let alone a sustained companionship, so memorable. David was more than a mere rogue or raconteur; his impatience with pomposity, his laser-eye for pretension would always leave its victims laughing, if at times uneasily. As we dined together at the Europa Hotel, Belfast, one evening in the mid-1970s, David happened to mention that it was his birthday. When I got our friend the pianist to ask if he had a request, he replied, 'Yeah. How about two minutes of silence?'

If it was all a way of hiding himself, of pricking his own pretensions before anyone else did, it worked. David's way of showing he cared about literature was to mock any writers with ideas above their station; Charles Glass, for instance, was made to rue the day he quoted Palestinian poetry in a *Spectator* essay on the Middle East. David would let himself be seen carrying only airport paperbacks and Pink Floyd tapes; yet a heavyweight novel and some Bach cello suites were among the travelling companions found in his hotel room after his death. Only a privileged few were allowed to see past the *furioso* to the *penseroso* Blundy.

9

So wide did David spread his largesse, and so colourful were the memories he left behind, that the store of Blundy anecdote matured into myth. It was no surprise to Lewis Chester, who meticulously researched his life for a tribute in the *Sunday Correspondent* magazine, to find that most of the stories – unusually, in David's profession – stood up to scrutiny. The gung-ho Blundy, for instance, as evidenced by David May, with whom he was 'missing, presumed dead' for four days in southern Lebanon in 1978. 'I remember waking up in the middle of the night and the Israelis were blitzing over our heads. Blundy had this huge flashlight on. We were right at the top of the block so it could be seen for miles around. I said, "Christ, Blundy, what are we doing, trying to get ourselves killed?" He said, "Oh, sorry, Dave, but I just can't find my bloody matches."' Or the waggish Blundy, bored by a briefing from an Israeli general in the company of the war photographer Don McCullin: 'He produced a clockwork toy which leapt uncontrollably all over the maps on the briefing table. Then, when the general gave him a dark look, he couldn't shut the damn thing off.'

One of the few reporters actually liked by photographers, David came to haunt McCullin, who couldn't figure him out. 'He was a strange person who'd come up to you sideways and look at you like some old crow, as if he wasn't sure whether or not you might be a delicacy to nibble at.'

Many of the best Blundy stories concerned expenses, a rich seam of journalistic anecdote, rarely better than the tale that he was assigned to try living on nothing for a week amid London's homeless, then turned in bills totalling £120. Another favourite concerned an executive attempt to turn him into a deskbound sub-editor, writing headlines, which had him shouting across the newsroom: 'What's a shorter word for Wednesday?' On closer inspection, however, both these stories turned out to be about Denis Herbstein, another *Sunday Times* newsroom contemporary. In death as in life, Blundy had even managed to corner other people's anecdotes.

But it was a mistake made only by a lofty few to consider this unkempt, gangling figure some sort of shambling court jester, fool enough in his middle age to think combat zones a measure of journalistic virility. David's irresistible sense of satire, which would quickly overmaster any dread temptation towards *gravitas*, in fact hid a profoundly thoughtful and concerned reporter. To his *Sunday Telegraph* colleague, Alexander Chancellor, he embodied 'that romantic idea of journalism which places friendship and loyalty among journalists higher than any loyalty to a particular employer; and insists that fun is such an essential ingredient that, without it, good journalism cannot exist.' To Chancellor, in fact, Blundy's 'most irritating' quality was to be 'intensely conscientious while pretending that he wasn't.'

Against the odds, perhaps, David's mature work was enhanced by these conflicting elements in his gipsy soul. His main priority, once the facts had been gathered and the words drafted in roughly the right order, was to make sure that his story was *interesting* – preferably, if appropriate, entertaining. The cardinal sin, to be avoided at all costs, was being boring. This is something of which no one could ever have accused the man, throughout his life, in print or in person. He was the most vivid of journalists, and the most glittering of companions, who left a charmed trail of admirers in his wake, both male and female, all over the world. The death of a man so full of life was, quite literally, impossible to comprehend. As the news spread, there was a powerful consensus that there must have been some mistake; that agency reports could not be trusted; that old Dave would somehow make it through. Like the man himself, we refused to believe it until we had seen it for ourselves.

Born on 21 March 1945, David Michael Blundy grew up in south London, at the Elephant and Castle. Subsequent myth had it that his father was an East End rag-and-bone man. Fred Blundy's antiques and 'quality furniture' business in fact covered some two acres of Newington Butts. The family lived above the shop, and many an ornate *objet* would find a temporary home in the living room – a temporariness which, as his friend Ian Jack observed, 'found many an echo in David's adult life'.

The youngest of three children by thirteen years, the boy was a favourite among staff and family alike. Apprehensive, perhaps, about being older parents to David than to his siblings, Brian and Pauline, Fred and Norah Blundy stretched themselves and their resources to see that their youngest got a good start. He was, for instance, the only one of the three children to be privately educated – at City of London, one of Britain's most academically ambitious public schools. By the time he was fifteen David's name was high both in the A stream and on the headmaster's blacklist for lateness. He was renowned for cruising West End pubs and coffee bars when he should have been doing his homework. It all seemed to have caught up with him one morning when he told the English master that he had left his essay at home.

'That's all right, Blundy,' came the canny reply. 'Your home's not far from here. Nip back and get it!'

The fastest essay ever written was then produced behind a locker in the changing-room, and handed in barely an hour later. 'Was it on that morning,' wondered Reg Bolton, one of his classmates, 'that a journalist was born?'

Natural ability rather than application won David a place at Bristol University, where within a month he had abandoned law and switched to psychology. On discovering that wisdom was based, as he put it, 'on the torture of rats', he then dropped out – but was allowed to return the following year to read English, alongside his girlfriend, Ruth Mansley. 'There was a James Dean side to his lean-and-hungry good looks, and a Jacques Tati side,' says a friend from the time, the poet William Scammell. 'Lecturers never knew whether they were dealing with a Tom Lehrer or a Tom Jones.' Marvell's poem 'To His Coy Mistress' (the reading of which caused some bafflement at David's memorial service) was the subject of his dissertation as he scraped a decent degree, despite moonlighting as editor of the student magazine.

Offered a graduate traineeship by the Thomson organisation, then owners of *The Times* and the *Sunday Times*, David was assigned to one of its more distant outposts, the *Evening Star* in Burnley – where, within weeks, he was again miserable. 'It's hard to be funny about it at the moment,' he wrote to Ruth, still at Bristol. 'I've had three days of intensive clod-hopping, bog-trotting, rube, hick, chaw-bacon (*Roget's*

Thesaurus) sentiments crammed down my throat in Mayors' parlours, committee rooms and the *Burnley Star* office ... I have had my fill of the submerged tenth, the swinish multitude, the hewers of wood and drawers of water, the great unwashed.' Burnley didn't think much of Blundy, either. 'This is sheer, unadulterated trash,' read one memo from the news editor. 'I sincerely hope that you will never, I repeat never, produce anything like it again.'

Assigned to cover a football match, he evinced a lifelong boredom with sport by writing instead about the sunset over the Lancashire moors, and took to his bed for a week with a complaint rarely heard in Burnley – 'a touch of sunstroke'. Keith Fort, then chief reporter on the Burnley paper, now editor of the Lancashire *Evening Telegraph*, unsurprisingly uses the word 'faltering' to describe David's start in journalism. 'Then one day I asked him to see if he could find a story in three coachloads of women who were coming down from Wigan to contest a Bingo final. It was then that we realised that Blundy was something special. His piece really shone.'

Amazingly, the piece survives in the erratic Blundy archives – complete with exclusive interview with Kenny Ball – and I was tempted to use it to start this collection. Then came the voice in my ear. 'To-o-ny ... *Tony* ... what are you trying to do to me? Thanks a *lot*, Tone.' The main problem in compiling this memorial volume to David Blundy has been constant interference from the man himself, steering me this way and that, reminding me that he liked to be thought *a serious person*. 'So do you, Tone, come on now. Would I do something like that to you?'

Of course he would. But Blundy, as usual, had his way, and TOP STARS AND A FLUTTER AT THE 'HOMELY' CABARET CLUB must remain a fond private memory for his family. David's few months at Burnley did, however, see the tercentenary of the birth of Jonathan Swift, marked by the recent English graduate with the lively satire which *does* begin this book; already at work in it are the eye and ear which were to particularise both the man and his writing.

Desperately oppressed by the north, and impatient to make it to Fleet Street, David negotiated a transfer to Thomson's

Evening Post, in Hemel Hempstead, where Ruth soon came to join him. In 1970, when he was 25, she gave birth to their daughter Anna. Though the couple had already agreed to part, they got married at Finsbury Town Hall and enjoyed a boat ride together to Greenwich before going their separate ways. From such honest if unlikely starts do the strongest relationships grow; his ex-wife and daughter, in their different ways, would remain the mainstay of David's life long after Ruth had remarried. (Her second husband, Ricky Chatto, became a firm friend.)

While the *Evening Post* insisted on much the same diet as Burnley – car crashes, court cases and council meetings – its enlightened features editor did give David more scope to stretch his wings. The Blundy archives even include a fashion piece, suggesting that skirts might rise a little higher this year. He wrote a soap opera under a (female) pseudonym, and pronounced at length on subjects ranging from the church via marriage to witchcraft (p. 28). I chose the latter again because of the dry, sardonic voice I can hear in such details as: 'They dance in the nude at Mrs Bone's because, she says, it helps break down class distinctions ... Nudity is a fairly recent innovation from the Continent.'

No journalist should be held accountable for his apprenticeship years – 'Come off it, Tone, leave it *aht*' – but David was already showing the eye and ear for detail which would distinguish all his subsequent reporting, whether wide-eyed in the United States or shit-scared in a war zone. No politician or soldier, terrorist or hoodlum would speak beneath his byline without our knowing precisely what they looked like, especially what they were wearing – David being a devout subscriber to Polonius's theory that 'the apparel oft proclaims the man'. When he and I reported the downfall of the Ulster Assembly together in 1976 from a Belfast even scarier than usual, he insisted on describing the 'bulges' beneath the armpits of several of our interviewees. In the next day's *Sunday Times,* they appeared as 'bugles'.

It was Michael Bateman who had brought Blundy to London from Hemel Hempstead, as his assistant on the *Sunday Times*'s diary column, 'Atticus', then a major spread filling the back page of the paper's front section. David quickly displayed a natural diarist's eye for the absurd, and a talent to disarm the wariest of interviewees. From the stepmother of the then Prime Minister, Edward Heath, he elicited the remarkable information that 'Ted is very considerate, and never goes out without telling me where he's going. He never forgets birthdays and rings Daddy once a week. No matter how tired he is, he comes in and says goodnight. He does get moody sometimes. One night he came home in a mood and without a word he tucked Maggie May, one of our beagles, under his arm and went straight up to bed.'

Beyond an instinct for an irresistible quote, David always had the useful journalist's knack of making something out of nothing. Sent to do a simple sketch of William Whitelaw's Cumbria constituency, he was arrested by Special Branch heavies for snooping too close to the then Northern Ireland Secretary's home. Bateman thus became the first in a long line of newspaper executives obliged to talk Blundy out of trouble – which proceeded, all his life, to follow him around.

Though he had quickly made a name as the paper's sloppiest dresser – to whom jeans, sneakers and leather jacket were some kind of uniform – David was always in fact quite vain about his appearance, going to some lengths to achieve the crumpled look in clothes which had cost him plenty. But when the headmaster of Eton rang up, to complain that he found it impossible to believe that the dishevelled person in his office could possibly be a representative of the *Sunday Times*, even the easygoing Bateman urged Blundy to take remedial action. An expedition to Chelsea resulted in the purchase of an exceptionally lurid green suit, which led to a famous exchange in the lift with the editor, Harold Evans:

'David, I thought I told you to get a suit?'

'I did, Harry.'

'Well, why don't you wear it then?'

'I *am* wearing it, Harry.'

Evans was at the time under some pressure from Lord Thomson to smarten up his staff, with special reference to the hair-length of reporters who might be sent out to see Cabinet ministers. In David's case, he confesses, it reached the point where he had to decide between firing him and telling him to get his hair cut. 'I risked it – and David turned out to be an exceptional reporter, full of industry and wonder.'

Evans gave him a trial in the newsroom. 'There could hardly have been a greater contrast between Blundy's less than banker-crisp appearance and the lucidity and accuracy of his reporting.' Reluctant to be typecast as a lightweight, a jumped-up diary reporter, David fought his way onto the Ulster rota and began to show the combination of nerve and persistence which became his hallmark. He would laugh more than anyone when telling of his first secret meeting with Provisional IRA men in the supposed no-go area of the Falls Road social club; his hands shook so much as he bought the first round that he drenched the terrorists in beer. His personal dress code made no concessions, either, for the officers' mess in Armagh, where troops assumed this tall, shambolic figure to be some sort of undercover agent (who blithely signed mess chits in the names of IRA leaders). 'He had this little-boy-lost approach,' remembers Colin Wallace, then an Army information officer at Lisburn. 'As a result, people would tell him much more than they would otherwise have done. It was a brilliantly effective technique.' Like the Wallace who later came to haunt governments, David began to produce scoops which, though denied at the time, have been endorsed by subsequent history – notably a detailed account of the activities of British military *agents provocateurs*.

Only one of his articles from Ulster, a magazine survey of a 'typical' week's carnage, finds a place in this book. The rest, however potent at the time, is a melancholy catalogue of death and destruction no longer likely to inform, let alone entertain, the reader. Besides, much of David's work there was shared with others. The biggest stories brought out the team fever then fashionable on the *Sunday Times* – as was true throughout his subsequent career – and I have felt obliged to reject all joint or multiple by-lines. David was in on some of the biggest stories of his day, from wars to famines, political scandals to assassinations, and was a pivotal member of any reporting team. Given the impossible task, however, of reducing more than two million words to less than 90,000, my selection has been based on the belief that this book is a memorial to an individualist, whose work inevitably grew better as he grew older.

During 1976 David escaped briefly to an exchange job on the *Boston Globe* (p. 43), where a profound fascination with cars saw him buy an absurdly long, if battered Oldsmobile. His letters to Ruth and Anna were peppered with drawings of it, stretching over the page; the discrepancy between the clocks in the front and the back he explained by bragging, 'This car is so big that the back seat is in a different time zone.' When he returned to Ulster (delighted that I had been landed, in his absence, with the fiendish slide-rule economics of proportional representation), its bloodthirsty merry-go-round had become too familiar. That taste of the new world had whetted his appetite for broader horizons.

After five newsroom years, through which we shared the bum assignments and the untidiest desk, David and I simultaneously moved on to the United States – he as New York correspondent of the *Sunday Times*, I as Washington correspondent of the *Observer*. In September 1979 we met beside the pool of the Washington Hilton for what turned out to be one of the most memorable, all-day lunches of both our lives. We couldn't believe it. A few years ago we had both been trainees at Hemel Hempstead; now we had carved up America between us, for the two leading newspapers of the day. When, as the late James Cameron used to put it, would we be found out?

In that department, at least, David soon had an involuntary breathing-space. Thanks to its management's dispute with the print unions, the *Sunday Times* ceased publication indefinitely almost as soon as he arrived. There was just time, after a brief flirtation with New York, to make his first visit to Central America. The rest, for what turned out to be a year, was a reluctant silence; but on he worked, regardless. Together we journeyed to a political picnic in New Hampshire, launching the 1979–80 presidential campaign of Governor Jerry Brown of California. So furious was David that I had a paper in which to report the bizarre goings-on, and he didn't, that he made one of his rare excursions into freelancery and filed a piece to the *Spectator* (p. 49).

17

It was also during the *Sunday Times* closure that he obtained the tête-à-tête with Elizabeth Taylor on page 53, used in an unpublished, 'ghost' edition of the magazine. La Taylor, at the time, was refusing interviews about the joys of being a Washington wife, so David cunningly sought one with her husband, Senator John Warner, whose longterm presidential ambitions were in need of some European publicity. So remorselessly did he ply the Senator with questions about strategic arms negotiations – not, at the time, one of David's specialist subjects – that he was finally invited, as he had hoped, to continue the interview back home. Once introduced to Mrs Warner, the Blundy charm ensured that she rode to her husband's Virginia barbecue in David's uniquely squalid hire car. When a million-dollar earring came off on a sharp bend, and its owner scrabbled around beneath the passenger seat to retrieve it, she emerged triumphantly clutching an abandoned item of female underwear.

Another Blundy interview with Taylor subsequently appeared in the magazine, once publication had resumed, but it was a pale shadow of this typically quirky piece of reporting. To David, a lifelong student of the bizarre, America was a journalistic adventure playground in which his sense of the absurd could overdose. Although he bounced around the campaign trail with as much gusto as anyone else, politics fundamentally bored him; his *joie de vivre* is much more on display amid the rogue's gallery of hoods, molls, aides and TV exotics who people this collection. Of the pieces I have culled from his first stint there, only one is directly political. It earned its place (p. 67) because the aside he teased out of Lyn Nofziger, Reagan's press spokesman – to the effect that President Carter had 'the clap' – itself became a campaign issue for a few days. Only Blundy, one suspects, could have wrung such a response from an official who should have known better; only Blundy, perhaps, would have printed it, unafraid of the consequences; and few more richly deserved the delight of being responsible for the latest 'Reagan gaffe' to bounce round the world and back.

Readers who study the datelines will note that David was himself, meanwhile, bouncing around Central America and the Caribbean, larding his largely lightweight output from the US with the heavier-duty, front-line reporting he came to prefer. It was again during the *Sunday Times* closure that he single-mindedly chased the remarkable story of the mass suicide at 'Jonestown', Guyana, and came up with a world scoop in the shape of the tape-recordings made as it happened. For reasons of space, only his vivid preface is reprinted here (p. 105), minus the transcripts of the tapes; even he, however, would admit that a year off, plus the challenge of his first major magazine piece, have his prose style trying a little too hard. The consciously wrought English is as restless and hustling as its author. For a man with so remorselessly philistine an exterior, it is endearing to note the Shakespearean reference in the first paragraph, and the use of such un-Blundyish words as 'mulcting', 'crepuscular', even 'abraided' (which my OED traces to Spenser).

Over the next three years he reported from a dozen Central American countries, and became the only journalist in living memory to *choose* to spend his vacations, even Christmas, in Haiti. His particular fascination with El Salvador led to perhaps the most distinguished article of his career, when he uncovered a cynical massacre on the Honduras–Guatemala border (p. 123). David would enjoy a second lease of life in these parts of the world, returning to the US for other newspapers; but he was meanwhile offered a very different challenge which was to inspire his most outstanding work.

At the end of 1981 the *Sunday Times* transferred him from the US to the Middle East, with the title of Chief Foreign Correspondent. To a man whose own lifestyle had perfected a brand of designer chaos, the perpetual shambles that was Beirut and surrounding areas immediately seemed some sort of spiritual home-from-home. Few journalists of his generation captured that complex, fast-changing scene so vividly, braving life and limb for what journalists call 'colour' material to spice the dull political rhetoric. Most at home in the least homely of places – a desert outpost, a besieged hotel, a hijacked airliner, a terrorist hideout – David derived from the Middle East the adrenalin to forget his own woes and chronicle those of others. He would say, of course, that he hated the place, that he was again suffering mightily for his art. But he knew there were few better locations on earth for his kind of journalism. 'I'm never going back to that shit-hole again,' he would declare each time he reported back to base in London, where a day or two would see him find a thousand reasons for an urgent return.

His role as Chief Foreign Correspondent also took him for the first time to Africa, where he began by reporting events in Zimbabwe powerfully enough (p. 225) to have his passport and notebook seized by the authorities. Here too, in 1985–86, he found himself becoming obsessed with an unlikely pair of contemporary figures, Bob Geldof and Colonel Gadaffi, who became the subjects of the two books he co-authored. Desperate though he was for the respectability of hard covers, David's attention span was too short to last the distance, and his personality is hard to find in either *With Geldof in Africa* (with Paul Vallely, 1985) or *Qadaffi and the Libyan Revolution* (with Andrew Lycett, 1987). His journalism, by contrast, was at its multifaceted best with a character like Geldof, who gave him a chance to combine ironic observation (p. 244) with loftier displays of *gravitas* (p. 249). Geldof himself would later testify: 'Blundy was a great guy. He rambled around life just having a look and he really enjoyed it . . . When we were in Africa, the nearer we got to the heavy stuff the more he enjoyed it. The trouble with Blundy was that he was too bloody tall. I never saw him duck once.'

Like the handful of his remaining colleagues from the Evans era, David did not long survive the *Sunday Times*'s midnight flit from the Grays Inn Road to Wapping. After sixteen years on the paper, he at last managed the leap of existentialist faith involved in a star transfer to the *Sunday Telegraph*, who sent him straight back to Washington. Back on the North and Central American beat, but deprived of old alliances down the phone to London, all his professional insecurities resurfaced. He worked as hard as ever, naming the terrorist organisations behind the Lockerbie bombing amid mandarin reporting of the Reagan White House; but it was barely eighteen months before he jumped at the chance to do the same job for a new newspaper, the *Sunday Correspondent*. Peopled by many of the *Sunday Times* diaspora, it offered him a greater chance of the *esprit de corps* so necessary to his morale, but so hard to maintain across thousands of miles. It was on behalf of the *Sunday Correspondent*, after only a few weeks of routine Washington 'thumb-sucking', that he headed back down to El Salvador on 15 November 1989.

As we watched him lowered into the ground a week later, within quipping distance of Karl Marx, there was a strong compulsion to hang around for a chat after the crowd had moved on.

David was the fourth journalist that year to have been killed in El Salvador, and the third from his vintage *Sunday Times* era to have given his life for his work: in 1973 Nicholas Tomalin was killed by a random heat-seeking missile on the Golan front of the Yom Kippur War, in 1977 David Holden was murdered in mysterious circumstances in Egypt. Journalism has a built-in advantage over other professions in giving its dead stylish farewells; but the lavish space accorded David's departure was prompted by more than merely its violent and premature nature – by more, even, than the futility of dying amid a distant punch-up about which no one in Britain much cared.

He would have been embarrassed – and mightily chuffed – by the wave of emotional tributes which washed through a long weekend of upmarket British newspapers. His editor at the *Sunday Telegraph*, Peregrine Worsthorne, described him as 'a Graham Greene type of journalist, more at home in wild and dangerous places than in the corridors of power.' Wrote his friend and long-time foreign editor at the *Sunday Times*, Cal McCrystal: 'No grave will inter his reputation as one of Britain's best narrators of war and other social and political ineptitudes. No editor who knew him will bury his or her grief. No journalist will dispose of his memory.'

In the same breath, sensing Blundy reading over his shoulder, McCrystal added: 'Were he to have known that these sentences would be written about him, he would have guffawed over his double Martini and flicked the olive at the hagiographer.' The journalists with David when he was killed could not have known – nor would he himself have believed – that over the next several days he would be hailed not just as one of the

21

most admired journalists of his generation, but as one of the most loved. The news of Blundy's death burnt up telephone lines across the world, so many and so fond were the friends he had made in its furthest-flung corners; the hardest of newshounds were surprised to find themselves weeping rare tears, then feeling a compulsive need to confess to them in print.

Faced with the same wretched assignment, David himself would have been more circumspect. He largely eschewed the journalistic first-person, preferring to let his minutely observed dramatis personae speak for themselves. Though an elegant writer, the directness of whose style concealed considerable craft, he disapproved of 'fine writing' per se, regarding long words as no substitute for facts and most adjectives as an admission of failure. Capable of rational self-analysis only *in extremis*, he would nevertheless have arrived at the stunned conclusion that a newspaper paragraph was not worth dying for. That he himself had done so lent an unreachable depth to the grief which overcame his friends.

To anyone who had known this outwardly shambling, chaotic, unkempt figure, his rangy physique as tall as many of his midnight stories, there could have been few prospects more incongruous than a final resting-place among the grandees of Highgate cemetery and a memorial service amid the solemn elegance of St Martin-in-the-Fields – followed by a party at, of all places, the Reform Club, to which he himelf would most likely have been denied admission.

Dave would have been more at home in the Zanzibar, a New York-style watering-hole in London's Covent Garden which he frequented long after it had ceased to be 70s-chic. He would have fidgeted his way through the heartfelt encomia of his sometime superiors, stylishly satirising the entire proceedings within minutes of making a relieved exit.

It was a fittingly gothic tribute to him that so many people stood around, as David himself would certainly have done, wondering if this many people would be turning out for *their* memorial service.

'No,' said one such, 'you've got to have died young and tragically.'

'No,' said another, 'you've got to have been David Blundy.'

BEGINNINGS

A journey into the jaws of Hell

*Jonathan Swift, England's most
scathing satirist, was born in Dublin
on November 30, 1667. David Blundy
celebrates the tercentenary of his birth
with a satire he calls Book 13 of*
Gulliver's Travels

Whereupon we travelled to the northern regions of this land,
walking with difficulty, for our clothes were heavy with in-
cessant rains and the sky became overcast with a corpse-like
hue until the sun could not pierce the thick damp mist that
encompassed us about.

Coming to the topmost point of a high ridge, we cast our eyes
down into a valley almost hidden by a cloud of great blackness,
yet through a rift therein we could descry tall mast-like objects
pouring forth an abundance of black and acrid smoke as if from
the mouth of Hell itself, and many low dwellings made a
sluggish trail along the valley.

One of my companions did here promptly die of a convulsive
fit most unpleasant to behold, brought on by the devilish sight
and pungent air of this place.

Wishing most heartily to descend into this sooty region, but
my companions holding back with shrieks of woe, I flogged
them heartily until they would descend with me.

Waylaying a short, brutish fellow of surly aspect I asked of him the name of this place, and what manner of friends existed therein.

'Yelnrub,' he muttered, 'fairest city of the north.' We passed quickly on, for, upon the whole, I never beheld in all my travels so disagreeable a person or one against which I naturally conceived so strong an antipathy.

Thus did we arrive, and, after a lengthy sojourn in the town, I discovered certain facts which might interest a reader who has stomach for the strange and obnoxious aspects of humanity.

First, it took long and painful studies before I could master their tongue, the natives being blunt of manner, low of speech and stubbornly taciturn.

The most I could at first decipher was a repetitive enunciation of such syllables as 'Ay noah' and 'Ay reet' which made but little sense, and there was much talk of brass, though very little of this metal to be seen, the town being predominantly fabricated of stone and cast iron.

The natives work at strangely curious occupations, many being treadle loom wafters, or other such names which I was not skilful enough to apprehend, who labour in large and odious edifices called mills, which for smell and intensity of noise I would not enter, and which produce the dun coloured smoke so beloved of the natives.

Indeed, such is their liking for blackness that many of them choose to spend their lives under the ground, emerging only at night, and burrowing like moles for black, dirty objects which they subsequently burn to produce more quantities of their beloved smoke.

Both mills and burrows are to be closed by the enlightened government of the land, which pleased me greatly, but caused the natives no little consternation, and I am led to believe they are wholly out of their senses.

I shall touch but lightly, out of respect for the sensibility of my reader, on the eating habits of this people.

The boiled, flabby intestine of the beast of the field greatly delights them, and they are no less pleased with the congealed blood of such beasts liberally spiced with fat – which they consume with much smacking of the lips.

26

Whilst not making smoke or living under the ground, the natives indulge in pursuits which caused me the greatest astonishment.

The men stand in their hordes to watch a round object moved with the feet on a large expanse of ground – a custom which caused them such jolliment that they frequently hit and kick each other, which I take to be a token of endearment among the natives.

The women of the town far excel their men in mental ability, having a great liking for abstract mathematics. They sit for many hours intent upon a person who reads out vast lists of numerals, and the women make abstruse symbolic marking on the paper before them.

On the day of my departure, the highest personage of the town, or arch fiend as my companions named him, did bestow on me the greatest honour, granting me the pleasure of a journey in the ceremonial barge along a heavily stagnant, murky and odorous canal, from which I saw many vistas of mast-like objects and much smoke.

By this time my companions – one of them had been kicked and beaten almost to death by the natives, as a sign of their friendship – were whimpering with terror, believing in their wild imaginings that we had reached the very jaws of Hell itself; but of course I knew this to be far from the truth as we set off for the golden city of Nrubkcalb.

Evening Star, Burnley
30 November 1967

The power that saved crops and a marriage?

There is a young man in Tooting, London, who is not impressed by the power of witchcraft.

He asked the local witches to turn him into a disc jockey in three months, and he got not magic but sound, sympathetic advice. The High Priestess told him to 'work hard and be patient'. 'We really aren't prepared to work on issues like that,' said Mrs Ray Bone.

A young wife was more successful. She asked the witches to bring their power to bear on an affair between her husband and his secretary.

The witches obliged, and, according to Mrs Bone, the secretary contracted a mysterious illness a few weeks later, just long enough to lose her job and the husband.

Nice for the wife, but a little hard on the secretary, perhaps. 'We didn't know our power would work in that way,' said Mrs Bone.

Mrs Bone is 57 and she has been a practising witch for 27 years. Initiated into the craft in Cumberland, she worked for many years in the St Albans coven with the late, celebrated occultist, Dr Gerald Gardner, meeting in a country cottage near Watford.

She left St Albans in 1962 – 'The witches became more mobile, and we divided up to form splinter groups elsewhere' – and now she commutes between two covens in Cumberland and London.

Talking to Mrs Bone, it is difficult to believe that witchcraft has been one of the greatest fears of mankind; that witches have been killed in their hundreds of thousands for alleged crimes against the established Church and society; that in the 16th century William West, the lawyer, defined witchcraft as in 'league with the devil' which involved shaking 'the air with lightnings and thunder, causing hail and tempests', 'sporting, banqueting, daliance and diverse other devilish lusts, and lewd desports and showing a thousand such monstrous mockeries.'

Ray Bone wouldn't agree with all this. The most spinechilling thing about her appears to be her address in Cumberland: Witchwood, Blinderag, Cockermouth; and far from 'devilish lusts and monstrous mockeries,' the work at her coven in Tooting is remarkable only for its mundanity.

About 13 people, men and women, attend covens at her house in Tooting every lunar month. 'They are a fair social cross-section,' she said, 'two teachers, a solicitor, a businessman and so on.'

They begin a normal evening of witchcraft by drawing a circle on the ground with the ceremonial sword, and saying a rite according to the season of the year.

Then the witches develop their power with ritual dancing and chanting. 'We begin slowly,' said Mrs Bone, 'rising to a climax.' When they achieve an 'ecstatic state' and their mental and physical energy has reached its peak potential, they claim that this power is converted into magic and concentrated on the business in hand.

At the end of the evening the witches have a thanksgiving meal of cakes and wine – 'this might be interpreted as a parody of Christian communion, but this is definitely not the case,' said Mrs Bone – and go back to their suburban homes.

They dance in the nude at Mrs Bone's because, she says, it helps to break down class distinction. The teacher and the solicitor become equal in witchcraft. Nudity is a fairly recent innovation from the Continent.

If the craft derives from a pagan fertility cult, nudity would seem to be a reasonable custom to follow. 'Anyway, no orgies take place in this coven, although I can't speak for the rest,' said Mrs Bone.

The coven's work usually comprises requests for help. They deal with any problem they feel is morally acceptable.

The magic which gave her the most satisfaction was the part she believes they played in curing a man of a fatal lung disease after doctors had given up hope. 'He is still working today,' said Mrs Bone.

For her, witchcraft is a religion and craft; more exciting than carpentry perhaps, but similar nevertheless. It is something you have to learn to do properly; it involves study of the proper rituals, knowledge of herbal cures, and is, she claims, a sort of community service.

Mrs Bone believes that she is acting in the ancient tradition of the craft; it is only surprising to see a rural activity transposed so successfully into 20th-century London.

Just as there are cabinet makers and French polishers, witches often have some special ability. Mrs Bone is good at cures and domestic problems.

Mrs Wilson's forte appears to be the weather, if only because there are more farmers in the Isle of Man than in Tooting.

Mrs Dominique Wilson is High Priestess of a coven in the Isle of Man. Her husband, a commercial airline pilot, is also a witch, and when I spoke to her she was preparing to fly – BEA – to an esoteric conference in Paris.

She was born to French parents in Vietnam and she grew up in the craft. 'In the atmosphere of Eastern mysticism in Vietnam witchcraft never seemed a strange religion to follow,' she said.

Mrs Wilson says that she can, on request, produce good weather for local farmers. 'Once a farmer came to me and asked me to work for fine weather during the harvest. The coven accepted the request and there were 15 days of sun while he harvested his crops.'

People often ask her to produce fine weather for their holidays, but if the farmer wanted rain, he would take priority.

She also claims to have had a hand in curing a man of cancer as far away as California.

The power of a witch works in strange ways. So strange in fact, that it is difficult to prove or to disprove. It seems to lie outside the pale of scientific test, and no witches I spoke to had made any attempts to have their power corroborated by objective experts.

Mrs Wilson says that their power is a natural force like electricity, which they have learned to harness and direct.

'It is very dangerous to play around with,' she said. 'I wouldn't give you details of my ritual because your readers might attempt to copy them; and just as you wouldn't dream of wiring up your own house without knowledge of electricity, you shouldn't dabble in the craft. It can be dangerous; inexperienced people have blown out their minds.'

Like Mrs Bone, Mrs Wilson worked for a time with Dr Gardner, whom she compares to a dynamo as far as occult power is concerned. 'He was fantastic; we could do twice as much work when he was in the coven.'

Mrs Bone also pays lip-service at least to the 20th century when she describes the power of witchcraft. She says it is a highly developed form of 'positive thinking'.

'Supposing you had a limp,' she said, 'and you asked us to cure you; during the ritual we would form a mental picture of you walking along without the limp; we form mental pictures of the event we hope to achieve.'

Their magic does not produce immediate, direct results. To other people their work would seem to be coincidence; it gives the normal course of events a gentle nudge in the right direction.

Mrs Bone said: 'If you are a Christian and you pray for certain events to happen, and then they do happen, you would believe that your prayers had something to do with it.' There again, you might not.

The witches maintain that their powers are always used carefully and righteously. 'The first law of witchcraft is "Do not harm",' said Mrs Wilson. 'The second is "obey the laws of the society in which you live".' Although some witches, no doubt, disobey their own laws, there is no reason to say that this applies to the majority.

Evidently it is difficult for a witch to do real harm. 'People might ask me to get rid of an enemy,' said Mrs Bone, 'but for the power to be potent enough to kill, the witch has to feel personal hatred. She has to be a very angry witch indeed.'

31

One witch claims more credit for stopping the German invasion of Britain during the last war than the combined allied forces. But, on the whole, the witches seem to be content with working on small, local issues.

'We do not attempt to change the course of history,' said Mrs Wilson, who, with her Vietnamese background, might be best employed attempting to stop the war in Vietnam. 'We have never thought of trying to do that,' she said. 'I suppose the problem of distance wouldn't be insurmountable.'

There has been a surprising resurgence of interest in witchcraft in Britain, at a time when the National Health Service, education and the urbanization of the countryside would seem to count against it.

The decline in Christian belief, the increasing interest in superstition and mystical religions have provided the right soil for the growth of the craft. Dr Margaret Murray's anthropological researches into the origins of witchcraft, tracing it back to pagan religions and Druidic belief, gave the craft a new respectability a generation ago.

There are, on good authority, about 40 active covens in the British Isles. The witches themselves are very hard to find. After a recent series of fairly lurid newspaper articles, the witches have taken up the brooms and swept themselves under cover.

Although one occultist maintained the press reports did witchcraft a service by getting rid of the charlatans, they put the witches on the defensive.

They have a serious problem of communication with the general public. In the popular imagination they are either crones with long hats, cauldrons, cats and broomsticks, or sophisticated perverts, holding midnight orgies and gambolling naked through the woods.

There are, of course, white witches and black ones. The people I spoke to were positively shining white, but a black witch would hardly be prepared to reveal her colours to the press.

The craft does tend to attract the wrong sort of people – the abnormal and the sensation-seekers who might join for the sake of nude ritual and novelty alone.

The bona-fide witches are aware of this and profess to have a strict screening system for new entrants; they are also on their guard against phoney witches: 'The ones who scrape the barrels of the world's religions and piece together some sort of ritual which they believe to be the true witchcraft,' said Mrs Bone, who has spent 25 years researching the subject and has come up with what she believes to be a genuine picture of true witchcraft.

'The books on the subject were mostly burned during the middle ages,' she said, 'and much of the knowledge has been passed down by word of mouth. It is difficult to get hold of the ancient rituals.'

Whatever the alleged crimes of the witches, past and present, from devil worship to sexual misbehaviour, there can be no doubt that the witches are more sinned against than sinning.

Their long history is marked by widespread and vicious persecution; they became the scapegoats for national and local misfortunes. The expression 'witch-hunt' has come to mean the general persecution of minorities.

Legislation against witches has been in force in Britain from 690 to 1951, when, with the Fraudulent Mediums Act, a confession of witchcraft became as dangerous as a confession of atheism.

A witch can no longer be prosecuted for witchcraft, but persecution is a different matter. 'As the Christians were thrown to the lions so the witches are thrown to the press,' said Mrs Bone.

A witch who used to be high priestess of the St Albans coven, and is still believed to practise the craft in the area, refused to make any statement to the press. 'The life of one of my friends has been ruined by a recent newspaper article,' she said. 'You are all tarred with the same brush, just seeking for sensation; that's all I've got to say to you.'

Mrs Bone and Mrs Wilson are the exceptions perhaps. Far from being averse to publicity, Mrs Bone allowed herself to be photographed in the nude for the *Daily Telegraph Magazine*.

'Personally, I have found the press very courteous with a very few exceptions,' she said.

She has never attempted to disguise her religious beliefs, wrote 'pagan' on an official form when she went into hospital – 'They tried to get me to put atheist or C of E, but I refused on principle' – and runs an old people's home in Tooting with the licence and blessing of the local authority.

Mrs Wilson also says that people in the Isle of Man accept her belief in witchcraft quite openly.

Her child attends the local school, and once when the headmaster asked the child to read the morning lesson Mrs Wilson rang him up to remind him that the family were witches. 'Oh sorry,' he said, 'I forgot.'

Evening Post
28 April 1969

Just another week in Belfast

Alain le Garsmeur arrived in Belfast on the Sunday evening and was driving down the Falls Road towards the city centre when two youths with hoods pulled over their faces ran up to his car and stuck a revolver through the window.

Le Garsmeur is a *Sunday Times* photographer. Only a few hours before he had been eating his Sunday lunch at home, in peaceful Highgate, London. He was understandably alarmed and bewildered.

Belfast is only an hour's flight from Heathrow. It is another British city. Yet there were hooded men with guns walking in the street and a fullscale battle was in progress. Hi-jacked cars and lorries on fire had been dragged across streets to form barricades for stone-throwing youths. There was the crackle of rifle fire as gunmen opened up on the Army. Soldiers with blackened faces and full riot gear crouched in doorways.

Le Garsmeur, convinced that at best the smart rented car would be burnt at the barricade and that at worst he would still be in it, made a seemingly futile gesture and showed his press card. The effect was startling. 'That's all right then,' said one of the two youths and gave him an armed escort through the barricades.

Next day the unfortunate Le Garsmeur met a British Army soldier in the middle of a street riot who showed considerably less respect for the press. For no apparent reason, the soldier grabbed his camera and threatened to smash it. Le Garsmeur protested strongly and the soldier compromised – by ripping out the film. Next day Army officers gave fulsome apologies for the soldier's 'over-reaction'.

In the atmosphere of Belfast that week it was perhaps understandable. Sunday turned out to be a bad day, even by local standards. It was the eve of the fifth anniversary of internment – imprisonment without trial which was introduced in 1971 and ended earlier this year – and a traditional day for Republican protest. Nevertheless, the ferocity of the violence which erupted that Sunday afternoon took police and Army by surprise. The Saturday night and Sunday morning had been, according to the clipped English voice of the Army press officer, 'jolly quiet'.

The Army and police run a 24-hour press information service on violent 'incidents' in the Province. Sometimes, confusingly, they give out different information about the same incident, but on the whole the system works smoothly. Army officers have developed their own abbreviated language and talk of a 'member of the SF being VSI with GSW in the RVH'. This means a member of the security forces is very seriously injured with gunshot wounds in the Royal Victoria Hospital.

The press officers sit at a semi-circular table with a bank of telephones. Before them is the large, illuminated operations map of Northern Ireland on which violent incidents are denoted by coloured dots. On Saturday night and Sunday morning the map was fairly clear: a man mending a dog kennel in his front garden had been shot in the buttocks and the arm by a passerby; there had been a couple of armed robberies; petrol bombs had been thrown at a police station and into someone's backyard; and a man reported that his motorbike had been hi-jacked at gunpoint.

Twelve hours later a rash of dots appeared across the Army's illuminated map as harassed press officers rattled off the list of incidents which, by midnight, numbered more than 30. On Sunday night there were 17 shooting incidents in the city. A soldier was shot in the leg in the Donegal Road. Five soldiers were injured in a shooting in the Falls Road. Three soldiers were injured in the face when a sniper's bullet hit the barrel of one of their rifles and disintegrated.

Men and even children with guns were cropping up everywhere. One young lad who took a pot shot with a revolver at an Army post in the Markets area was possibly hit when the Army returned fire with high velocity rifles. 'Damn silly of him,' said an officer. 'Couldn't possibly have hit us at that range.' Next day a police patrol spotted a child, not more than five years old, staggering along with a ·22 rifle. The child said he had found it on some waste ground and it was promptly confiscated.

The person who had perhaps the most unpleasant night was Westminster MP and leader of the Social Democratic and Labour Party, Gerry Fitt. In the early morning a mob broke into his house and started charging up the stairs towards Fitt, his wife and daughter. Fitt, in pyjamas, stood at the top of the stairs and kept the mob at bay with his revolver until, after a considerable delay, the Army and police arrived. Fitt was badly shaken and taken off to hospital suffering from shock. 'I really thought, that's it, I've had it,' he said next day.

The gunmen and rioters seemed to knock off just before dawn, Monday, and we drove past the smouldering barricades to the Conway Hotel on the outskirts of Belfast. Eight years of Troubles have now changed the whole face of the city. Almost all the hotels have closed and last year the Europa, the favourite haunt for the press, was finished by the 29th bomb. The Conway, despite a bomb which demolished a large part of it last year, still stays open, although it looks less like a hotel than a high security prison.

Guests go through a steel gate in a high, wire-mesh fence to a wooden hut where they are searched by a security guard; then across a floodlit compound, past the bombed ruins of the main part of the hotel, to a door with a one-way mirror; this is opened electronically by another security guard. When the compound was patrolled by large dogs, which failed to discriminate between guests and terrorists, the experience was even more unnerving.

Monday morning the local commercial radio station, 'Downtown', was giving its uniquely dramatic bulletins. Instead of reports of faulty traffic lights on the A3 it advises drivers how to avoid riots, barricades and roads blocked off by the Army.

The city's local newspaper, the *Belfast Telegraph*, ran banner headlines saying 'Gerry Fitt – My Night of Terror' and 'Orgy of Violence', but struck a note of real terror with a reader's letter hidden away on an inside page. A Mr Charles Neeson wrote: 'I would like to reply to the savage who hacked, slashed and cut my brother Con to death on the corner of Manor Street last Sunday night.'

The city has had a lot of practice at recovering from violence. The men simply clamber over rubble, past the smoking wrecks and barricades and go off to work. Women push prams past soldiers who stand on corners and lay flat out on the pavements with their SLR rifles at the ready.

The city settled into a grim routine of rioting, hi-jacking and shooting while the Army press desk recited the litany of violence. On Monday afternoon there were six shootings in one hour: three shots fired at an Army foot patrol in Andersontown; 10 shots fired at a patrol near a Methodist church in the city centre; two shots at an Army base; three separate attacks on another.

Late on Wednesday night we made a grand tour of the trouble spots from Andersonstown, down the Falls Road, up the Protestant Crumlin to Catholic Ardoyne and down the Protestant Shankill to the Catholic Unity flats area. The city was uncannily quiet, like an English country town on a Sunday evening.

A crowd had gathered by the side of the Lagan, the dirty and often foul-smelling river that runs through Belfast, to watch a body being dragged out by the police and dumped unceremoniously in the back of an estate car. The crowd soon thinned when the police explained that the man had been drunk and had just toppled into the river.

Soldiers who had sweated under their riot gear and heavy flak jackets in 90-degree temperatures that week, and had been attacked nightly in the streets, also came under verbal attack from some Protestant politicians. They were blamed for not cracking down on the violence and it was mentioned, ironically, that next weekend marked the seventh anniversary of the day in August, 1969, when Jim Callaghan, then Home Secretary, ordered the troops on to the streets of Belfast for the

38

first time. And a lot of good it had done, grumbled both Protestants and Catholics.

The soldiers on the ground were also fed up. For some it was their third tour of duty in Belfast and if there had been excitement at first it had soon worn off. They also noticed little change for the better.

One group of 29 soldiers from the Royal Artillery lived in miserable conditions at a cramped and dingy mission hall in the Markets area of Belfast. They had worked long hours, taken abuse from angry crowds and watched barricades being built before their eyes. The instructions from Army head-quarters stated that as far as possible soldiers should keep a 'low profile' during street demonstrations, and clear up barricades after the crowds had gone home.

A large part of the Army's task is building up intelligence files on Catholic and Protestant terrorists. Such routine intelligence work is composed of reports on one man's movements, who another met in a certain bar, which car a woman is driving and how many milk bottles were delivered to a certain house.

On Thursday we made a routine patrol with the soldiers, growling round the seedy back streets in a 'pig' – an armoured car which gives a false sense of security, as the thick metal sides and doors would not stop one of the IRA's RPG 7 Russian-made rockets or even a high velocity rifle shot. As it happened, the tour was uneventful. A small boy threw what looked like a sweet at the back of the retreating pig and the soldier looking through the narrow window slits reported on a suspect IRA man. Their intelligence seems to be good and one wall of the mission's operation room is covered by photographs, a rogues' gallery of suspected terrorists.

It was also a bad week for the men at the top. At Stormont, to the East of the city, Merlyn Rees, Secretary of State for North-ern Ireland, in his official helicopter, landed on the lawn outside the mock Gothic castle which serves as the seat of British power in Northern Ireland for long, anxious meetings with his civil servants. Meanwhile, in Andersonstown the barricades went up again.

On the west side of the city, in the centre of a beautifully landscaped but heavily fortified Army compound, sat the man with the weightiest problems of all, Lieutenant General Sir David House. He is in charge of the British Army in Northern Ireland. A general's job in Northern Ireland is a complex and subtle one. He is not called upon to lead his men to victory up the Falls Road, but to engage politicians in less glorious skirmishes in sub-committee rooms.

Sir David, with his rimless glasses and fastidious manner, seems more like a headmaster than a general. He is normally quite remote but that week took the rare step of seeing journalists in his office behind an ominous steel gate on the first floor of the HQ building. The General was clearly irritated. The press had got it all wrong, he said. 'They keep saying the Army should take a harder line but there is nothing more we can do. It will take more people killed and a few more weeks like this one and perhaps the attitude of the politicians will change because their policies just bloody well aren't working.'

The week was in fact dominated not by high level rows but by an incident so brutal that the rest of the violence paled before it. On Tuesday afternoon a terrorist escaping from an Army patrol was shot and killed. His car ran out of control and crushed two young children and a baby, all members of the Maguire family, to death against an iron railing. The dead driver of the car was Daniel Lennon, a Provisional IRA volunteer from Andersonstown. The death of the children was not destined to become just another incident. Next day an Andersonstown housewife, Betty Williams, collected more than 6000 signatures from outraged mothers on the Catholic estate and started, overnight, the Mothers for Peace movement.

Andersonstown is in the front line between the British Army and the Provisional IRA, who have their strongest Belfast contingent in this sprawling, squalid housing estate. The area has bred such IRA hard men as Seamus Twomey, now the top man on the IRA's Army Council, and Maire Drumm, who was vice chairman of Sinn Fein, the Provisional's political wing. But most families resent both the intrusion of the British Army and the activities of the Provisionals. They had never dared to make known their feelings publicly before.

Most reporters thought the peace movement would dwindle into oblivion before the end of the week. But, happily, they were wrong. The first Peace Rally, which took place in Andersonstown that Saturday by the railings where the children had died, was a startling success.

Ten thousand women turned up, dressed in their Sunday best. Among them was a plucky group of Protestant women from the Shankill Road who said it was the first time they had dared to enter a staunch Republican area since the Troubles began in 1969. They were given a rapturous welcome by Catholic women from Andersonstown and the Falls Road. The women sang hymns and said prayers in soft, rather timid voices against the background of raucous heckling from a group of young IRA sympathisers who stood on the roof of a garage nearby.

As the women walked to the Milltown cemetery, where the children, and Belfast's IRA martyrs, are buried, they had to run the gauntlet of another, larger group of Provisional supporters who taunted and occasionally assaulted them.

It was perhaps even more encouraging that the events of the week caused at least second thoughts in the minds of some committed Provisional IRA supporters. In Andersonstown we met a formerly important IRA man who often used to boast of his military prowess and his actions against the British Army. He is committed to the IRA's long term aim – a United Ireland – but had begun to have doubts about their military campaign. 'The killing of the children was a tragic accident and no member of the IRA would ever want that to happen. But the violence last week and the random shootings bring them no advantage. For the first time it seems to be mindless violence.'

The violence, however, continued. On Sunday night a small boy told a security guard at a bus depot in Ardoyne that his ball had just bounced over the wall into the depot and could he have it back. As the kindly guard opened the gates four masked men rushed in and planted incendiary devices in 11 buses. Just before midnight a jaunty Army explosives officer arrived at the depot, which was bathed in a sickly green light. He strode among the buses, a shot gun under his arm like a country squire, blasting away at detonators. All the bombs were duly disarmed. The Army was in exuberant mood and celebrated both an actual and psychological victory over the enemy. They

41

said that earlier that evening at a local Republican drinking club there had been a premature and inaccurate announcement over the public address system that no buses would be running next morning because the Ardoyne bus depot had been razed.

That week saw a marked change in the type of warfare taking place in Belfast. On the Monday, Tuesday and Wednesday the Army had had more shots fired at them than at any time since the Troubles began. However, by the end of the week Northern Ireland had left the front pages of the English newspapers and the Army press office settled down to its normal diet of incidents. ·

Sunday Times Magazine
19 December 1976

One man's
week

Monday

A sign at Logan International Airport says 'Boston, the Liveable City.' I'm not so sure. Crime is rife and people take it, depressingly, for granted. A bank in downtown Boston put a sign up today: 'Closed due to hold-up.' The Boston Globe sent me off to a local supermarket to cover a routine crime. A security man had been shot by raiders and the manager, who had had a gun held to his head, was visibly shaken. Three women step round the pool of blood and shout: 'Ain't you serving anyone?'

Tuesday

It is snowing and the temperature has slumped to near zero. People are putting on their thermal underwear and I am wearing two pairs of trousers. Dinner with a feminist at a feminist restaurant in Cambridge, Boston's answer to San Francisco, where, in summer, students play the cello on street corners. The waitress is called a waitperson and in the crowded room the only spare seats seem to be at a large table where two women are already sitting. The waitperson asks them if they mind if a man sits there. They do. We find somewhere else and eat food which is brown and macrobiotic. My spirits rise when the waitperson gives my companion the bill and she pays.

43

The waitperson, who had frowned when I wanted sugar instead of honey in my herbal tea, now suddenly asks: 'Are you into nitrous oxide?' This is evidently the new drug experience. She says her friend carries a cylinder of it in her car boot and stops for the odd mind-blowing whiff.

Wednesday

A friend takes me on a conducted tour of Boston's red light district, known as the 'combat zone.' The strip clubs are said to be the finest in America. I don't want to see the worst. Stripping was banned in the city until 1970 and Bostonians are making up with quantity rather than quality.

At the Two O'clock Lounge four girls strip simultaneously. At Jerome's two girls, introduced as Lustful Linda and Cheeky Cheryl, run up and down a long stage shedding their clothes. The lights are dim but not so dim that I can't recognize a very senior and strait-laced Boston businessman huddled over his Budweiser. He is in good company. The owner of one club is a PhD in anthropology and the floor manager is a lawyer.

Thursday

Lunch with Bill, an FBI special agent I recently wrote about. The FBI is apparently as sensitive as a young starlet and Bill tells me agents paled when they saw the piece. I called one agent 'plump,' an understatement, and this led to a major inquiry. J. Edgar Hoover would have had every agent in the Boston bureau weighed to find the guilty man.

Friday morning

The presidential primaries are looming and candidates are as thick as snowflakes on the streets of Boston. At 7.30 a.m. Jimmy Carter, one of the Democratic candidates, has a fund-raising breakfast at the Copley Plaza which has all the seedy splendour of a British Rail hotel in Liverpool. Despite the hour and the freezing cold Carter pulls in a room full of sober Boston business men in dark suits. I very nearly shake hands with a

Secret Service agent instead of Carter. They both look like male models for Austin Reed. The difference is, I discover, that Secret Service men are the ones with little radios stuck in their left ears, like National Health hearing aids, and who keep talking into their left sleeves where they keep their microphones.

Carter stands against a painted backdrop of Venice and launches, with a rapid drawl, into his economic theories, while we eat scrambled eggs. He says that zero budget control will cut back federal spending. This doesn't go down well on the press table. 'Ass-hole,' mumbles a bleary-eyed reporter. 'What's zero budget control, godammit?' Nobody can help him. Carter also says that the one thing he alone can bring to the presidency is his experience as a Georgian peanut farmer. There is a stifled explosion of mirth from the press but quiet respect from the rest of the room. On the table in front of me a photo of Carter beams up from a small packet of peanuts.

At 9.30 the press grab their peanuts and Carter buttons and rush off to catch another Democratic candidate, Birch Bayh, at the Boston Parker House. Bayh is doing well with the labour unions but has trouble, according to an aide, with his recognition factor. In other words, voters don't know who he is. To help them remember Bayh once composed a little ditty to the tune of 'Hey Look Me Over.' One verse went: 'My first name is Birch and my last name is Bayh.' Bayh talks fluently about economics and gets bogged down on Angola. He also shows that President Ford doesn't have a monopoly of clumsiness by sending his microphone flying three times with dramatic gestures. Alert Secret Service agents wrestle it to the ground.

I am with the Globe's political correspondent, Curtis Wilkie, a Mississippi man with a strange, slow drawl like a record played at 78 rpm. He recalls once being wrestled to the ground himself, by Ford's over-alert Secret Service agents who mistook him for an assassin. 'Ah spent seven hours in the Nashua slammer,' says Curtis. He is more sullen than usual because he has been forced to follow Henry 'Scoop' Jackson who is not renowned for his wit: 'Scoop is so boring he once gave a fireside chat on TV and the fire went to sleep.'

Friday evening

Yet another presidential candidate, George Wallace, is having a big do at the Statler Hilton. Wallace, who has no problem with recognition factors, draws a big crowd. The Governor organizes his rallies like Sunday Night at the London Palladium. The audience is warmed up by Grampa Jones on a banjo, a priest gives a fiery invocation and a boy scout salutes the flag. Then an aide says: 'The Governor is near at hand,' and Wallace is wheeled up a ramp behind a bullet-proof podium.

His eloquent and often funny attack on bureaucrats, the press, intellectuals and federal judges is interrupted by one of his supporters who attacks a Secret Service agent. Scuffles break out all over the hall. 'They are all just undecided voters,' says Wallace. As the crowd piles out the mood is ugly. Some young supporters set upon a student because, they say, he looks like a Communist. As he looks a bit like me I beat a hasty retreat.

Saturday

I have a toothache, something that fills Americans with dread. I go to a dentist who refers me to a root specialist who wants to call in an oral surgeon. The original dentist says I should wait until I get back to Britain and charges $5 for this good advice.

Sunday Times
8 January 1976

U S A
1979–1981

Picnic among the ruins

A picnic in a small field next to a large graveyard in Nashua, New Hampshire, last Sunday marked a crucial moment for the American Democratic Party. As Jerry Brown, a Presidential 'hopeful' and Governor of California, put it, 'This is really the beginning, the beginning of the Democratic primary.' Democrats sat in the sunshine sustained by hot dogs and stirring talk about how they should 'toil in the vineyards of the party' and the importance of 'unity and cohesiveness' in the 1980 campaign – sentiments belied by stickers plastered over the wall of a barn which told the true story. 'Viva Jerry Brown,' said one. 'We love Miz Lillian,' and 'Support Kennedy in 1980,' said the others.

The three rival factions, Brown, the President's mother Miz Lillian and the supporters of Senator Edward Kennedy, sat on the dais together smiling tightly at each other as men in stetson hats played rousing country-and-western tunes. It was supposed to be Brown's big day, his first political offensive in the state which has the first primary next February and where, he hopes, his anti-nuclear stand and his campaign for a constitutional amendment to balance the Federal budget might touch the hearts of liberals and fiscal conservatives alike. He has yet to make much headway with the extremely conservative New Hampshire newspaper the *Manchester Union-Leader* which described him last Sunday as the 'Californian snowflake'. Although Brown's political organization in the north-east is reputedly meagre, he had drummed up a small but vociferous contingent from the farm workers' union, most of them very pretty girls in their late teens and early twenties, who waved banners and chanted his name with the zeal of Hare Krishnas as he arrived at Logan airport in Boston.

The large press corps indulged in heavy speculation about whether he would bring his close personal friend, the rock star Linda Ronstadt, with him or perhaps appear on roller skates but the Governor appears alone and on foot, a small, lean figure dressed in a black suit, white shirt and striped tie. His visit began to go downhill almost immediately. He was enveloped by press and supporters and shoved up against the airport wall, his microphone worked only spasmodically, a girl supporter was hit on the head by a TV camera and burst into tears. Within earshot of the Governor a network TV reporter began his live face-to-camera report with the words: 'This is not so much a campaign as a circus.'

The media interest in Brown is intense, not so much in his policies but in the fine personal detail. On Sunday morning before the picnic he went to Mass at a Catholic church in Nashua, and afterwards a group of reporters grilled him on how much he had dropped into the collection plate. Brown, who has a reputation for being frugal, refused to reveal how much: 'I can tell you it was paper and it was more than one,' said Brown. 'Two dollars,' said a reporter promptly.

But whatever thunder there might have been in his arrival in the north-east was stolen by the more pressing issue of what Mrs Rose Kennedy was thinking out at the family compound in Hyannisport, a subject which dominated the press. The day before Brown came east the *New York Times* carried a story without sources, names or quotes which said that Edward Kennedy's mother, Rose, had changed her mind about not letting her son run in 1980 and had told him to go ahead. This is a pretty insubstantial story by any standards. The Senator himself had no comment to make about it and his aides said, 'Much is being made of very little.' It was enough, though, to take Brown off the front pages and put Kennedy in his place.

50

The Democratic Party seemed last weekend to be in the grip of mothers in their eighties. First Rose, 89, then Lillian, 82, who turned up to represent 'My Jimmy who y'all might know is President of the United States.' Her white hair cut in pudding basin style, she was led onto the podium by her secret service agents to make a speech which 'her Jimmy' will regret for many months to come. Lillian is normally adroit at the soft, folksy utterly innocuous speech and she started off true to form: 'I know each and every one of you know what Jimmy is doing and what he has done and what he will do,' and then came the gaffe. 'As for Mr Kennedy he assures us that he is not going to run, and if he does run I wish him all the luck in the world and I hope to goodness nothing happens to him. I really do.' If ever a remark ruined a Democratic picnic that was it.

There was a shocked silence then the sound of booing mixed with the groans of Carter supporters. Lillian made a quick recovery and tried to change the mood by talking about beagles, but the damage was done. The next day the *New York Post* devoted its entire front page to the headline 'Miz Lillian's Ted Shocker'. Carter's mother 'screwed up and I mean really screwed up', as one Carter supporter put it. The President himself was making a barely visible appearance in some sort of promotional film being screened under a tree by a hot-dog stand. His only audience was one small boy. Suddenly our own Mr Callaghan flickered onto the screen and urged the President 'to carry your responsibilities with spirit'. The small boy wandered off.

Exactly on schedule the Brown group dashed across the state to another Democratic picnic in a wood just near Dover on the New Hampshire coast. He spoke about MX missiles which he opposes, the environment which he supports, about 'the psychology of inflation' and he urged Americans to wake up and stop being prisoners of their past perceptions. A small audience listened silently and applauded tepidly. Most of the Democrats wandered off out of earshot, but in one corner of the leafy glade a group was having an animated discussion, not about Jerry Brown or the psychology of inflation but the burning question of whether Edward Kennedy had stopped eating ice cream – another *New York Times* exclusive – in order to slim down for the 1980 campaign. 'You know what', said a Washington reporter, 'I'm not so sure he's ever eaten goddamned ice cream, so how can he stop?'

Spectator
15 September 1979

How Liz got her unlikely new role

The candidate was addressing a huge crowd of Republican faithful as they gnawed their fried chicken on the lush green lawns of a Virginia estate. Suddenly, a few hundred yards away, a small, plump woman with a walking stick and a billowing tent-like caftan appeared under a tree. The crowd broke off from the dissertation on the excesses of Federal taxation and dashed for the tree. 'Oh, Liz, how is your bad hip?' 'I can't believe it, you're gorgeous,' they warbled.

The effect of Liz Taylor, known rather primly here as Mrs Elizabeth Warner after her sixth husband, on Virginia politics is electrifying.

Although the 38-22-34 figure that won her millions of admirers 20 years ago had sadly thickened to almost matronly proportions, she still looks stunning as she stands with her raven hair and violet eyes wearing primary colours against the drab landscape of the other Republican wives in prim and pastel shades.

She is largely responsible for rocketing her husband John from the Washington bureaucracy to a 3000-vote lead in the Virginia senatorial election.

Liz and John met in the summer of 1976 during the Queen's visit to America for the bicentennial celebrations. And Cupid appears to have been the social secretary at the British Embassy in Washington. The Embassy heard that Liz wanted to go to a dinner they were giving for the Queen, but that she didn't want to go alone. The Embassy asked her if she would accept John Warner, head of the Bicentennial Committee, as an escort. Liz agreed; and love blossomed over the post-prandial brandies. John invited her to his ranch in Middleburg, Virginia, where she had a go on one of his children's bicycles and unromantically hurt her leg. 'John was very solicitous,' said a friend.

His friends and enemies thought the marriage was an act of political suicide. Virginia is a notoriously prissy state, where women are expected to keep their place – and their first husbands. Strangers are resented.

On the face of it Miss Taylor had everything going against her. She has divorced four husbands (one of them twice). She is a converted Jew. She is British, smokes, drinks and has been known, in the style of *Who's Afraid of Virginia Woolf?* (for which she won an Oscar), to yell at her husband.

Warner once left her sitting on a bench in an hotel during a campaign swing through Virginia. Liz was besieged by autograph hunters and escaped to the ladies' lavatory, where she sat fuming. Warner burst through the crowds and into the lavatory to rescue her. Her voice pierced the door: 'Johnnnn. I am not here because I want to do-do.'

She sometimes looks distinctly unglamorous. One photographer caught her at some Republican function sitting barefoot, legs splayed, hunched over a hamburger. 'I hate people watching me while I eat,' she told a reporter. 'You're always sure you'll drip something down your chin or something.'

Her political credentials are also suspect. She used to be a Democrat and went around with Billy Carter during his brother Jimmy's election campaign. But for the love of John she converted to Republicanism.

But the crowds and the television cameras do not come out to study her politics – which is fortunate, because her speeches are short and usually go like this: 'Thank you all for coming here. I sure am glad to see all those Warner stickers. I'm not going to try to sell you on John Warner. John Warner speaks for himself and stands on his record. He has spent 10 years working for other people, not for money and not for fame but because he cares about people. He cares about you, about your children and about your grandchildren. He wants to do what he can to make this world a better place. That's why I feel so strongly about him. That's all.'

Asked why she wants John to be a Senator, she has another little speech: 'We're all just little grains of sand. But if all of us tiny pieces of sand get together we can make a stone. That stone can become a boulder and that boulder can become a huge body.'

Despite all this, Liz is a smash hit almost everywhere she goes. The campaign staff tell the story over and over again of Liz's visit to an old people's home in Hopewell, Virginia. An old man in a wheelchair looked up at her and croaked: 'It's you. It's Cleopatra.'

At a home for retarded children Liz genuinely won hearts, and a little boy clung to her so tenaciously he had to be gently prised away.

Aides grow dewy-eyed when they talk about her. 'She is, how can I say, so *ordinary*,' said one. 'She is a real trouper,' said another. They tell the moving story of how one day John and Liz had been campaigning separately in different parts of Virginia when they met accidentally in the centre of some small town. 'They both jumped out of their cars and rushed up to each other and hugged, right there, in the middle of the street.'

She has thrown rubber footballs through hanging toilet seats at the Arlington country fair; been auctioned as a cook to benefit the handicapped; flown in small planes, which she hates; visited hospitals and workshops for the retarded. In one swing she travelled 20,000 miles through Virginia by car, plane and Greyhound coach.

She has entered the weird heartland of American politics. One evening she found herself addressing the Galaz Moose Lodge and presenting a prize for its 41-year sponsorship of the annual Old Time Fiddler's Convention.

If that were not bad enough, the power failed. More than 5000 Old Time Fiddlers in the audience grew restive, plucked at their banjos and shouted complaints. Then Liz, in black-and-white-striped pants walked on to the stage. There was a sudden hush. 'She looked real fine, like a tiger,' said a Fiddler. 'She sort of glowed in the dark.'

She has been plagued by Liz Taylor look-alikes who attend the function that Liz doesn't. A member of the Central Intelligence Agency went to one Warner reception and saw across the room a raven-haired woman, laden with jewellery and wearing a tent-like caftan. He pushed through the crowds. 'Are you Liz Taylor?' he asked. 'No,' said the woman, 'but I'm sure glad you thought I was.'

Husband John is an extremely lucky man. Where most politicians would plead with Miss Taylor to make a single appearance on their behalf and almost certainly get turned down, he has married her. Through Liz alone he gets huge press coverage for appearing at the Virginia Peanut Festival. Liz got her photograph in the *Ladies' Home Journal* as she sat on a tractor – and of course John got a mention.

It has been tough luck on Liz's Democratic counterpart, the wife of Andrew Miller, Warner's opponent in the senate race. Her name is Doris. And she has not appeared in the *Ladies' Home Journal*. 'I am not good looking,' Doris has said defensively. 'She (Liz) is not a US citizen. I know Virginia very well and I love it. I've led a very dull life, really, with one husband and three babies.'

The Democrats claimed to have conducted a poll which showed that the average voter considered Mrs Elizabeth Warner 'a big drag'. The Warner camp on the other hand feared that Liz was taking too much publicity and eclipsing the candidate himself: requests for interviews with Liz were turned down abruptly by the Warner campaign people. 'Who are you interested in, the candidate or his wife?' they would ask. 'His wife,' most people said. 'Yeah, guessed as much,' they said.

The candidate himself used to be Secretary for the Navy in the Richard Nixon administration, which is not exactly a vote grabber, and then headed the group which organized the American Bicentennial celebrations in 1976. He then retired to his horse-breeding ranch in Virginia to prepare for a political career. He is very rich. He has $7½ million, mostly from his ex-wife, a member of the enormously wealthy Mellon family. He inherited the Republican nomination by a quirk of fate after the actual nominee, Richard D. Obenshain, was killed in a plane crash.

Without Liz he is rather unimpressive. On the eve of the election we met him campaigning outside Rosslyn metro station in Virginia. Liz was in hospital and couldn't appear. Whereas she stands out in a crowd, Warner, despite his size and rugged good looks, tends to blend into the background. Commuters seemed reluctant to talk to him and shake his hand, and some were virtually frog-marched towards him by his aides. The TV networks had failed to show up and Warner was grumpy and unsmiling. 'I want you to know that Mrs Warner wishes she could be here today,' said Mr Warner's Press aide. 'In fact her recovery is being hampered by the emotional strain of not being with him. But he phones her up, gosh, three times a day at the very least.' We asked Warner if he was going to visit Liz in hospital that night. 'No,' he snapped.

'What Mr Warner means is that he will visit Mrs Warner if he can, but because it is the night before the election his schedule is extremely tight,' explained an aide.

Liz had suffered as she stumped thousands of miles around the Virginia hustings on John's and the Republicans' behalf. During the campaign of Republican John Dalton, who was running for Governor, she did her share of hand-shaking. At one reception a man squeezed her hand so hard it broke a blood vessel. She had it bandaged up and continued shaking with her left. She developed the condition called bursitis – it is what causes 'tennis elbow' – in her hip, and for a time hobbled around painfully with a stick. She caught an ear infection and some bad colds.

She rose from her sick-bed to go to Richmond for Dalton's election party. 'I broke my hand, I broke my hip and I busted my ear and my ass for Dalton, and I'm not going to miss the victory party,' she said.

But her worst injury to date was at a chicken dinner reception towards the end of John's campaign. As Liz and John toured the kitchens, he spotted a tray of fried chicken, picked up a piece and gave Liz a bite. Seconds later she clutched at her throat and gasped. A piece of bone two inches long, had stuck in her throat. 'She's lucky,' said a radiologist at the Richmond hospital where Liz was rushed. 'This could have lodged in her larynx and killed her.'

She went back into hospital when her throat became infected and once again rose from her sick-bed to be at her husband's side and share in his election night celebrations. She stood there smiling gamely despite a medical condition described by doctors as 'very weak, with painful spasm in the chest and arms'.

Both Liz and John feel the media have been less than fair to them. When Warner was Secretary for the Navy he was called 'the worst thing to happen to the Navy since Pearl Harbor'. It has also been pointed out that Liz's marriage is bad news for the tiny settlement of Kasane in northern Botswana. That is where Liz honeymooned idyllically with two of her husbands, both of them the actor Richard Burton. She had such a good time she promised to donate $350,000 to improve the local hospital. Since her divorce and remarriage, she has scaled the offer down to $43,000 because, she says, her marriage to John has changed her tax status in the US.

She has also been the target of bitchy comments, largely from other, far less attractive, middle-aged women. Her double chin, the size of her waist and degree of downward shift in her voluptuous bosom have been discussed more frequently and with more interest at Republican coffee mornings than husband John's predictable conservative policies. In fact Liz is looking better than she appears in some magazine photographs, where the fold in her chin and sag in her bosom are accentuated. She can still dominate any Virginia party with her natural sexiness.

In a rare interview with a local Virginia paper she discussed her looks. 'I have lived every second of my life. I have never lied about my age. I am proud of being 46. It is nothing to hide. I am happy. I am content. I don't want to starve myself because my looks don't matter that much to me. John is interested in having a happy human being, not a model type beauty.' 'I can say she is prettier inside than she is outside,' said John. 'Why thank you, John,' said Liz.

Sunday Times Magazine
1979

Jordan's high life
turns sour

The most exclusive place in New York used to be about 16ft below ground on 54th Street just off Broadway. Only the top celebrities would be invited in through a door at the back of Studio 54, the chic discotheque, down a staircase and along a passage past lockers and peeling pink paint.

Then other doors would open to give a glimpse of this Shangri-La of the late Seventies. One room was laid with astroturf and contained a duckpond upon which real ducks swam and quacked. Another was like a master bedroom and another like a miniature discotheque.

On June 27, 1978, one special guest, it is alleged, was Hamilton Jordan, now chief of the White House staff. It was an unlikely setting for Hamilton, who seems more at home propped on a bar with a six-pack of Billy Beer, brewed by President Carter's brother. But that night, according to the discotheque's co-owner, Steve Rubell, Jordan had more potent stuff: 'two toots' of cocaine, an illegal drug, which he snorted into each nostril.

Jordan's social life is occasionally less than decorous. He was accused of spitting three ice cubes down a woman's dress in a Washington bar and of peering into the cleavage of the Egyptian ambassador's wife while muttering about the pyramids.

Jordan admits he went to the Studio 54 club but denies having had cocaine. 'The charge is junk, the witnesses are junk

59

and if it weren't for the Ethics in Government Act the case would have been thrown in the garbage,' said a Justice Department official angrily.

But the US attorney-general, Benjamin Civiletti, said he 'could not yet conclude that the charges against Jordan are so unsubstantiated that no further investigation . . . is warranted.' At the end of last month he appointed a New York lawyer, Arthur Christy, as a special prosecutor to look into the Jordan case. Christy, a large man with a black moustache, is used to rather tougher cases – the prosecution, for example, of the Mafia godfather, Vito Genovese, for narcotics violations. Last week Christy was shelving all his other business at his Fifth Avenue law firm and recruiting a special team for the Jordan case, 'I can't say a word about it, Dave,' he said. 'This Ethics in Government thing is a whole new ball game and I don't know how long it's going to take. At the moment I want to get the hell out of my own office and set up a kind of headquarters.'

Although both Jordan and the president are riding high in the opinion polls at the moment they are watching Christy's investigators with trepidation. If he finds any evidence that Jordan snorted even a single 'toot' it will mean his resignation and a severe blow to the White House.

The man they can thank for all this is Steve Rubell, a short, slightly balding 34-year-old. Last week, in the early hours of the morning, Rubell scurried into Studio 54 accompanied by his two bodyguards. He was quickly surrounded by well-wishers. 'Hi, Stevie!' they said. 'How you doing? How's it going, Steve baby?' Steve was kissed, cuddled and patted on the head. 'Good,' said Steve. 'Great. Terrific.'

At 4 a.m. Rubell climbed into the disc jockey's pulpit above the dance floor and addressed his motley flock. The disco beat stopped and even 'Rollerina,' a man who wears women's clothes, ornate spectacles and roller-skates, cruised respectfully to a halt. 'I want to announce that this is the first anniversary of the police raid on 54,' said Rubell. 'The drinks are on the house.' In fact Steve has little to celebrate. He is unlikely to be around for the second anniversary.

Last year the US attorney's 'organized crime strike force'

found that Rubell and his partner, Ian Scharger, had been skimming hundreds of thousands of dollars from the club's earnings. They have pleaded guilty to both private and corporate tax evasion, which carries a minimum sentence of ten years, and they come up for sentencing next month.

They are also under investigation for narcotics offences and the state liquor authority has sent them notice that it is revoking their licence. Unless his army of 15 lawyers can pull off a last-minute coup it seems that Steve's discoing days are over.

The rise and fall of Rubell will make one of the grubbier chapters in the history of New York's high society. A few years ago he was an amateur tennis player and the owner of a chain of steak restaurants. In 1977 he took over a disused television studio on 54th Street. He brought in sophisticated lights and a sound system so powerful it made the floor tremble. And he paid public-relations people a hundred dollars a time for bringing big names through the doors of Studio 54.

Soon top people in show business, fashion and society were seen and photographed boogying the night away at 54. The writer Truman Capote was a regular ('it's the best nightclub in the world ever,' he said). So were Liza Minnelli, Mick and Bianca Jagger, Margaret Trudeau and the top model, Cheryl Tiegs. The artist Andy Warhol was often seen palely loitering.

Some of the guest were less interested in the decor than the bizarre menu of drugs to be sniffed or swallowed with the compliments of the management. What they did not know, however, was that Rubell and his staff kept a list of their names and favourite drugs – a list now in the hands of the US Attorney's department.

'Those scum-bags!' said a fashion designer and regular visitor to the basement. 'How could they sink so low?'

Business was good in 1977. Rubell told the magazine New Yorker: 'The profits are astronomical. Only the Mafia does better.' These profits failed to appear in the tax returns. In 1977, for example, Rubell reported a net taxable income of only $47,000 (£22,000) and paid only $8,000 in tax. But when the police strike force struck last year it found a separate set of books hidden in the basement which showed that 54's undeclared profits were indeed astronomical. The police also found almost a million undeclared dollars in a safe-deposit box at Citibank on Fifth Avenue.

Although Rubell and his partner pleaded guilty they did not go down gracefully. In a desperate attempt to plea-bargain, Rubell said he had information so vital to the national security that if the government dropped its case he would reveal all. The government refused. Then Rubell made his allegations against Jordan.

Rubell danced merrily into the early hours on Friday. He says he is a victim: 'This is the price you pay for being a media success.' When reminded that he did pay less tax than he should have, he looked hurt: 'Now you're trying to turn it into a moral issue.'

Sunday Times
23 December 1979

Benny the Squint,
Big Nose and pals

American criminal history was made last Friday, when, for the first time, a New Jersey court proved what the world has always assumed – organized crime exists in the United States. The shock for crime writers, film makers and policemen is that is not called the Mafia.

Investigators spent two years listening secretly to the conversations of such New Jersey citizens as Little Pussy Russo, Benny the Squint, Jimmy the Brush, Nicky Dirt, Big Nose, Pee Wee (who is only 4ft 7in high) and Ruggerio 'the Boot' Boiardo, who is 90 years old. They revealed that the organization is called, somewhat mundanely, 'the Thing,' or 'this Thing of ours.' 'They never said "Mafia" – not once,' said a member of the Justice Department. Neither was the Italian original of 'Our Thing' ever mentioned: Cosa Nostra.

The indictment read: 'The defendants did knowingly, wilfully and unlawfully conspire as members of a secret nationwide organization known by its members as "This Thing of Ours" . . .'

John Degnan, New Jersey's attorney general, said when the case began: 'We are telling the people of New Jersey and the United States that we are now prepared to prove in a court of law the existence of a national criminal conspiracy.'

The four men found guilty of conspiracy, illegal gambling, loansharking, extortion and robbery are all from New Jersey, which calls itself the garden state. Its lush pastures have provided lucrative grazing for members of organized crime since the days of prohibition. It was a haven for the crime bosses, who had politicians, judges, prosecutors and policemen in their pockets. It is still a favourite dumping ground for the bodies of those who run foul of 'the Thing' in New York and Philadelphia.

The top man, according to state officials, is the wrinkled and ancient Boiardo 'the Boot,' whose other title is 'capo-regime.' He organizes crime from a magnificent stone mansion standing at the end of a long drive lined with life-sized, luridly-painted statues of himself and his family. A huge crystal chandelier hangs in his kitchen and he has an equally large incinerator in his back garden.

A murder charge against Boiardo was dropped after his lawyers argued successfully that he was too ill and senile to stand trial. However, in tape recordings he sounds robust enough as, with a voice like gravel, he instructs an underling to 'hit' the son of an associate.

The New Jersey families are linked to a nationwide confederation of 26 families for whom crime pays. Their profits are estimated by the FBI to be about 25 billion dollars a year – untaxed, of course. America's biggest legal corporation, Exxon, makes a mere two or three billion dollars a year profit.

The New Jersey case will become a text book for federal agents, criminologists and those with a more gratuitous interest in the Mob. Investigators bugged restaurants, private houses, clubs, bars and even a lamp-post in a street where criminals were known to loiter. And hundreds of hours of sometimes muffled conversation provided a rare insight into the moves of organized crime, which got a boost from Edwin Stier, New Jersey's director of criminal justice, when he said it was a common mistake to dismiss the people who ran it as stupid thugs. 'I would match the good organized criminal against any corporate executive. They run huge business empires under the most trying circumstances.'

Like other corporate men, the gangsters talked about profits and losses, investment and business expansion. They bemoaned the inefficiencies of their staff and the difficulty of getting well-qualified recruits. But there was an 'incentive' to hire the right man. As one said to a colleague: 'You get some nice good kids that you can trust. Don't bring me a kid you say is good, because if the kid's no good you're gonna go with the kid.' New members had to prove themselves by making a 'registered hit' – the murder of someone chosen by the organization. If they carried out the task satisfactorily they became 'made men' or 'wise men,' or, as was sometimes said in the tapes, 'a man of respect.'

The investigation began when a building contractor called Richard Bonhert borrowed $75,000 from a loanshark and found he was being charged $½m in 'Vig' or interest. He went to the police, who persuaded him to record conversations with the Mob using a specially designed, sound sensitive jock strap. In one conversation Little Pussy instructs Louis Ferrari what to say to Bonhert if he should refuse to pay his Vig instalment.

The expletives in the tape transcripts have been deleted by the attorney general and replaced by dots.

'Little Pussy': 'Now all we're gonna do is tell you in a nice way. Next week you can go run any place you want because we're gonna break your . . . legs and put you in the hospital. And every time you come out you go back in.'

Louis learnt his lines and was almost perfect in the next day when he met Bonhert.

Louis: 'Hey, he ('Little Pussy') said he's gonna break your . . . legs. He's gonna break your legs and put you in the . . . hospital and the day you come out he's gonna break your . . . legs again. You understand? The hospital, with broken . . . legs all the time.'

Then Louis continues with the classic line: 'Let me tell you something, Dick. We like you personally as a person. You know what I'm talking about. You can't tell these people that kind of an attitude because you won't last 24 hours. They don't give a. . . .'

● *Note From Blundy to Foreign Editor: A message from Mr Boiardo – 'Hey, you . . . If you'se don't use my boy Dave's stuff in de paper then you'se is going to the hospital with your . . . legs broken. Then you come out then they is broken again and you'se goes back into the . . . hospital, even though I like you personally as a person. Warm regards, The Boot'.*

Reagan laughs off 'heart attack' but gives palpitations to friends

A soft and ample paunch thrust pugnaciously over the armrest of my seat on Ronald Reagan's campaign plane. It belonged to the governor's long time aide and crony, Lyn Nofziger, who has the permanently dishevelled look of a Bowery bum. 'Do you know what I'm doing?' he asked. 'I'm having a good time and I'm drinking.' He was indeed, deeply; from a large glass of the Bombay gin which United Airlines had stocked for his personal comfort.

This was not at all the atmosphere of gloom, even despair which, it has been reported, has shrouded the governor's campaign of late. Nofziger was exuberant: 'We've got the White House on the run. We hit them on the Middle East last night. Then before they knew what to say we hit them with the "Stealth bomber". Those assholes don't know where to turn.'

It had been a remarkable day during which Reagan, far from blundering, had shown his prowess as a powerful stump speaker. At noon on Thursday, he gave a rousing anti-Carter speech to businessmen in Jacksonville, Florida, then flew through an electrical storm to New Orleans where, on the creaking deck of a Mississippi paddle steamer, he gave another stirring oration.

At New Orleans airport, the governor loped athletically down the aircraft steps, to be greeted with the surprising news that he had suffered a heart attack en route from Jacksonville.

His phantom heart attack began, it seems, when a woman

phoned the radio station WNIF in New York with the bad news, then hung up. Although Wall Street experts believed it was the work of a speculator, Nofziger had a different interpretation. 'I'll tell you who started it,' he said. 'The White House. Now I'm going to start another rumour. Write this down, Jimmy Carter has the clap.'

All this raucous, almost bar-room good humour, cannot mask the fact that Reagan's campaign, if not his heart, is suffering severe palpitations.

After his nomination as Republican candidate in July he was leading Jimmy Carter in the polls by a healthy 45 to 31. Then the gap closed with Reagan 39 to Carter's 38. He intended to surge ahead in the final two months of the presidential race with swingeing attacks on Carter's vulnerable record. It did not work out quite like that. To Reagan's fury the newspapers were filled with his own indiscretions and 'misstatements'.

First, there was the shambles over US relations with Taiwan during the trip to China of his running-mate George Bush. Then Reagan dismayed Republican moderates by calling the American war in Vietnam 'a noble cause', and expressing doubt about the Darwinian theory of evolution. He accused Carter of campaigning in the birthplace of the Ku Klux Klan, which was both inaccurate and unfair.

A current joke about Reagan's performances: 'Today Ronald Reagan issued a clarification of yesterday's apology for his misstatement the day before.' As his former campaign manager John Sears said: 'If you are making your opponent the issue, then you should not be spending most of your time explaining why you are not an idiot.'

Most of Reagan's aides – Nofziger, Ed Meese, who runs the campaign, Bill Casey, the chairman, and Mike Deaver, another top man – are cronies from his California days. Then there is Richard Allen, who is tipped to be national security adviser in a Reagan administration. Allen is intelligent and hardworking. Last week he crafted two excellent Reagan speeches. Unlike the rest he has had Washington experience. He was President Nixon's deputy assistant for international and economic affairs and held a senior position under Henry Kissinger on the national security council.

His extra curricular activities, however, leave some room for doubt. Whilst an official under Nixon he was also a $10,000 a month consultant to financier Robert Vesco who was, at that time, allegedly looting hundreds of millions of dollars from the Geneva-based Investors Overseas Services.

Late on Thursday night, in the campaign bus on the way from Washington's Dulles Airport, Allen told me how both he and the governor had been misunderstood, especially by the British press whose coverage of Reagan had been, he said, immature. 'The correspondents have not sent full and accurate reports of Reagan's speeches back to their head offices,' said Allen. 'That means that the British editorial writers only have caricature impressions. You may quote me – if you do so accurately.'

Allen also said the British press portrayed Reagan as a cowboy, using photographs from his old films. That, he said, is a disgrace. In June, Allen met Margaret Thatcher who, he said, showed a deeper appreciation of the governor's finer points.

At last, on Thursday, the Reagan campaign slogan 'The time is now' proved to have some validity. His blistering attack on Carter for leaking highly secret details about the Stealth radar resistant aircraft for political purposes, grabbed the headlines and put Carter on the defensive. The continuing 'Billygate' investigation fed the Reagan offensive and these were just bonuses to Reagan's central attack on Carter's management of the economy.

The ebullient Nofziger even doubted if the Reagan goofs did any damage. 'The conservative Reagan constituency, and that's not small, got worried when moderates like Bill Casey, Anne Armstrong (former US ambassador to Britain) and Bush took the leading roles in the campaign. They wondered where Reagan was going. They liked those remarks about Vietnam, evolution and the Klan. It was like revaccinating the Reagan constituency. The media might write us off. But wait and see. Let's drink to that.'

Sunday Times
7 September 1980

Cash from ash

It was a typical evening at Earl and Dolly Truax's house in the small town of Battle Ground, Washington State. There was a large pile of fine, gritty dust on the kitchen table. Earl, a retired railwayman now in his 70s, sat in his red apron and spooned little heaps of ash into glass phials. His youthful second wife, Dolly, deftly popped corks in the top. She nudged Earl with her elbow: 'Come on, dear. Don't lose your concentration.'

Earl and Dolly were on the production line of their lucrative new business, Truax Industries. Hundreds of ash-filled phials stood in a box in the corner ready to bounce from the ear lobes or rest upon the bosoms of ladies in Washington, Oregon and California.

On a clear day Earl and Dolly used to be able to see, 30 miles away, the 9,677-foot tip of America's most celebrated volcano, Mount St Helens. They were not aware that deep below their feet giant, continent-sized plates which form the earth's crust were slowly shifting, getting hotter and building up an enormous explosive head of gas. In March this year the volcano began to rumble and the crater bulged, ominously. On 18 May at exactly 8.32 a.m. the top of the mountain blew off. The explosion was estimated to be 500 times more powerful than the atomic bomb dropped on Hiroshima. It took away 1,300 feet of the mountain. Clouds of ash, made of pulverized rock, rose 12 miles into the sky, while an avalanche of hot mud, rock and gas roared down the slopes and through the valleys.

Thirty-four people were killed and 28 are still missing. The scale of the devastation was staggering. It spewed out 1.5 million tons of debris; 5,900 miles of road were buried under ash; 150 square miles of timber were flattened. Volcanic ash landed by the ton in Idaho 300 miles away. It also descended on the front drive, roof, garden and the two cars of Earl and Dolly.

At first Earl, who was proud of his new ranch house and its neat gardens, was furious. 'Goddammit,' he said. 'That ash irritated me.' He clambered on to his roof and began sweeping it off. Then Dolly had a flash of inspiration. 'Honey,' she said to Earl. 'If we put that ash in bottles it would be a fine souvenir.' 'I think you could be right,' said Earl. He carefully gathered it up in buckets. They soon had a fine harvest of volcanic ash. Earl bought tiny spice bottles from Taiwan and Dolly attached key-rings, necklaces and ear-rings. They began hawking their wares at $2.95, $4.95 and $7.95 respectively to the avalanche of tourists that rolled into the area. Truax Industries had begun.

The intrepid Dolly tracked north towards the volcano along Interstate 5 towards Toutle River, which had taken the brunt of the eruption. There she gathered pieces of light pumice stone. She bought bottles of rattling plastic eyes from Japan and stuck two on each piece. It was the new Earl and Dolly line – 'Pumice Kids'.

Just after Mount St Helens exploded there was an eruption of a different kind among hundreds of people in Oregon and Washington – greed, or put more kindly, the old American instinct to make a fast buck. Chuck Jones and his wife Polly started up a company called Vulcanology Ltd. They brought out a Mount St Helens calendar and four volcano books, of which their latest, *Fire Mountain*, is hot off the presses at $9.95. 'We feel we are at the quality end of the market,' said Chuck. 'A lot of these junk souvenirs are going to go.'

Others found talents lying, like lava, deep inside them. Rory Hooper, a logger, was moved to write a poem about Mount St Helens and sell it at a dollar a sheet. 'Some can cuss and hate her,' wrote Hooper in reference to the mountain. 'Some can say she's bad. But I will always love her, For what we used to have.'

71

Another local man, Lawrence Dawson, rushed into print with his poem called 'Smoking Mountain' also on sale at Chet's place – 'Boats and Worms' says the sign – at Silver Lake on the road to Mount St Helens. People at Chet's feel Dawson has the poetic edge and his verse has a Miltonian ring to it, although no one quite understands what he means.

Rick Bartlett of Spirit Lake Highway wrote a quick ballad to Harry Truman, the 84-year-old who lived with 16 cats at a recreation lodge near Spirit Lake about five miles from the mountain. Harry became a national celebrity when he barked angrily at television crews: 'No one knows more about this mountain than Harry, and it don't dare blow up on him.' Harry and his cats are now missing, presumed dead. His camp lies under feet of steaming mud. But Bartlett is determined to see he lives on with his ballad on a 45 rpm record produced hastily and cheaply by a company in Vancouver, Canada.

Harry has spawned his own souvenir industry, with plates, mugs, posters and paintings showing his grizzled old face. But the real souvenir fall-out begins as visitors approach Mount St Helens along Interstate 5. At Exit 14 there is a barren piece of grass populated by a handful of makeshift shacks. There is a hastily constructed sign which says 'Official Viewpoint'. A steady stream of tourists was flowing in the mountain's direction and some stopped to have an 'official' view. Fifty-one-year-old John Wilcox, who owns the food concession and sells 'Volcanic Hamburgers' – ordinary hamburgers with mustard – showed them where the mountain was, pointing into an impenetrable mass of cloud. 'There she is, or she would be on a fine day.'

One of Wilcox's friends, who has also leased a few square feet of land from the local upholsterer at $100 a month, sells the usual range of Mount St Helens T-shirts, 'Mount St Helens registered belt buckles', plastic pens full of ash, Earl and Dolly's ear-rings and a plaster figure of a naked woman speckled with ash. In a shack next door Peter Kraakman sells pears and peaches 'grown on genuine Mount St Helens volcanic ash'. Not actually from this eruption, he points out, but ash from the one 134 years ago.

Wilcox says it has been a good summer, with about 500

tourists dropping in for a Volcanic Hamburger or a cup of coffee most days. Next summer, he says, will be great. 'People won't be afraid to come here, and we're setting up a Ferris wheel, a merry-go-round and a helicopter pad.'

His optimism is supported by the Washington State Tourist Board, which estimates that tourists will spend a staggering $300 million in the area over the next three years. 'We're going to make big bucks,' says Wilcox.

As you go down Route 504 towards Mount St Helens, the road is lined with little souvenir stands. Every gas station has its display of souvenir T-shirts, hats and badges showing photographs of smouldering volcanoes. Drews Grocery Store in Toutle sells two-pound bags of ash for $1.98; bits of pumice are 25 cents. Twenty-one miles from the peak you reach the 'red zone', where the police have blocked the road. It is a relief to find there a schoolteacher called Blair Barner – a man who is not making a buck from the devastation.

Barner had just built a spacious house on the banks of the Toutle River and was looking forward to the fine salmon and steel-head fishing. Then the mountain exploded. The mud poured down the river and into his house to a depth of four feet. Tourists who stop at the roadblock wander across into Barner's house to gaze at his mud-encased refrigerator and mud-filled bedroom and, occasionally, to fall into a small but treacherous hole in his floor. Hundreds of people come into his house every day, chat with Barner, take a photo and wander off. It is the best free tour in Washington State. But that very day temptation was gnawing at Barner. 'People say I'm crazy not to charge people a dollar to come in,' he said. 'Maybe I am. This place could be a gold mine.'

One man who would not have thought twice about charging two dollars is Joel Andrews a few miles down Route 504 at Silver Lake. Andrews is fast becoming the Rockefeller of the Mount St Helens tourist industry. 'I admit, I have got this all wrapped up,' said Andrews, who used to have a Hawaiian Hamburger concession, selling ordinary hamburgers with a slice of pineapple in them.

He quickly moved into 'Mountain Hamburgers' and with partner Larry Halstead he started Andrews Concessions Inc.

He was the first to come out with mass-produced items made to his specifications by a company in Iowa. He has a small factory in a shed where he makes the moulds for smoking volcano ashtrays. His site, on the banks of Silver Lake, is also an 'official viewpoint' and tourists were excited to see, 20 miles away, a smudge on the horizon. 'That,' said Larry Halstead, 'is Mount St Helens.'

Their range of souvenirs is dizzying and, Larry admits, near the bottom end of the market. He sells the 'Rockter Scale' – a spring stuck on a piece of rock which trembles even in a light breeze – Christmas balls with ash inside, candles shaped like volcanoes, 'Poff, the Magic Mountain Flick Book, a thumb-powered pocket movie', a silver commemorative coin, books, T-shirts, letter-openers, paperweights containing the all pervasive ash, a lurid picture of Mount St Helens painted in oils on a metal saw, and bumper stickers in dubious taste.

Larry and Joel offer boat tours on Silver Lake for a clearer view of the black smudge, and tours in the back of a pick-up truck to the borders of the 'red zone'.

But for up-market tours visitors should go to Rocky's Place, a tiny airstrip in Toledo a few miles away and another wooden shack which is Rocky's control tower and headquarters. A group of elderly ladies was sitting on a bench waiting for Rocky and his two staff pilots to take them up in single-engined Cessnas. As the planes are small and the air turbulence often enormous, these trips can be gruelling. 'Don't chuck up over me,' said the pilot. 'If you get sick do it over yourself.'

The plane bobbed through the air, avoiding the ash drifting from mountain slopes, over the grey mud and carpet of up-rooted trees towards the crater itself. It provides a view which moved President Jimmy Carter, who took a similar trip in an Air Force helicopter. 'There is no way to prepare oneself for the sight that we beheld this morning,' said Carter.

In their ranch-house in Battle Ground, Earl and Dolly are moved by emotions more basic than awe. Earl went up to the border of the 'red zone' the other day and a geologist who had returned from the crater told him there were new emissions of steam. Earl turned to a fellow souvenir vendor: 'I don't worry about no steam. That's money coming out of that volcano and it's going to land right in our pockets.'

Radio Times
19 December 1980

Jimmy the Weasel 'sings' Sinatra

'I'm King of the hill, head of the list, cream of the crop at the top of the heap,' croons Frank Sinatra in his recent hit song New York, New York. A week tomorrow, he will be. He has been appointed director and producer of the Inaugural Gala for the new President of the United States, his friend, Ronald Reagan. It will be a splendid affair. Sinatra has summoned some of America's top talent to Washington for Reagan's delectation: Bob Hope, Johnny Carson, Dean Martin, James Stewart, Charlton Heston, Donny and Marie Osmond.

Sinatra has always craved the respectability, and perhaps the influence, that accrues from friendship with a President. He almost made it 20 years ago with John Kennedy, but the relationship turned sour. He cultivated Vice-President Spiro Agnew and President Richard Nixon but the prize was snatched away by Watergate.

'King Frank I', 'Chairman of the Board', or 'Ol' Blue Eyes', as Sinatra is variously known, has almost everything else the world can offer. He has indeed done it 'his way'. The son of a bantamweight boxer from Hoboken, New Jersey, his career as singer, entertainer and film actor has hardly faltered, but for a brief dip in the late Forties. At 65, he still evokes adulation.

He reigns over the entertainment world from his opulent home at Rancho Mirage in Palm Springs, southern California, lavishing largesse on his friends, showering $100 chips on waiters and porters. He has a helicopter to whisk him to his private jet. He is cocooned by aides and armed security guards. His temper, once notorious, has mellowed somewhat; but he likes his privacy. The sign on his gate once said: 'If you haven't been invited you better have a damn good reason for ringing this bell.'

Ronald Reagan could have rung Frank's bell anytime and been confident of a warm reception, for the two men have been friendly for ten years. In 1976, Reagan took a day off from his election campaign to attend Sinatra's wedding to Barbara Marx, his fourth wife, at Rancho Mirage. Reagan's nominee as US attorney general, William French Smith, is also close to Sinatra. Exactly a month ago, on the day after Reagan announced his appointment, Smith flew to Rancho Mirage for Sinatra's 65th birthday.

When Sinatra applied recently to the Nevada Gaming Control Board for readmittance to the gambling scene he was asked to give a personal reference. He gave the best: Ronald Reagan, President-elect of the United States. 'The governor is not disturbed,' said a Reagan aide, comparing it simply to a credit-card reference.

Perhaps Reagan's aides did not know why Sinatra lost his gaming licence in the first place, although the facts are on record and well known. In 1963 he was accused of playing host at a Nevada casino, the Cal Neva Lodge, to Sam Giancana, reputedly the Mafia boss of Chicago.

But Reagan and his attorney general cannot be unaware of the dozens of stories linking Sinatra with members of organized crime. They date back to 1947 when Sinatra visited Havana, Cuba, and met 'Lucky' Luciano, the exiled Mafia leader.

Some of the names linked with the singer since then would be decidedly out of place on an Inaugural Gala guest list. They appear instead on the files of the FBI's organized crime squad. They include Aladena (Jimmy 'the Weasel') Fratiano, a self-confessed Mafia murderer; Joseph Barboza, another self-confessed killer; Raymond Patriarca, Mafia boss of New England, now in prison; Carlo Gambino, alleged *capo di tutti capi* (boss of bosses), now dead; Willy Moretti, and Rocco and Joseph Fischetti, all cousins of the late Al Capone.

None of such well-publicized associations seems to have bothered Reagan and his aides unduly. But in the past week, an embarrassing spate of fresh reports about Sinatra's gangland connections have caused many people to question the propriety of the new President and his attorney general endorsing the reputation of a man who, at the very least, keeps questionable company.

'Let party-goer Smith review the FBI's Sinatra file. Then let him tell the Senate to what extent he thinks it proper for a friend of mobsters to profit from being the chum of the chief executive and of the man who runs the department of justice,' wrote William Safire, the respected conservative commentator, in the *New York Times*.

According to *Newsweek* magazine, Sinatra is now the subject of a New York federal grand jury investigation for allegedly receiving $50,000 in 'skimmed' profits from the bankrupted Westchester Premier Theatre in Tarrytown, New York, where Sinatra gave several concerts. (Grand jury investigations are secret, and the legal authorities will neither confirm nor deny this.)

A photograph taken in the theatre's dressing room in 1976 shows Sinatra with a group of known gangsters. Smiling almost as widely as Sinatra is Jimmy the Weasel, who has since become the most informative witness on Mafia activities that federal investigators have ever dealt with. Sinatra has his arms around Gregory De Palma and Thomas Marson, who, together with Richard Fusco later pleaded guilty to 'skimming' money from the theatre. Joseph Gambino was sentenced to ten years imprisonment in 1977 for income tax evasion, extortion, conspiracy and racketeering. The senior member of the party was the late Carlo Gambino, Joseph Gambino's uncle.

In the past few months, Jimmy the Weasel has been 'star witness' in many criminal proceedings against his former friends. Next month, a book about his exploits will be published. Now 67, he spoke cheerfully on US television last week about murdering five people (two with a garotte) – and about Sinatra:

Fratiano: 'Jilly Rizzo [a male friend of Sinatra's] told me that Frank [Sinatra] wanted the legs broken of some guy that was writing a story about him in the paper or in a book. . . .'

Interviewer: 'Did you ever break his legs?'

Fratiano: 'No, we couldn't find him.'

Both Rizzo and Sinatra have refused to comment on this. But it will be galling indeed for Sinatra if the spectre of his Mafia friendships should again deprive him of the respect of the most powerful man in the world, just as the prize seems firmly within his grasp.

Twenty years ago, Sinatra's relationship with President Kennedy was wrecked by a gangster's moll. Sinatra had stumped with Kennedy in the primaries, solicited contributions, and staged Kennedy's Inaugural Gala.

He did the President another favour: he introduced him to a former girlfriend called Judith Campbell. Now Mrs Exner, she claims in her book *My Story* that the introduction led to an affair. A few weeks later Sinatra did exactly the same favour for Sam Giancana, and for a time Campbell was then simultaneously dating the President and a leading mobster. There is no evidence that the link was used by the Mafia, or by Sinatra, to bring pressure on the President. That it existed at all was bad enough.

There is evidence, however, that the US attorney general, the President's brother Bobby, did not pursue the Sinatra/Mafia connection as fervently as some of his investigators would have wished. In 1962 and 1963 the justice department prepared several long reports on Sinatra's ties with the underworld. They were sent to Bobby Kennedy, but no further action was taken. 'Bobby would always tell us "peel the banana, attack the respectable associates of the Mafia," but when we tried to go after Sinatra rigorous new standards went up,' said a former official.

But, it seems, the President realized his indiscretion. In 1962 Kennedy announced that he would be Sinatra's house guest in Palm Springs. As Sinatra prepared for the visit, even building a new wing for the President, the White House suddenly announced that Kennedy would stay at Bing Crosby's house instead. The mortified Sinatra had lost a friend. Kennedy never invited him to the White House again.

Perhaps piqued by this rejection, Sinatra had a political change of heart. He had been a lifelong Democrat – his mother was a party organizer in New Jersey – but in 1970 he switched to the Republicans, becoming co-chairman of the committee to re-elect Ronald Reagan as governor of California.

In 1972 he plunged enthusiastically into Richard Nixon's re-election campaign. And the following year he got his reward when Nixon invited him to sing at the White House.

Meanwhile he faced a select committee on crime, after a convicted Mafia killer, Joseph Barboza, alleged that Sinatra had acted as a front for members of the mob. Sinatra was truculent and aggrieved. He glared at the congressmen and said: 'This bum [Barboza] went running off at the mouth . . . I resent it.'

The hearing ended well for him. He received compliments and apologies from the congressmen and only a mild rebuke from one committee member who suggested that as Sinatra was such a fine performer he should be more careful in checking out his investments.

Now, with another 'bum running off at the mouth' in the shape of Jimmy the Weasel, Sinatra may already feel that he has pushed his friendship with Ronald Reagan too far, too fast.

The gaming licence application on which he quoted Reagan as a referee would allow him to become entertainment and public relations director of Caesar's Palace in Las Vegas. According to the investigation division of the Nevada gaming commission, the casino is owned by Desert Palace Inc., which is owned by Caesar's World Inc., which is owned by Clifford S. Perlman. Perlman was recently asked to withdraw from the casino in Atlantic City, New Jersey, because, New Jersey investigators alleged, he had contact with an underworld financier.

On Friday, Sinatra withdrew Reagan's name as a character reference. 'Circumstances have changed since Mr Reagan's name was submitted as a reference,' said Sinatra's attorney.

Sunday Times
11 January 1981

Lovely Rita's acts of congress give Washington the shudders

The lady looked as the wife of a US congressman from a conservative southern state should – pretty, yet demure, as she stood in a knitted lilac dress and matching shoes by an ornamental pool in Dallas, Texas, last Wednesday.

It took a keen eye to spot signs of the sex scandal now bursting over the nation's highest officials in Washington. The body under that knitted dress was perhaps a little too curvaceous, the face too pretty. Embedded in the ruby red nail polish of one finger was a little diamond, a present from the Playboy king, Hugh Hefner. And a small black wire protruded from the back of her dress. It was a remote microphone.

Rita Jenrette, estranged wife of a former congressman, John Jenrette, who was convicted in the Abscam bribery scandal, was about to tell yet another television crew her story of drugs, drink and affairs of state that never make the public record.

Congressmen sweated and state governors trembled as she threatened: 'I am going to name names.'

Rita and her revelations were eagerly received by a public that enjoys nothing more than a juicy scandal on Capitol Hill. She has also revealed large expanses of her ample body in the pages of Playboy magazine, dressed, though barely, in a negligee and black stockings. 'I was told I look like Marilyn Monroe,' she said. 'I didn't mean to take my clothes off but when I got into the studio I just did. I don't think it's tacky though, do you?' Indeed not.

The photographs of Rita deshabillée were counterpointed with more chaste pictures of her from her husband's congressional days – receiving a smile and a handshake from former president Jimmy Carter and attending a White House reception with Carter's wife.

Rita has been talking more than undressing on a Playboy-sponsored national tour that is presidential in its scale. She has talked about a bizarre act of congress – making love late one evening on the steps of the Capitol; of cavorting in hot tubs with distinguished Washingtonians; of a Congressman who slipped her an illegal drug during an attempted seduction; of another who frequented Washington's massage parlours and encouraged his wife to join in; of the weekend love-nests of South Carolina dignitaries.

And she has talked endlessly about her husband John – his drunkenness, his frequent infidelities and, ultimately, his conviction for taking bribes.

Rita has risen spectacularly in the past week to join that exclusive group of women who kissed the mighty, then told – for substantial and usually undisclosed fees. (Rita is certainly not disclosing hers, though she is expected to make well over $100,000 from *Playboy* and from her book, which will appear in two weeks.)

First there was Judith Exner, who two-timed the late President John Kennedy with a leader of organized crime. Elizabeth Ray told all about Congressman Wayne Hays, who had employed her, on a substantial federal salary, as his secretary even though she said: 'I can't type. I can't file, I can't even answer the phone.' Then Wilbur Mills, the long-serving congressman from Arkansas, saw his career collapse in ruins because of his relationships with 'the Argentine firecracker', a striptease dancer called Fanne Foxe. Now there is Rita.

She arrived in Washington from Texas in August 1975 as a 25-year-old researcher for the Republican national committee. On her first day she met Jenrette, a Democratic congressman from South Carolina. He was a striking figure, she said, in green, orange and yellow plaid jacket. He came quickly to the point. 'Hi,' he said. 'How would you like to go to the Virgin

Islands with me? We'll lie in the sand nude all day and make love all night.'

The startled Rita declined. A month later Jenrette came up with another, albeit less glamorous, proposition, to go to a reception at the Romanian embassy.

'Yes, please,' she said, and their romance began. They lived together, then married, then regretted it. Rita should perhaps have been warned by Jenrette's messy divorce from his first wife, who cited 23 co-respondents. She says she knew the honeymoon was over when she woke up one morning to find Jenrette lying on the floor wrapped in the embrace of a woman 'old enough to be his mother.' In the next five years, she says, she caught him in similarly compromising positions about 14 times.

Jenrette was not only susceptible to pretty women. He also succumbed to the financial proposition of an Arab sheik representing a company called Abdul Enterprise who offered him a substantial bribe. As Jenrette quickly discovered, he was a victim of the elaborate FBI Abscam operation. He was video-taped accepting the bribe, and was convicted.

Rita did not help his case when she discovered $25,000 hidden in a shoe in his bedroom closet. She handed the money over to her lawyer. Some of the notes came from the FBI's Abscam bribe.

Rita is making the most of what may be a brief blaze of notoriety. According to the Washington columnist Jack Anderson, she may soon be eclipsed by a new scandal which will catch another crop of congressmen in *flagrante delicto*. This time the star is a blonde and shapely lobbyist called Paula Parkinson.

Paula is hiding away in Texas, writing the inevitable book. Her lawyer told Anderson: 'This is big. Very big.'

Sunday Times
8 March 1981

The city where children fear to play

I met 'Chicken' George by chance last Wednesday as he played baseball in a public park on Atlanta's South Side. He was not very friendly. 'What you want?' he said. 'F . . . off!' Like most black teenagers in Atlanta these days, he does not like strangers. A group of his friends approached somewhat aggressively, and he shouted out: 'Watch out, you gonna get abducted.'

Chicken George Bell had every reason to be suspicious and afraid. His 14-year-old brother Jo-Jo (Joseph) had been missing from home for a week. On Friday Jo-Jo's photograph was flashed on to every television screen in America. He had become statistic number 22 on the Atlanta police department's list of missing and dead children.

Twenty of the black youngsters on the list – 18 boys and two girls, aged from seven to 15 – are dead, all murdered, since July 1979. Two more 10-year-olds are now officially missing: Darren Glass and Joseph Bell. For Jo-Jo's mother, Doris, it is like a death sentence. 'We're all mixed up,' she said yesterday. 'It's like a disease going round.'

'He was street-wise, real cool,' said Beverley, one of Jo-Jo's friends. Chicken George says, hopefully, that his brother 'might be with his kin'. Most of Atlanta's 20 murdered children were 'street-wise', coming from poor black families on the South Side.

Most of them were from broken homes or lived with foster

parents. Many hustled in the streets to earn an extra dollar. Like Jo-Jo, who used to work at weekends in the fish market, many had spare-time jobs. They were confident and in some cases tough. It did not protect them.

Last week, for the first time, Atlanta's murders became a national issue. Yesterday Vice-President George Bush made an official visit to Atlanta's mayor, Maynard Jackson, and the police task force set up to crack the case. On Friday President Reagan announced a $1,500,000 (£650,000) grant to help pay for the police investigation, which is costing $250,000 a month.

Last Tuesday Sammy Davis Jnr, Frank Sinatra, Burt Reynolds and Roberta Flack arrived for a fund-raising concert. On Friday there was a vigil in Washington for the Atlanta children and a march in Harlem, New York.

Understandably, some blacks see a national conspiracy in it, although without a shred of evidence. They link the Atlanta murders with the killings of six black adults in Buffalo, New York State, four of whom had their hearts cut out, and even the shooting of black leader Vernon Jordan.

Atlanta has no lack of good will, and Americans have started to wear green ribbons in sympathy for the dead children. But the killings continue. On Wednesday the twentieth victim. 13-year-old Curtis Walker, whose body was hauled out of the South River on March 6, was buried. Like one other victim, he was clothed only in his underwear, and like three others he was killed by what the police call 'gentle asphyxiation' – some object held over the mouth and nose.

The police have processed 20,000 tips from the public, have phoned 150,000 people, and interviewed thousands. They have used hypnosis, voice analysis, and the latest computer techniques for sifting information. They are being helped by 40 FBI agents and homicide experts from six cities.

But the only thing every killing has in common is that the police have no idea at all on who did it. They believe there is not one killer on the loose in Atlanta but several, perhaps as many as 14. There are substantial links between only seven of the deaths.

On Thursday night Officer Danny Sailers from the Atlanta Police Department cruised through Zone Five, the city's downtown area. There is now a 7 p.m. curfew on all children under 14, although its value is limited as most victims were abducted before sunset. The streets were eerily deserted.

'I normally have to brake a dozen times to avoid kids,' said Sailers, as we drove through a black housing project without seeing a single child. He shares the anxiety and frustration, having worked for days on the case of 11-year-old Patrick Baltazar, victim number 19. Patrick disappeared in broad daylight.

For lack of hard evidence, rumour and fear abound. Most blacks think the killer, or killers, are white. Most whites think they are black: 'What honkey [white man] could persuade a black kid to go with him?' said a former Atlanta policeman. One street rumour is that the killer is a policeman. Some think a woman is responsible, or a homosexual, or a religious cult. Others believe that a whole group of white racists is responsible for all the killings.

Mothers said their children would not even walk to the local shops on their own. A teacher said that one 13-year-old at her school was seen toting a 0.38 revolver. Marvin, a 10-year-old, carries a large knife whenever he leaves his housing project.

Given this level of suspicion and anxiety, it is perhaps surprising that there is no sign of racial tension in Atlanta. The city is balanced fairly evenly between black and white, and during the turbulent Sixties it advertised itself as 'the city too busy to hate'. This good humour has continued. 'Everybody is helping everybody else, black or white,' said the headmistress of a black school.

There is a danger, however, that the investigation will turn into what the *Atlanta Constitution* newspaper called 'a grotesque circus' as the city begins to dominate the national attention. Last week, for example, a group of psychics were imported by the *National Enquirer* newspaper and began poking around in the areas where bodies were found.

'I feel something in my feet. They are burning,' squealed one fat lady seer. More than 2,000 psychics have sent their contributions to the city's police.

Some believe the biggest circus is the Atlanta police department itself. The bodies of the first two children, Edward Smith,

14, and Alfred Evans, 13, were found one Sunday in July 1979 by a woman scavenging for aluminium cans. One had been shot, the other was too decomposed to determine the cause of death. But it was not until seven black children were dead and their parents held a press conference that the police formed the special team.

The horror is that the publicity created by the parents may have prompted other 'copycat' killers. Since July 1980, a distinct pattern in the killings has emerged. The cause of death has been asphyxiation or strangulation. Some of the bodies have been found in similar positions – laid out on their backs, arms extended above the head, the face turned sideways. Some of the bodies seem to have been carefully washed.

Only one victim, a 12-year-old black girl, Angel Lanier, showed any sign of sexual abuse. Most of the bodies were unmarked. Only one boy seems to have resisted, although some of the victims were fit and tough.

The police investigation has been marred by bungled evidence-gathering – the remains of two bodies were dumped in one bag, and bones and teeth have been left at the scene of the crime – and mix-ups between different departments.

The man who takes the brunt of all this – and has, perhaps, the most unenviable job in America today – is Atlanta's black police commissioner, Lee P. Brown. He has a PhD in criminology from Berkeley University, experience on the beat and a sound reputation with his men. But under the daily barrage from the press, public, and politicians, he has begun to lurk behind a fog of polysyllables. 'We have potential problem areas,' said a perspiring Brown last week, adding vaguely that 'we have a multi-jurisdictional organization.'

Jargon is not the only commodity on the increase in Atlanta, however. As the leads diminish, so the paranoia among blacks and whites, young and old, grows. When police officer Sailers stopped alongside two blacks, one of them said: 'Oh, no,' and started to run. 'It's okay,' said officer Sailers, 'I ain't gonna grab you.' This time, at least, the reassurance worked.

Sunday Times
15 March 1981

The 'Valium of America' backs old formula to hook Britain

On the night of Saturday, October 3, British viewers will, for the first time, see the most hallowed ritual of American television. It will happen exactly like this: there will be a raucous blast of trumpets. Then a huge man with a beer belly and florid complexion, called Ed McMahon, will shout, his voice rising to a crescendo: 'Heeeeeeere's Johnny!'

There will be thunderous applause, whistles and shrieks as the TV camera snaps to a gold, pink and blue striped curtain. (The ritual is so beloved that when NBC rashly changed the colour of the curtain, there was a national outcry. It was quickly changed back.) The curtain will swish aside and a 55-year-old man with greying hair and a conservative suit will step diffidently forwards.

He will stroke his nose with one finger, pull at his cuffs, touch his tie and rock slightly on his feet. So it will be, and so it has always been for the past 19 years the opening of the *Tonight* show, starring Johnny Carson.

The late Kenneth Tynan called him 'the Valium of America'. And the addiction to Carson is staggering. He has been watched by more people than anyone else in the history of television. Most nights of the week at 11.30 a devoted following of 15.5 million Americans stays up to watch him. His total audience during the show has been 60 billion people. He is paid more than anyone else on television – and perhaps simply more than anyone else at all. His contract for the *Tonight* show gives him more than five million dollars for four hours a week, 37 weeks a year.

That works out at almost $34,000 an hour. And it does not include the substantial profits from his companies, Carson Production Inc. and Carson Production TV, his appearances in advertisements, his Las Vegas performances and TV specials. He has a profitable clothing company and a large stake in the production of the De Lorean car, which is manufactured in Northern Ireland. His show alone provides the mighty NBC with 17 per cent of its net profit.

'God knows, I have all the material comforts,' Carson once said. This has not quenched his ambition. Although he is better known than almost anyone else in North America, to his irritation he is largely unknown in the rest of the world.

As Tynan said: 'The reason for this obscurity is that the job at which he excels is virtually unexportable.' Carson, however, is determined to try. The show now appears in Canada, Australia and New Zealand. He has sold 13 shows to London Weekend Television, and in October he will burst upon the British market. 'If Benny Hill can come over here I don't understand why the British won't understand Johnny,' said his publicist, Joe Bleedon.

Johnny, though, has a nagging fear about British reception of a show made specifically for Americans. 'We are going to refuse to pander to the British audience,' he said on Thursday's show. 'The show is going to be the same as it has, uh, always been. Isn't that right, old bean?' he said to Ed McMahon. 'Quite so, my Lord,' said McMahon. But Carson admitted: 'Part of the monologue might be vague for viewers in England. Sometimes it's vague for viewers here. From now on, during the monologue, we're going to put John Gielgud in a corner of the studio translating what medflies* and chicken McNuggets* mean.'

Last week I was permitted briefly to enter the inner sanctum of Carson Productions at the NBC studio in Burbank, Hollywood. I was shown Carson's parking space, his black Mercedes, and the armed guard who stands next to it. I was shown JC's coffee mug. During the taping of the show, I was given the best seat in the house – a mere five feet from the great man himself. Next to me was Carson addict George Slack, an elderly insurance salesman, and behind me was Audie Foot, who, in a desperate effort to attract a glance from his hero, wore a rubber chicken on his head.

The great mystery is how a chat show host has achieved extraordinary national eminence. Carson can be sloppy. He is lowbrow and fiercely proud of it. His show is not there to inform, he says, but to entertain. He dislikes having politicians on the show because he finds them boring, and relies on a familiar stable of showbiz stars and Las Vegas entertainers. On the whole, he dislikes British comedians: 'I find them unfunny, infantile, and obsessed with toilet jokes.'

During his interviews he relies, like President Reagan during his speeches, on printed cards. His monologue is written on a huge piece of cardboard 12ft long and 3ft high. He sometimes forgets the names of his guests and is hazy about what they do. The British actor Jim Dale had a miserable experience with Carson. 'He didn't know anything about me,' said Dale. 'He asked me something about what it's like to be English.' Some of his jokes bring groans from his audience, such as his 'Joke du jour' on Thursday: 'Martians land on the White House lawn and ask a guard if they can talk to President Reagan as they intend to wipe out planet Earth. "I don't know if we can wake him for that," says the guard.' Loud groans.

Occasionally, his interviews peter out into silence. But the ratings never flounder. As the dean of comics, George Burns, said of Carson, 'When it comes to saving a bad joke, he is the master.'

'He fashions victory from failure,' said Tynan. One of dozens of joke writers who have been hired and fired from the *Tonight* show described Carson's appeal. Every day he and the other writers had to deliver some 80 one-liners on to Carson's desk. He would select about 16 for his monologue.

'It comes down to who do you want to invite into your living room?' said the writer. 'The answer for Americans is Carson. He has mid-Western charm mixed with urban wit. He is sarcastic but still likeable, risqué but never rude. He is utterly predictable. He's at home with a vast variety of guests. He is simply brilliant.'

The Carson staff can already sniff victory in their British

invasion next month, when it is likely Carson will be slotted opposite the BBC's chat show host, Michael Parkinson. He is not considered a grave threat at Burbank. 'Who is this Parkington?' asked a Carson staffer. 'Do you mean Parkinson?' 'Yeah, that's him. Is he some kind of schmuck?'

*To understand Carson's jokes you need a crash course in Californian sub-culture. The *medfly* is a source of dozens of Carson cracks (eg: Governor Brown is killing them with his solar-powered fly-swat). It is in fact a fly which is threatening California's fruit crops prompting helicopter spraying in affected areas. A *chicken McNugget* is a small lump of chicken sold by McDonalds. Other mystifying words abound. *Jack in the Box*, *Bob's Big Boy*, and *Taco Bell* are names of fast food restaurants. A *Whopper* is a hamburger. *Senator Hayahawa* is a Californian politican, who frequently falls asleep in the US Senate. *Rodeo Drive* is the swankiest street in Beverly Hills. *Bel Air* is the richest neighbourhood.

Sunday Times
13 September 1981

Darwin in the dock

Federal district judge William R. Overton rubbed his eyes
vigorously with thumb and forefinger, like a man waking from
a bad dream.

In pursuit of an answer to the vexed question of human
origins, an assistant attorney-general had just thrown a question at Professor Harold Morowitz of Yale: 'According to the
second law of thermodynamics, is it possible to create life from
non-life in an equilibrium state?'

Morowitz, a world authority on the second law, glowered, as
if looking at a primitive life-form. Overton's patience cracked.

'Say what?' he drawled. 'What was that question you asked?'

'I don't have any idea, your honour,' said the assistant-
attorney, and sat down.

Overton's impatience was understandable. He had sat
through several days of philosophical and scientific evidence,
discussions about ultimate reality, primary and secondary
causation, 'punctuated equilibrium', pantheism and the
metaphysical foundations of modern empirical thought.

He can perhaps console himself with the thought that he will
surely make his mark on American legal history with civil
action LRC 81322, which began last week in courtroom 419
above a downtown post office in Little Rock, Arkansas. Twenty-
three local plaintiffs, backed by the American Civil Liberties
Union, are challenging Act 590, passed last March by the state
legislature, which would require school science classes to teach

biblical as well as evolutionary theories of the origin of man. Proponents of 'creation science' claim there is scientific evidence to show that the world was created in six days, according to a literal reading of the Book of Genesis.

A battery of 11 lawyers from the ACLU are fighting the Act on the grounds that 'creation science' is religion, not science, and therefore infringes the first amendment of the US Constitution which bans the teaching of religion in schools.

The view from Overton's bench must be extraordinary. On his left are the evolution witnesses, mostly men in crumpled suits with hair curling untidily about their ears and unkempt beards which they stroke and tug while giving evidence. 'Ain't never seen so many beards in the whole of Arkansas,' said a court secretary. In the body of the courtroom sits a grim contingent of religious fundamentalists, large men crammed into three-piece suits of dazzling hues. On Overton's left is a bench full of court artists. One of them has a huge tray of paints and seems prepared for the Sistine chapel. The artist from ABC TV is a lady who wears binoculars fixed to her spectacles and studies every magnified flicker of emotion on Overton's face. 'Know what I had to draw yesterday?' she said. 'The creation.'

On Tuesday, a man dressed in a gorilla suit appeared outside the courtroom carrying a placard with a question mark written on it. It was one of the more comprehensible statements of the week.

The case has obvious parallels with the celebrated 'monkey trial' of 1925 in Tennessee, when John Scopes was convicted for teaching the Darwinian theory, then considered blasphemous. But the issue is still a live one in Arkansas, which allowed evolution to be taught in schools only 15 years ago. A recent poll by the ABC television network showed that more than 70 per cent of the state's inhabitants believe literally in the biblical story of creation.

Little Rock (population 350,000), which is internationally known for the integration battles of the Fifties and the explosion of a Titan missile in its silo last year, has been gripped by feverish interest in the evolution-creation battle. In the back bar of the Sam Peck motel, opposite the courtroom, the country

94

and western music of Lynne and Red was drowned by a spirited discussion between evolution experts on hermeneutics and teleology. The girl behind the counter at the office products shop in the high street gave a lively discourse on the carbon dating of fossils. The local pest-controller came down solidly on the creationist side: 'I wasn't brought up to think man came from apes,' he said.

The battle has even trickled down to what must be the lowest form of entertainment in Little Rock. On Thursday night four local ladies wrestled in a vat of chocolate pudding. The bar where they performed is called The Missing Link. 'Come on down,' said the bar owner. 'Come and get splattered.'

But the issue is not confined to Arkansas. The creationists are a growing power in the land. Similar legislation to Act 590 is pending in 15 states and the movement is not restricted to the southern 'bible belt' where religious fundamentalism has been strong for more than a century. Cases have been brought by creationists in California and New York.

The fears of evolutionists were expressed in a recent article by the scientist and author Isaac Asimov: 'With creation in the saddle, American science will wither. We will raise a generation of ignoramuses. We will inevitably recede into the backwaters of civilization.'

The genesis of Act 590 is as murky as that of life itself. It appears to have been the result, not of a national effort by the fundamentalist movement, but of a series of flukes and accidents by a tiny number of believers. And that it passed into law is due not to the creationist fervour of the Arkansas legislature, but to its idleness.

The Act's creator is an X-ray technician called Paul Ellwanger from South Carolina. Neither a lawyer nor a scientist, he drew up a roughly-worded proposal which was honed into its present form by some more qualified creationist colleagues. Ellwanger then sent it off to the followers of a small organization run from his home called Citizens for Fairness in Education. It included a few people in Arkansas. 'They phoned me up at the beginning of February and told me they were going to get it into state law,' said Ellwanger. 'I said, "Don't be ridiculous. You don't have time this year." Then, blow me down, two months later it was law.'

The man who introduced it into the state senate is Senator Jim Holsted, an insurance salesman and creationist, who is under indictment for embezzlement. In the waning hours one night last March, it passed through both houses with barely a vote of opposition. 'I have been sick about it ever since,' said Senator Ben Allen, the pro tem senate president.

'I voted for it, but I hadn't read it and didn't really know what it said,' Allen said last week. 'We discussed it for about a minute. The assembly did not pay attention. Most of us felt it was meaningless, just a piece of junk, so why not vote for it. I am sick as hell.'

The new Democratic governor of Arkansas, Frank White, who is a fundamentalist, signed the act but says he didn't read it properly. So Act 590 became law.

Last week evolutionists of many hues joined forces to try to reverse the process. Methodist church leaders took the stand to argue that creationism is religion and should not be confused with science. They argued that if schools teach creationism, a fundamentalist view, then all other religions should also be taught.

A geologist who studied moon rocks for the US space agency, Nasa, argued the case for the carbon dating of fossils in testimony so obscure that one reporter emerged from court with a single word on his note pad: 'Rocks.' America's most eminent evolution scientists, including the celebrated Stephen Jay Gould, professor of geology, biology and history of science at Harvard University, poured meticulously argued scorn on the creationist case.

But the award for intellectual pyrotechnics must go to Dr Langdon Gilky, a leading theologian from the University of Chicago. Tugging his beard, raising his eyes perhaps to a divine presence somewhere over Judge Overton's head, Gilky gave a discourse which will be admired in university common rooms for years to come. 'What is the meaning of religion?' asked the state attorney, somewhat unwisely. Gilky took a deep breath and sprinted off into definitions of ultimate reality,

96

the ex-nihilo interpretation of genesis, gnostic heresy, cyclical time, Popperian theory of scientific falsification, primary and secondary causality. In one remarkable sentence, Gilky mentioned Copernicus, Galileo, Newton, Descartes and St Thomas Aquinas. He referred frequently to Aquinas with the familiarity of an old friend. Judge Overton sat still, as if frozen in time, interjecting occasionally . . . 'Hang on there a moment, doctor. Ahm makin a coupla notes.'

At some points in cross-examination, Gilky became snappy: 'I have not said that everything in religion has to do with ultimate origins. I have said everything to do with ultimate origins is religious. That's completely different.'

'What do you mean by "why"?' he snapped at one point. 'I mean "why",' said the puzzled state attorney. 'Such a "why" question refers to primary cause as defined by Galileo and Aquinas and is not relevant,' said Gilky.

After giving evidence, he sipped a gin martini in the Sam Peck bar, tired but jubilant. 'I think the only person who could have made me sweat in there would have been A. J. Ayer. Ayer [the British logical positivist] would have said I was talking as much rubbish as the creationists.'

The creationists in court were neither persuaded nor impressed by Dr Gilky. 'I'll tell you what that was,' said a fundamentalist butane gas delivery man from Arkansas. 'That was cotton pickin' bullshit.'

The creationists began their evidence in support of Act 590 on Friday afternoon with an assertion that there was nothing necessarily religious about God. Norman Geisler, a theological professor from Dallas, said that God was religion only when accompanied by faith and could otherwise be dealt with as philosophy and history. He acknowledged under cross-examination that he believed in UFOs as 'satanic manifestations for the purposes of deception'.

Another state witness is Professor N. C. Wickramasinghe from University College, Cardiff, who flew to Little Rock yesterday. A colleague of the astro-physicist, Sir Fred Hoyle, he will argue that the Darwinist position is weak, non-factual, and indistinguishable from theological argument. 'In the state of our knowledge of life it is arrogant to say the creator is ruled out,' he said on the phone from Wales on Friday. 'I believe that evolution is one of the greatest evils of the twentieth century. By the way, what's the weather like in Arkansas? Is it cold or what?'

Wickramasinghe is one of the delights to which Judge Overton can look forward this week. Overton left the court on Friday looking weary, his mind humming perhaps with rival arguments about the pros and cons of the second law of thermodynamics.

He must look back with nostalgia on his more clearcut cases, such as the kidnapping of a drug dealer by a hillybilly gangster called Bumgarner, whom he sentenced to five years in jail. The case moves into its seventh day tomorrow. And as the *Arkansas Gazette* pointed out, that is one more day than the creator took to produce the entire universe, according to the creationists.

Sunday Times
13 December 1981

Ah well, it's back to the HP sauce

David Blundy, who has spent the past 3½ years as our New York correspondent, returns to the London office in the New Year

I seem to have aged 30 years in a split second. Returning from the Creation trial in Little Rock, Arkansas, I bent to pick up my suitcase loaded with such weighty tomes as Cosmos by Carl Sagan and the Arkansas Hogs by Matt Bradley and a muscle in my back snapped like a guitar string. Divine wrath, the fundamentalists would say.

Now I am lying on my back helpless as a turtle. My eminent New York physician is unsympathetic. I cannot go to him and he will not come to me. 'Relax,' he says. 'This could take four weeks. Have a lot of hot tubs.' How do I get into the hot tubs? 'Like a dog,' he says. 'Head first.'

It's a lousy way to finish three and a half years as New York correspondent. As I drift on powerful painkillers the Christmas muzak pouring out of the easylistening station on the radio makes me nostalgic. I remember the same tapes in 1978 in the Pegasus Hotel in Georgetown, Guyana. God Rest Ye Merry Gentlemen made a strange accompaniment to interviews with the survivors of the Jonestown massacre. Last Christmas it poured out of the loudspeakers by the pool of the Prince Hotel in Port au Prince, Haiti, until a Swiss pilot called George, maddened by Jingle Bells, ripped down the control box.

New York is not a bad place to be ill in. I can look out of my 24th-storey window at one of the world's finest views, from the Empire State building which is illuminated red and green and wreathed in cloud, across the aluminium spire of the Chrysler building to the thin wedge of the UN building by the East River.

I am succoured by American television. I cannot understand why the British are so snobbish about their measly three channels. In New York I have about 28. Even at two in the morning I can watch Mary Tyler Moore reruns, four or five old movies, a movie in Spanish, obscenities on a private cable channel, a 24-hour news show or just watch the Reuters wire service rolling across the screen. There is a personal message channel on which someone could if they wished send me condolences about my back.

Recently I was eating hasty pudding (a glutinous mixture of pumpkin, breadcrumbs and ice cream) in the Harvard Club with my colleague Walter Isaacson from *Time* magazine. The beady eyes of an elephant shot by the late president Teddy Roosevelt stared down from the wall. Around me are the beadier eyes of the bosses of American corporations, past and present advisers to presidents, ancient cabinet secretaries. It has the ambience and power of a British club at the turn of the century and I will miss it, not least because Isaacson, as the member, has to pay.

Isaacson is going on about how none of the foreign press covered the American election last year as well as Alexis de Tocqueville, author of Democracy in America, covered the country in the 19th Century. A pompous observation, but true. However, would de Tocqueville have fared so well on a modern American campaign which for its mind-numbing qualities could have been designed by the late Jim Jones?

Isaacson and I crisscrossed the continent sometimes twice a day, freezing with George Bush in New England, sweltering with Reagan in New Orleans, motorcading with Kennedy in Chicago, snoozing at John Anderson in New Hampshire.

The food was awful but there was a rich diet of handouts, speech transcripts and the occasional 10 minutes of banalities from the candidate himself. It is sad but understandable that the coverage of campaign 80, including *Time* magazine's, had the consistency of hasty pudding.

I have limped painfully to meet a friend in the delegates' lounge of the United Nations and sit opposite a revolting pea green tapestry of the Great Wall of China, I have tried to love the UN but failed. The recent election for secretary general involved not a single moment of public debate. The members of the Security Council would not reveal how they voted or why. The word subsisted on largely misleading information from non-attributable sources.

I have a final personal gripe with the UN: I wrote that the now ousted secretary general Kurt Waldheim had, as a perk of office, a charge account at Bloomingdales, the fashionable Manhattan store, and received this blast from his assistant Brian Urquhart: 'That's bloody nonsense. Why don't you check your sources and facts? Waldheim doesn't even know what bloody Bloomingdales is.'

Chastened, I printed an apology and then checked my facts again. I can reveal that according to the United Nations office of procurement Waldheim's wife Elizabeth has a charge account at Bloomingdales. The bills are sent direct to the UN. So there.

I will miss going to central America and seeing my friend Father Earl Gallagher, a Catholic priest, in the remote village of Guarita on the border between Honduras and El Salvador. It is through Gallagher, a bearded, jovial man from Brooklyn, that news of the massacre of peasants and refugees in the border area reached the outside world.

Gallagher's robust faith has withstood being mortared, bombed and machine-gunned from helicopters provided by his own country to El Salvador, threatened with death and seeing the mutilated corpses of many of his parishioners. Last week I heard a depressing rumour that Gallagher had been beaten up and perhaps forced to flee. He lives far from any telephone or even any road so news take time to filter through.

Although this is statistically impossible I leave New York city without a single harrowing tale of personal violence. I have not been shot, stabbed, raped, beaten, or even threatened. I have not been mugged, my apartment has not been robbed. The whole lot will probably now happen on Sunday morning.

I have walked the streets in the early hours without incident. Even New York cab drivers have been invariably polite. I have never been ripped off. I lost my wallet in a diner near Times Square and a man with a face like an FBI wanted poster ran up to me and returned it.

I have learned to love the place and will miss it deeply. The other day a radio reporter in Arkansas asked me what I missed about Britain. On the spur of the moment only two words came into my mind: HP sauce.

Sunday Times
27 December 1981

CENTRAL AMERICA AND THE CARIBBEAN

The Jonestown Tape

Exactly a year ago, 913 members of a
religious sect were found poisoned at
their jungle settlement in Guyana,
South America. Among the dead was
James Jones, the once-dapper prophet
who had led his flock from California
to 'Jonestown', his jungle promised
land. A US Congressman had been
visiting Jonestown to investigate
reports of brutality; Jones ordered his
murder, and then in a monstrous rite –
the often-rehearsed 'white night' –
goaded his followers into drinking
cardboard cups of cyanide-laced
Flavor-Aid. The first words of the
mass-suicide ceremony activated an
automatic tape recorder, which ran
until all sound ceased. . . .

The throne he sat in was a crude affair of barely-upholstered
wood, set on a dais of rough planking above the floor of the
open-sided pavilion. But from it, beneath the slightly mis-
quoted aphorism from George Santayana's *Life of Reason*,
'Those who do not remember the past are condemned to repeat

105

it,' James Jones exercised over his thousand subjects an ascendancy as despotic, as cruel and as absolute as any Cleopatra's. By November 18 last year he was no longer the sleek young polyester-suited evangelist who had wooed – and won – the politicians of California, dined with the First Lady, Rosalynn Carter, and flown in the private jet of the Vice President, Walter Mondale. For the pudgy, pale, profusely sweating man slumped before the microphone that was both fetish and instrument of rule, his made-up world had catastrophically imploded; and the void it left was too terrible to contemplate.

Perhaps the followers who gathered round him in response to a loudspeakered 'Alert, alert, alert!' at five o'clock that afternoon knew that their leader was plagued by mysterious fevers and was sustained through days of obsessive activity and nights of fitful sleep by massive doses of tranquillisers and stimulants. Perhaps they noticed that their sometime spruce and confident 'Dad' sat limply in the muggy Guyanan weather, a trickle of black dye from his sideburns echoed in the dribble of saliva from the corner of his mouth.

If they did, it made no difference to his power over them. At the alert, familiar to them as the beds from which its predecessors had so often kept them, they trudged wearily from their huts and clustered about James Jones in a great semi-circle. The old and sick – all but one or two deliberately or accidentally overlooked by hut-mates or relatives – were helped along by the Jonestown 'nurses'; the reluctant or merely lazy prodded along by the settlement's security squad, hefty young men no less menacing for being armed mostly with crossbows.

It had been a difficult day for them all. Not only had there been newspapermen, but lawyers, and a consular official, and interfering 'concerned relatives' trying to entice their fellow-Templars away from Jonestown, and above all a congressman from Washington 'investigating' the stories that had been written about 'Dad' back in the States from which they had made their exodus more than a year before.

Not only had these unwelcome visitors eaten good pork and chicken from the community stock while they, its owners, subsisted every other day on rice and gravy or beans; not only had they had to overcome their weariness – they worked every

106

daylight hour of every day – to smile and dance and sing for the intruders; not only had a good 20 or more of their community actually been persuaded to leave – mostly white people, including one whole family – but, in the finish, one of their number had actually attacked the congressman with a knife and would have killed him had he not been dragged off, cutting himself badly in the struggle and covering the visitors in his blood. The congressman, with this outrage to convey to the world, was even now going aboard his plane. And now this. Unsettled and exhausted, they waited to hear what 'Dad' had to say.

The reels of the voice-activated TEAC tape-recorder beneath the throne began to turn. The soft, persuasive voice gave them a short preamble, peppered with quotations familiar from previous alerts. They cheered. They cheered even when James Jones said: 'If we can't live in peace then let us die in peace.' But they were quiet through what he next told them.

'What is going to happen here in a matter of a few minutes is that one of your people on that plane is going to shoot the pilot . . . and down comes that plane into the jungle. And we had better not have any of our children left when it's over because they are parachuting here on us. I have never lied to you, never ever lied to you. I know . . . he will do it. So my opinion is that we should be kind to children and kind to seniors and take the Potion, like they used to take in ancient Greece. Step over quietly; because we are not committing suicide: it is a revolutionary act . . . There is no way we can survive.'

Almost any other group of a thousand people anywhere in the world, even among the extreme sects that have flowered so luxuriantly in Midwestern and Western America, would simply have turned their backs on this preposterous suggestion and walked away, or led their fevered preacher gently away to lock him in his hut. But for the People's Temple the suggestion was not preposterous, and its members barely faltered in their obedience to their Father, James Jones. It was in any case something they were used to: the subject of their suicide in just such circumstances (they knew who Dad's 'they' were – the CIA, the Guyanese Defence Force, fascists, mercenaries and the like) had been discussed often, and the act itself as often rehearsed in alerts like this one, which they called 'white nights'.

Every one of them had, at least once in the recent past, drunk the grape-flavoured Potion and syringed it into the mouths of their children, without knowing whether it was genuinely laced with cyanide of potassium or merely the innocuous instrument of one of Dad's 'tests'.

By this means, and others which a subsequent Congressional report described as 'the recognized strategies of brainwashing ... practised with engineered precision', had James Jones established, over a period of nearly 25 years, an absolute psychological control over the members of his sect. In the mid-Sixties he could uproot them from Indiana and lead them halfway across America to the promised land of California. A decade later, insisting that their persecution was about to begin, he could fly them en masse across half a hemisphere to their refuge in the Amazonian jungle. As the trusting voices on the Jonestown tape affirm, he could take them all, man, woman and child, with him to the grave.

It could be said, with a kind of crooked truth, that James Jones and his People's Temple were in Guyana and self-condemned to their terrible end only because the press would not leave them alone. Jones had said as much himself, often, warning his people as far back as 1972 of an incipient campaign against the Temple by the 'Fascist Press' which would lead to all the horrors – torture and murder by the CIA or FBI – his paranoid imagination could invent.

The straight truths within the crooked one were of a somewhat different order. There had been, in 1972, a series of articles by Caroline Pickering in the *Star* of Indianapolis – where the first People's Temple had been set up in 1957 – and the *Examiner* in San Francisco, where the Temple flourished for more than a decade after the mid-Sixties flight out of Indiana. They were sceptical of Jones's claims to be God's heir on earth and hinted at the despotism with which he ruled the Temple. They called for an inquiry into the Temple's – and Jones's own – operations in and from its base in the northern Californian town of Ukiah; and Ms Pickering also made direct private appeals to such eminences as Senator Birch Bayh of Indiana.

But until late November last year, when the sudden grim prominence of Jonestown sent other newspapermen scurrying to their files, Ms Pickering, her articles and her appeals were totally ignored. Ignored, that is, by all but James Jones who, in a state of acute anxiety, set two of his inner circle of confidants, Terri Buford and Michael Prokes, to work in the Ukiah public library to find somewhere else for the Temple to set itself up, far from the oppressive inquisitiveness of the press. Guyana attracted their attention because, like the People's Temple itself, it was mainly populated by blacks, was vaguely 'marxist' or at least socialist, and conveniently conducted its business in English. It offered, as the Temple purported to offer, uncritical hospitality to the refugees of capitalism – especially if they could pay for it. The Temple could certainly pay: its proposal to spend $1 million in clearing and farming leased land in the jungle was quickly accepted by the Guyanese; and in 1974 the People's Temple pioneers, under Mike Touchette and Philip Blakey, began to build their paradise.

'Don't bother telling anyone about what goes on here,' Jones had once told his legal officer, Tim Stoen. 'It's too bizarre.' Considering this confidence, which was well founded on an elaborate system of 'insurances', it is surprising that the only other seriously hostile press treatment of the People's Temple should, in 1977, have triggered the exodus of almost the entire membership to the bolt-hole in Guyana. By that time, it is true, there were enough defectors from the Temple to interest ambitious journalists somewhat removed from the circles of power in which Jones had, by legitimate public relations, by flattery and intimidation, by favours (like the guaranteed delivery of a disciplined 'rent-a-crowd' of voters for useful political candidates), by near-blackmail and by highly-organized letter-writing campaigns, purchased a very considerable indulgence.

In the ordinary way such journalists would quickly have come up against the wall of credibility which Jones had built for himself as city big-wheel (he was by this time, thanks to the influence of Tim Stoen who also happened to be the deputy District Attorney of Mendocino County, chairman of the San

Francisco Housing authority), public do-gooder and wielder of the kind of political clout respected by police and press functionaries. But an unforeseeable turn of events far from the Californian shore allowed Marshall Kilduff, a hustling reporter on the San Francisco *Chronicle*, actually to publish the kind of exposé of Temple methods that Jones had hoped would never see the light of day.

Kilduff had spent a considerable time compiling a dossier of 'odd' information about the Temple, most of it from defectors, and about Jones's performance as chairman of the Housing Authority. But when he proposed to write about it he was turned away with assurances that his suspicions were unfounded.

At *New West* magazine Kilduff at first came up against the same stone wall. But later that year *New West* was taken over by Rupert Murdoch, the Australian press magnate, who gave Kilduff the go-ahead for an inquiry. Had he known how the Temple would react, perhaps he might have drawn back: he and Kilduff were deluged with protesting letters from the congregation – 600 in a single day at one time – as well as one from Lieutenant Governor Vincent Dymally of California, who opined that it would be 'unwise' for *New West* to pursue its intention. But Murdoch had not been drawn into the Jones circle of influence.

Kilduff's article, 'What's going on behind his church's closed doors', appeared in August 1977 and gave a detailed account of the ritualistic beatings of adults and children, the bizarre sexual activities, the mulcting of members, the intricate network of informers and the threats of reprisal for defection that constituted the Temple system and had kept its congregation so docile and cohesive. By the time *New West* was on the news stands James Jones was already 5000 miles away in Jonestown; and the mass migration of his followers into the new promised land was well under way.

The irony of this flight was that it was unnecessary. Behind the refugees their insurance system held up wonderfully: no American newspaper of any influence picked up the Temple story; none of Jones's political friends recanted; Mayor George Moscone of San Francisco (since then shot dead by a disgruntled citizen) who, many said, owed his election to the Temple block vote, announced that there would be no investigation by the city authorities since the District Attorney could find 'no evidence' sufficient to prosecute any Temple member.

By then the thousand People's Templars were squeezing themselves into the cross between an old age home and a holiday camp that Touchette and Blakey had built, amid 20,000 acres of jungle, to house 50 to 100 people in somewhat spartan comfort. They were coming into a fatal inheritance.

The system James Jones so feared to see exposed had its roots in a small middle-American town of much the same size as Jonestown and, perhaps, with some affinities of character to it. Lynn, Indiana, is sternly religious in the 'born-again' tradition, intolerant of deviations and minorities and the home of a thriving industry – coffin-making. There, in a crepuscular loft set about with gaudy pictures of the Good Shepherd and his grisly death, 12-year-old James Jones preached his first hellfire sermon in 1943, to a congregation of younger children. There he developed a taste for the prophetic style associated with Pentecostalism and earned a small reputation as a healer of ailing pet animals. There he saw his shrewish, defiantly unconventional mother slighted (she wore trousers, smoked in the street and swore) and learned to despise his bar-fly father. And there he laid the first claim to membership of an underclass he was both to support and to exploit all his life: darkly-complexioned, he fancifully declared himself of Cherokee descent.

Perhaps it was this that separated him from his Lynn contemporaries (who mostly went into banking, teaching, farming or insurance), and found him, at 16, married to pale, skinny Marcie Baldwin, five years his senior and a nurse in the hospital near Indianapolis where he worked as a porter. His colleagues were poor and black; and he got on with them surprisingly well. At the end of an abortive year at Indianapolis University, it was among the poor, black neighbourhoods of that town that he earned his living, selling South American spider monkeys from door to door and recruiting a congregation for the Methodist church of which he had become,

111

after a bizarre encounter with the local superintendent of that church, the unordained supply pastor.

His ministry there was neither long nor, in Methodist terms, fruitful. The congregation of whites did not like the new, black membership; they did not like Jones keeping monkeys and chickens in the vicarage; they did not like his 'offensive' and 'fanatic' preaching style; and they did not like to hear him say he had had God as a fellow-passenger on the Philadelphia train one day. They threw him out in 1954, and closed his church as if it had been desecrated. Undismayed, he founded his own church, rebuilt his following and, in 1957, set himself up in a lavishly converted former synagogue in North Delaware Street, Indianapolis. This was the first People's Temple.

Jones's 'politicization' had, by his own account, preceded these religious adventures. There is a fragment of evidence – an FBI 'trace' – for his claim to have joined the Communist Party in 1953. By that time he was certainly preaching, to general disapprobation of which dead cats thrown into his church were the outward sign, a kind of proto-communism smacking more of Robin Hood than Marx. He never competed with the new, Brooks Brotherly, evangelical establishment, with its anodyne reassurances about the rightness of the American way. He railed against the rich and comfortable, against bigotry, against the endurance of the unendurable. On the whole he practised what he preached: there was a soup kitchen for down-and-outs, a clothing hand-out for the poorest, two nursing homes for the old and sick. He also adopted a multi-racial family – a Korean and two blacks.

In a fragment of autobiography found after the mass suicide, Jones claimed that 1953 was also the year in which he first conceived the idea of 'revolutionary death'. The execution in the electric chair of the spies Julius and Ethel Rosenberg did much to damage the idea of America as 'the best hope of mankind' all round the world. For Jones it was of special horror.

'I wish I could have died then. Hell, you can only have so many revolutionary deaths . . . so, hell, death isn't a problem for me any more. I was in this goddam miserable coma . . . I don't know why I lived.'

From this time on he was always to describe himself to his adherents – if not to the men of business and city politics with whom he was later to hobnob – as 'communist' or 'socialist'. But it was not this that drew packed houses at the Temple services. Jones's pulling power depended largely on the regular performance of miracles – spectacular cancer cures, the revitalization of the hopelessly wheelchair-ridden, astounding clairvoyance. In carefully theatrical settings these manifestations of divinity impressed all but obdurate sceptics. They were all fakes. Jones's inner circle of women, those of them who survive, testify to the nature of spewed-up 'cancers' (chicken livers), wheezing and paralyzed black ancients (one of the inner circle, made-up) and 'mind-readings' (information supplied by the inner circle).

Prophecies are, as is well known, an easier matter: only those that are fulfilled are remembered. No immediate consequences therefore followed for Jones when the world was not engulfed in thermonuclear war on July 15, 1967. His people had forgotten his prophecy, made in 1964 'by divine revelation'; or forgiven it, being satisfied enough with what the prophecy had led to. That was when James Jones had led his people out of the snowy winter wilderness of Indiana to the promised land of northern California, bearing before him – a banner with strange device – a copy of *Esquire* in which were pinpointed safe havens in atomic war.

Ukiah was not one of these, but near enough to be plausible. There the People's Temple established itself in a new building and began to stiffen its depleted congregation with a new class of member. Many original members had stayed in Indiana: those in the pilgrimage were old and wholly dependent on the Temple; or, having given all their possessions to it, had no choice but to follow their investment; or, like the Parks and Touchette families, were both loyal and desirous of sunshine. The new people (in addition to the orphaned, the indigent and the inadequate, who were as poor and black as ever) were mainly white, and intelligent, and idealistic.

Tim Stoen, the successful deputy District Attorney, arrived in a Porsche, which he donated to the Temple. He brought his

113

girlfriend, Grace (later his wife), as well as a lot of useful influence in San Francisco city politics. Later, as Jones's adversary, he more than anybody else was to provide the spark for the explosion of the 'powder keg' at Jonestown. He had signed a paper 'lending' his wife to Jones for the purpose of childbearing – these 'confessions' were standard guarantors of obedience in the Temple – but when she had a son, John-John, Stoen claimed fatherhood and, eventually, obtained a court order for John-John's custody. In Guyana, Jones would not give him up: John-John died with the others.

Philip Blakey, an English public schoolboy from a farming family, arrived in California to marry Debby Layton; and they, too, were to play a key part in the Temple's fate. Philip was one of the pioneers (he was on the Temple's ship *Albatross* on November 18, and survived); Debby, escaping from Jonestown in April last year, was branded as a murderess by her brother Larry because she had not been able to help their mother in the cardiac seizure that killed her. And Larry, anxious to kill Debby, was one of Congressman Leo Ryan's assassins.

The entry fee for these and people like them was, simply, everything they owned or earned; and they chose to pay it. Others had no choice: an unknown number of children – perhaps as many as 150 – were simply handed over to the Temple's care, together with their welfare cheques, by probation officers and welfare agencies in Ukiah and San Francisco. Nobody is sure how many of them took the Potion.

By the early Seventies the Temple was in full swing and Jones's political career was flourishing. Each provided 'insurance' for the other: nobody with Jones's record of good works could be other than advantageous for a politician to know – and nobody that friendly with politicians, police and press would need to fear that nasty revelations about his good works would be believed.

The political friendships were not always what Jones made them out to be (the much-advertised acquaintance with Rosalynn Carter boiled down to a routine dinner after a campaign rally: when told of Jones's death, she said, 'Who?'). But the nasty revelations, unbelievable and unbelieved right up to the end, were a true bill. Blood-curdling punishments were used to enforce obedience and loyalty. Children, informed upon for some minor breach of discipline, would be taken at 2 a.m. before a microphone and beaten with a board, perhaps 75 or more times, while their screams echoed and re-echoed around the Temple's public address system. Adults might be caned, or set to fight each other until 'right triumphed', or simply beaten into bloody submission. They were set to performing sexual perversions before the assembled congregation, or made to submit themselves to Jones's own vaunted sexual energies.

In the developing obsession with 'revolutionary suicide' (first mentioned to Grace Stoen in 1973 – 'Everyone will die – except me. I've got to stay behind and explain why we did it . . .'), they were eventually to become participants in rehearsals for a 'white night'. The first of them, already recognizable in all essential details, was on New Year's Day of 1976. The shaken Templars, nerves abraded by some outbursts of hysteria and the fake shooting of a runaway, thanked their 'Dad' for testing them when he told them the 'poison' was innocuous – minutes after they had drunk it.

There were some near misses for the rising public figure, friend of City Hall and Police Headquarters. In the winter of 1973 he was arrested in Los Angeles for making a blatant homosexual advance to a policeman in plain clothes (Jones himself was unashamedly bisexual), and charged with 'lewd conduct'. Bailed the same day for $500, he tried to donate $500 to the police the next day – and the matter was not heard of again. A municipal court judge, at the City Attorney's Office request, dismissed the case and ordered the record to be sealed and destroyed. No one now knows – or will divulge – how this fatal suppression was achieved – fatal because an open record of the arrest for lewd conduct would have prevented the award of custody to Jones of all those children.

Once the Temple as a whole migrated to Jonestown, life there became exceptionally difficult. Grossly overcrowded – the thousand occupied land and buildings intended for 50 or 100 – with a population hopelessly imbalanced by the large pro-portion of the aged and the very young, they were subjected to all the familiar brutalities and in addition worked continually in the fields, dawn to dusk seven days a week, on a diet inadequate even by the standards of the Guyanese peasantry. And then there were the 'white nights', and meetings, and church services. None of them was in any condition to resist doing what he or she was told.

Jones himself, although he occupied a separate, comfortable hut with his mistresses Maria Katsaris and Carolyn Layton and had his wife Marcie close by, fed well and enjoyed plentiful supplies of his favourite tranquillisers and stimulants, was faced with administrative problems that might have daunted a man entirely free of paranoid fears and the obsessive behavioural characteristics which occupied so much of Jones's time. The short-wave radio was never silent; laboriously coded messages were transmitted back and forth between Jonestown, San Francisco and the Temple outstation at Georgetown, the Guyanan capital, 24 hours a day. Jones controlled the Templars' listening, fed them with doctored news, supervised punishments (one was confinement in a metal box buried in the ground, 24 hours at a stretch; children were lowered into a dark well and pulled into the water by a waiting assistant) and conducted all meetings, services and 'white nights' himself. Much better and more stable men would have cracked under the strain.

There were desertions – Grace Stoen in 1976, Tim Stoen in the following May, Debby Blakey in April 1978, Jim Cobb at about the same time. Their stories attracted little attention back in the US.

But one man listened. Congressman Leo Ryan heard from a friend in 1977 that the man's son, Bob Houston, had died in an accident the day after resigning from the Temple (he was not the first to whom such coincidentally swift retribution had come). Ryan made up his mind to see for himself what was going on. The Temple migration was complete by that time and the obstacles put in his way multiplied alarmingly, not least because Jones's own considerable defensive skill had been augmented by that of the flamboyant lawyer (and professional conspiracy theorist) Mark Lane. But Ryan persisted. The visit was eventually agreed. On November 17, 1978, Ryan and his party – nine journalists, four 'concerned relatives' of Temple members, organized by a defector, Deanna Mertle, and Jones's lawyers Mark Lane and Charles Garry – set off in chartered aircraft for the Port Kaituma airstrip near Jonestown.

They were well fed, entertained by dancing and a concert. And they were impressed. The next day, after a night at Port Kaituma village, they returned to a Jonestown made even jollier by the overnight warning to its inhabitants by their security guards: 'Smile more tomorrow.' Jones, sharply interviewed by the press, behaved oddly, pleading a fever and 'cancer' in apology. Edith Parks, grandmother of a family which had been planning escape for some time, approached Ryan and asked to be taken out. Ryan confronted Jones. The pretence shattered. Jones screamed at his members, 'I am betrayed; it never stops!' He pleaded with the adamant Parkses. Other families saw their chance: 20 people asked Ryan to take them with him as Jones cried hysterically, 'I've given my life for my people . . .'

The departure, strained enough by these events, turned to disaster as Don Sly, one of Jones's aides, tried to stab Congressman Ryan. Pulled off by Mark Lane, Sly cut himself badly and covered everyone nearby in his blood. The party made what speed they could back to the airstrip.

As they stood waiting to board their aircraft, a tractor and trailer drew towards them. There were puffs of smoke from behind the trailer. Six people were killed – Ryan, two defectors and three journalists. Most of the others were wounded.

Back in Jonestown, the loudspeakers said: 'Alert! Alert! Alert!' Marcie Jones and Larry Schacht, the medical officer, were making up a tub of Flavor-Aid.

Sunday Times Magazine
25 November 1979

Gunfire takes over from reggae music as Jamaica's new sound

The Wong family lives in some style in Kingston, Jamaica. Their grand mansion in the Beverly Hills section of Kingston, with its five bedrooms, accompanying bathrooms and ornamental swimming pool, has one of the world's great views: from the Blue Mountain, across the city of Kingston to the Caribbean. The sun shines almost all the year.

It is the sweet life that lured wealthy Europeans to the island. Noël Coward lived here; Ian Fleming wrote his James Bond books from the Golden Eye Villa, blinds drawn so that he would not be distracted by the natural beauty of the scene outside.

In the past six months Fleming would have had more insistent distractions. The Wong family are woken every night by the sound of gunfire. They now have a panoramic view of violence as it spreads through the ghettoes from Trench Town to Gold Street and into the slums of the dock area.

Beverly Hills itself is not the place it used to be. The Wongs are among the few survivors of the middle and upperclass families who formed a rich and flourishing colony. Many have left because their businesses went bankrupt. Others fled in fear. Magnificent villas lie empty, some of them stripped and vandalized.

Gunfire has become, more than reggae music or political slogans, the distinctive sound of the 1980 Jamaican election campaign. As the prime minister, Michael Manley, defends his left-wing People's National Party (PNP) against his right-wing opponent Edward Seaga and the Jamaican Labour Party (JLP), more than 500 people, according to the latest Red Cross statistics, have died in the campaign so far.

As next Thursday's polling approaches, the toll is rising. Fifteen were killed, mostly by gunshot, one by suffocation and another by poison, in the previous weekend. More than 50 died last week.

Violence has become the key election issue, taking attention away from the real problem: the disastrous state of the Jamaican economy, which has put a third of the population out of work and condemned an even larger proportion to grinding poverty.

The gunmen, most of whom emerge from ghetto gangs, are only dimly aware that the election has riveted the interest of the world's two major power blocks. Manley has become a Third World leader and, to the dismay of the United States, has formed close links with Fidel Castro's regime in Cuba. He has sought help from Russia, such left-wing regimes as Algeria and Iraq and such Muslim hardliners as Colonel Gadaffi.

The US sees Jamaica as a domino about to fall into the Communist world, taking with it the string of Caribbean islands that lie scattered across the approaches to the Panama Canal and shipping lanes through which more than half America's imported oil passes.

Relations between Jamaica and the US are occasionally lukewarm but mostly cold. Manley did support the West in United Nations Security Council votes on Iran and Afganistan. At the summit of non-aligned nations in Havana last year, he said the struggle against imperialism was stronger than ever.

Manley has contempt for the American view of the Caribbean. 'The US perception of this is nothing short of tragic,' said Manley recently. 'It is suspended somewhere between tragedy and comedy, a devil theory of history in which all sorts of wild imaginings go on that have nothing to do with reality at all.'

There are no wild imaginings about who the Americans want to see as prime minister of Jamaica. It is Manley's rival, Edward Seaga. He is a conservative, trained at Harvard, a former governor of the World Bank, who wants Jamaica to be a haven for investors from the capitalist world. Through Seaga Washington is hoping for a continuation of the 'Conservative sweep' which has brought right-wing or centrist government in the past year to St Vincent, St Kitts-Nevis, Antigua and Dominica.

Seaga, who makes frequent trips to the US, is represented by a public relations company in New York. One of the many rumours in Jamaica is that the Cuban ambassador is already packed and ready to leave, should Seaga win this week.

Such ideological considerations do not, however, catch the flavour of the Jamaican election. So here, briefly, is a day in the life of Michael Manley during the campaign last week. It began with the funeral of an MP from his own party, a former junior minister in the department of national security, Roy McGann, who was gunned down as he campaigned. The day ended, very nearly, with Michael Manley himself falling victim to the violence.

The crowd that gathered round McGann's open coffin had the mood of people at a political rally. Manley was cheered as he entered the church. The congregation gave the clenched-fist salute and shouted the PNP slogan 'Stand Firm'. Although the reason for McGann's death is murky, PNP supporters predictably claim that he was shot in cold blood by the police, acting in concert with Seaga's men. Manley's pleas for peace on Jamaican television that afternoon did little to assuage the anger on both sides.

The murder of McGann took the violence to a new peak. It was the first time an MP has been killed in Jamaica's history and it brought immediate reprisals. On the day of his funeral five supporters were shot dead in his own constituency.

That night, Manley drove to Spanish Town, about 20 miles from Kingston, for a rally in the main square. The setting was delightful. The sun sank over the Spanish and British colonial buildings and a statue of Lord Nelson dressed in a toga.

A crowd of hundreds, many reeling from the effects of rum and ganja – marijuana – cigarettes as fat as rolled newspapers, danced to reggae music. A man staggered out of the crowd, a bloodstain spreading across his bright yellow shirt. He had been mistaken for a supporter of the rival party and stabbed in the chest.

Manley arrived on the podium at about 10 p.m. to shouts of applause and a burst of heavy gunfire. For a man who cuts a dashing figure among statesmen in London, New York and Havana, it was a chastening experience. He was hurled into the dust by his security men and pinned there as police and army engaged gunmen in a 10-minute battle. 'This violence makes me haemorrhage inside,' said Manley. Such events are becoming routine. This is the third time he has come under fire – and his opponent has had an equal share of bullets aimed in his direction.

Supporters on both sides are well armed with pistols and high-velocity rifles, and both parties claim there is a sinister international conspiracy by the CIA or the Cubans (according to which side you ask) to arm their rivals. The truth may well be simpler: that the guns are brought in from the US with the proceeds of the illegal sale of marijuana, Jamaica's most lucrative agricultural produce.

The police are handicapped in their investigations by incompetence, lack of funds and manpower. A senior official at Kingston police headquarters said, rather sadly, that they could not so far track down the 'high up' politicians who pay the gunmen. 'Our under-cover men cannot afford to go to the clubs where they drink,' he said. 'You know a Coca Cola costs 2.50 Jamaican dollars (just over £1). How do you put that on expenses?' Related to pay rates, the point was indisputable.

Both parties hope that after the election the violence will abate, regardless of who gets in. They know, however, that the economic crisis will not. Jamaica is in debt to the tune of 3,677 million Jamaican dollars (£849 million). Manley managed to beg a few lines of credit so that the supermarkets would have food during the election months. After that the supply of imported goods will dry up.

Whoever wins this week in Jamaica will need more than a little international help to halt its plummeting economy. The feeling of the middle class is that Seaga has more chance of getting it, and he has already started negotiations with the

IMF. In the ghettoes there is still fierce loyalty to Manley, despite the poverty.

Last week there was still a natural exuberance, even in the ghetto. Between gun battles in Spanish Town a man, with bruises and cuts on his face from a political beating-up the night before, approached me in the square. He had, that morning, heard about the possible closure of Times Newspapers and was concerned: 'Don't worry yourself,' he said. 'Come and live over here. It ain't so bad.'

Sunday Times
26 October 1980

Victims of the massacre that the world ignored

Lolita Guardado was awoken at about 4 a.m. by a strange noise. There was the usual sound of the persistent drizzle pouring through the roof of closely packed palm leaves and through the walls of mud and sticks.

But outside, across the Sumpul river, she could hear men shouting. Groups of peasants gathered anxiously in the grey dawn to watch as Honduran soldiers formed a line on the far bank and ran to and fro, carrying stones from the riverbed. They built a low wall. Only later that day, after her family, friends and neighbours had been slaughtered, did she fully understand why they were there.

Lolita, her husband Genaro and their eight children are Salvadoran peasants. They lived, along with about 1,500 others, in Las Aradas, a settlement which lies a few yards inside the Salvadoran border on the banks of the Sumpul, the frontier with Honduras.

There were few comforts. Lolita was considered fortunate because at least she had a hut. Most of the others lived under trees, with sheets of plastic to protect them from the rain. There was no electricity, no clean water, no medicine, barely enough food and no road. But Las Aradas, they believed, had one virtue. It was so remote that they were safe from the violence between the left and the right that racks El Salvador. They had fled from their houses and land – away from the soldiers, the national guard, the secret police, the

123

right-wing death squads and left-wing guerrillas to this haven.

That morning a group of 300 peasant refugees, mostly women and children, had arrived after a three-day trek through the Salvador mountains. Few of them would survive the day.

As Margarita Lopez, a bright and pretty 16-year-old, was preparing tortillas for the new refugees, 300 Salvadoran soldiers from Chalatenango army base were already taking up position behind the nearest hills. Beside them, merging into the forest, were two olive-green helicopter gunships, each with machineguns and bombs. On the other side of the Sumpul, 150 Honduran soldiers stood behind their stone wall.

El Salvador and Honduras, although technically still at war after 11 years, were about to carry out their first joint military venture. The Salvadorans call it an 'operacion de limpieza' – a cleaning operation.

The decision to carry out the attack was made, according to Honduran sources, at a joint meeting between Honduran and Salvadoran military commanders at El Poy, a town on the border about 13 miles from Las Aradas.

The motive was clear. In the border area are the camps of the left-wing guerrillas, against whom the Salvadoran ruling junta has been fighting a bloody civil war. It is also one of the main channels for arms shipments from Nicaragua and Cuba. The Hondurans were keen to help because they feared both the war spilling over into their territory and their neighbour falling into communist hands.

The only flaw in the plan was that Las Aradas was not a guerrilla base. It seems not a shot was fired in defence by the people there. But for the Salvadoran military mind, the distinction between peasant and guerrilla is academic: they are, indeed, often one and the same.

Also, the guerrillas need peasant support if they are to achieve popular insurrection and more immediately they need the peasants to provide food and shelter when necessary. For The Salvadorans this made the peasants a fair military target.

The 'cleaning' began at about 10 a.m. on May 14 last year. Margarita remembers a deafening explosion of gunfire which would continue for the next six hours: 'the bullets came in fistfuls. They went through the walls of houses, people were falling and cattle were dying. The bullets were everywhere.'

Genaro Guardado heard the thud of bombs falling outside his hut. With his 17-year-old daughter, Ernestina, he grabbed five children, all under 12, who were standing outside, and ran. Rosabel Sibrian, a 22-year-old, saw the gunships buzzing low over the trees and heard the rattle of their machineguns. Then he saw soldiers standing round his friend, Amanda Rodriquez: 'She begged them not to kill her. They all opened fire. They shot her 11-year-old son.'

The troops had surrounded the settlement. The obvious escape route was across the river into Honduras – that was when the peasants learnt the function of the Hondurian soldiers.

The peasants 'ran to the river in flocks,' said Genaro. It was the beginning of the rainy season and the river was flowing deep and fast. Margarita ran into the water and found it came up to her neck: 'Children were drowning. The Salvadoran soldiers stood on the bank and fired at us. My two friends were killed next to me.'

As Genaro jumped into the water with about 70 people, his daughter Ernestina was shot dead in the back of the head. First he walked, pulling the five children, across to the other bank. He left them there and went back for Ernestina's body. Then, carrying the body, he walked up the bank towards the Honduran soldiers: 'They grabbed Ernestina and threw her into the river. Then they pushed us back into the river. We pleaded with them. Begged them. They just pushed us. They didn't fire their rifles, but they wouldn't let us through.'

He returned to the Salvadoran side, to face the guns. 'The Salvadorans fired from the hip and kept their guns low. I suppose they didn't want to shoot the Honduran soldiers. But they fired into the river.' Those who survived the crossing were herded together by the Salvadoran soldiers, who tied their hands and made them lie, face down on the ground. 'They beat us with their rifle butts. They kept asking, "Where do you keep the guns? Who are the guerrillas?"

'They took groups to one side and machine-gunned them. I had my children with me. Then a soldier cut my bonds. I don't

125

know why he did that. But I ran with my children. Only three others survived.'

Rosabel Sibrian, who hid between some rocks, says the main slaughter took place on the river bank, near Las Aradas: 'There were 50 soldiers and they gathered a big group together. Then they shot them. The people were screaming. Those who would not die were beaten on the heads with rifle butts.'

He says, and this is corroborated by other eye-witnesses, that the soldiers were aided by members of Orden, a paramilitary right-wing group, distinctive in their black shirts with skull-and-crossbones insignia. 'Some soldiers and Orden people gathered children and babies together,' said Sibrian. 'I saw them throw children into the air and then slash them with long machetes. They cut their heads off and slit their bodies in two.' One soldier told the mother of a child: 'We are killing the children of subversion.'

Sibrian tried to run downstream, carrying his baby son. Soldiers chased him and a bullet smashed into Sibrian's leg: 'I couldn't run with my baby any more. I left him beside a small ditch, then rolled away and crawled through the bushes. I thought the soldiers would kill him.' But, in one of the few acts of humanity carried out by the Salvadoran army that day, they did not. 'They picked him up very gently and carried him away. Later I heard they bought him milk in a local town. I think he is in a children's camp. I am trying to find him,' said Sibrian.

Lolita was not so fortunate. Just after the first bombs dropped at 10 a.m., she had lost sight of her husband. So with her brother-in-law, Angel, and three of her children, she made her way slowly upstream, hiding for long periods in the bushes until soldiers and paramilitary men had passed. She went for a mile along the Sumpul until the cordon of Honduran soldiers on the opposite bank had ended. Then at about 4 p.m. she started to cross the river.

She walked over the rocks and had just reached the water when she heard rapid firing behind her and felt 'a burning pain' all over her body. She fell backwards into the Sumpul. Her body lay in the water, her head resting on a rock. She had been hit by 15 bullets, in an arc from her thigh across the small of her back.

One bullet passed through her hand. Two of her children lay dying in the water beside her. One died quickly – a bullet had passed through his armpit into his chest; the other, shot in the testicles, did not. 'He lasted half an hour,' said Lolita. 'I couldn't move. I couldn't comfort him.' Her brother-in-law was dead, too. She lay with her suviving child three-year-old Ovidio, clasped to her breast. He had been hit in the leg and the scalp.

'Ovidio kept crying and shouting. He called out "Uncle Angel, Uncle Angel! Come. Come see my mother. Her leg is bleeding into the water."' He kept talking to his two brothers long after they were dead. He shouted at them: 'Why don't you talk to me?'

After dark, Lolita says that occasionally soldiers walked along the bank. She tried to hold Ovidio still and keep him quiet: 'The baby cried with pain, but I told him to be silent. I heard a soldier say: "Hit them. Hit them again." But another soldier said: "I have hit them already. Let's not shoot again. They will just die."

'I had a terrible thirst. The water was full of blood. It was the blood of my children. But I kept drinking water, drinking water.'

That night she felt an object bump against her in the river. Then it floated off downstream. It was, she says, the head of a child. The next morning a Honduran fisherman pulled in his nets. They contained the bodies of three dismembered children.

Lolita lay in the river until after dawn, when a group of four Honduran men saw Ovidio moving. They crossed the river and put Lolita in a hammock, then carried her to a Honduran's home. It was another 15 days before she received hospital treatment.

For the peasants, the behaviour of the army at Las Aradas was not new, just a little more extreme than usual. The Salvadoran soldiers have a single tactic to discourage peasant support for guerrillas – terror. Lolita and her husband had fled to Las Aradas after soldiers had decapitated some of their neighbours. The heads had been left neatly by the side of the road to ram the lesson home. Most refugees have stories of such appalling brutality it is difficult to believe that it became almost a way of life.

127

Officially they were all victims of a massacre that never happened. The government of El Salvador has denied that any killings took place at the Sumpul river on May 14. On June 25, the military leader of Honduras, President Policarpo Paz Garcia, said on national radio that the massacre did not happen. One of his army chiefs, however, Colonel Ruben Montoya, head of the third military region, denied that the Honduran army had taken part, while admitting that the incident took place: 'The Honduran troops did not help in the killings of civilians.'

At first the American embassy in Tegucigalpa, the Honduran capital, told reporters that there was no evidence to support claims of a massacre. But like the government, the Americans later changed their line, admitting 'something happened' at the Sumpul river that day.

At noon the day after the massacre, a Roman Catholic priest from the Capuchin order walked over the hills towards the Sumpul. If he had not, then the massacre might have become just peasant folklore. Father Earl Gallagher, 35, comes from Brooklyn, New York City. He has worked in Honduras for four years. Because of his prematurely grey hair and prowess at climbing the hills, he is known by the peasants as 'the old billy goat.'

He noticed that the river banks looked strangely black. When he got closer he saw why. They were covered in a thick carpet of buzzards. In the village of Talquinta he met his first survivor, a 10-year-old boy with bullet wounds in his mouth, thigh and shoulder.

'I heard the Salvadoran troops were coming back to kill the survivors,' said Gallagher. 'I felt I had to make it public and perhaps that would help them.' It did not help the little boy. A month later he fled from the Honduran army back to El Salvador, where he was killed.

Gallagher returned with a camera and tape-recorder and took down the stories of dozens of survivors. He could not visit the Sumpul itself because it was still patrolled by members of Orden, who shot intruders. Meanwhile, dogs and buzzards picked the bodies clean.

On June 24, Gallagher's report condemning the massacre

and the role of the soldiers of both El Salvador and Honduras was published as a joint declaration by the priests of Santa Rosa de Copan.

Gallagher immediately received death threats over El Salvador Radio. He was threatened with expulsion and condemned by the Honduran government. The then minister of foreign affairs, Eliseo Perez Cadalso, said on July 1: 'The church declaration responds to a well-orchestrated campaign with the purpose of destabilizing the convivial and highly democratic climate in which the people of Honduras live.'

Gallagher's report reached Washington, where the only person who paid attention was Senator Edward Kennedy. He had it placed on the congressional record on September 24, and said: 'I am deeply concerned by the reports of increasing hardship and often death that face innocent men, women and children who try to escape the escalating violence in El Salvador.'

But the world paid scant attention, inured perhaps by the daily stories of violence in Latin America. The Sumpul massacre was mentioned in a few newspapers which ran part of Gallagher's report. It was almost completely ignored by the American press at the time. 'Our thing was: it happened. Come and have a look. And nobody did,' said Gallagher.

The misery for the Sumpul Survivors and the 29,000 refugees who have fled El Salvador for Honduras did not end on May 14.

'They live in fear,' Gallagher said last week. 'Their only hope is international attention.'

He and other priests have compiled a list of incidents against refugees since the massacre. It runs into several pages, a litany of murder, rape and cruelty.

Hundreds of refugees have been handed to Salvadoran troops to face certain death. In the Honduran town of Santa Rosa last week an 18-year-old girl described her life in El Salvador. She lived near the Honduran border with her husband until soldiers took him away and shot him. She moved in with her four brothers. Last year, Salvadoran national guards took them out of the house and sprayed them with liquid from cans they carried. 'Their skin went black. Their eyes melted,' she said. Her brothers were pushed into a cornfield and killed with machetes.

Last week we spoke to Lolita, who now lives with her husband and five remaining children in an adobe hut deep in the Honduran hillside. Life for her is not convivial. She is afraid, and for good reason. The Honduran government has refused, at the urging of El Salvador, to grant Lolita or the other refugees 'refugee status'. This means their movements are tightly restricted and they cannot find work. They are constantly threatened with expulsion.

There are also signs that the Honduran government is growing more repressive. A week ago a colleague of Gallagher's, Father Fausto Milla, was arrested by security men. He was blindfolded and interrogated for three days. He had just returned from a human rights conference in Mexico City where he presented the testimony of Lolita and other Sumpul survivors.

The day we saw Lolita, she had been visited by a Honduran security man, who threatened her with expulsion back to El Salvador. 'They may as well kill me here,' she said. 'It's easier.'

Sunday Times
22 February 1981

The innocents caught in Lempa River massacre

Champagne fizzed and glasses tinkled at the residence of the British ambassador to Honduras last Tuesday evening as the diplomatic community celebrated the Queen of England's birthday. It is the high point of the social season in Tegucigalpa, the Honduran capital, rivalled only by the American Fourth of July festivities. The ambassadors of the United States and El Salvador exchanged merry banter with dignitaries from the Honduran government, and they stood stiffly to attention as they raised the glasses to the toast: 'Her Majesty, the Queen.' All seemed well in Tegucigalpa.

The beano at the embassy might be misinterpreted by the Honduran and Salvadoran poor as a symbol of international indifference to their plight. Only a few hours' drive from Tegucigalpa along unmade roads, through dusty, wretched little towns like sets from a spaghetti Western, lies the remote and mountainous border with El Salvador. Here the Salvadoran army is carrying out what can only be described as mass extermination of thousands of peasants living in the area where guerrillas of the Revolutionary Popular Block (BPR) are based, waging a bloody war with other anti-government forces against the Salvadoran junta.

A 10-day journey along the border area, and dozens of interviews with doctors, priests, Honduran soldiers, Salvadoran refugees and members of Protestant and Catholic aid organizations, provided overwhelming evidence of atrocities of

131

increasing brutality and repression by the Honduran army as well as the Salvadorans.

It was also clear that these were not the excesses of a few brutal and disobedient troops, but a co-ordinated military campaign by the Salvadoran military, assisted by the Honduran army with – according to some Honduran sources – the support of the United Sates.

One American priest who works with the refugees, Father Earl Gallagher, narrowly escaped death from an aerial bombardment as he helped fleeing Salvadorans cross the River Lempa into Honduras on March 18: 'That was my tax money paying for American bombs to drop from American helicopters on to my head,' he told me.

On Tuesday morning, just before dawn, I waited with two doctors, a Frenchman and a Honduran, and a nurse in a pine forest on a precipitous mountainside on the border between El Salvador and Honduras. Word had passed along the peasant grapevine that a small army of refugees, 500 in all, who had been hiding from the Salvadoran army for as long as five months, were about to cross into Honduras. The doctors were tense. Such an exodus is often accompanied by a full-scale air and ground attack by the Salvadoran and Honduran armies, like the one which almost finished Gallagher in March and the one that killed 600 people as they crossed the River Sumpul into Honduras last year, a massacre that outraged international opinion.

At about 6.30 a.m. an old man staggered out of the gloom of the forest. He was barefoot, leaning on a stick and supported on his other side by a colleague. The doctors rushed to help him and he sat on the ground weeping with relief.

Slowly the hundreds of refugees, two-thirds of them women, children and babies who had been on the march for weeks, eating only berries, a little rice and coffee, emerged cautiously into the clearing.

One woman, Saturnina Sanches, had been carried in a string hammock hung on a bamboo pole. Her leg was swollen like a balloon and she clutched her only possessions in a plastic supermarket bag – a gaudy portrait of the Virgin Mary and a sepia print of St Gaspar, a bearded man in a crown and strange tunic, who, she said, had guarded her during two months in the mountains. As we carried her up the slope she said she had broken her legs two weeks before, while fleeing from a Salvadoran bombing raid on a cave where she was hiding.

The momentary relief of the refugees was shattered as a squad of Honduran soldiers in full battle gear, grenades hanging from the webbing at their waists and automatic rifles at the ready, came crashing through the undergrowth. They pushed the man with the walking stick into a ditch, formed a cordon across the track, pointed their rifles and ordered the refugees to go back to El Salvador.

The French doctor, Gérard Bruneau-des-Ouillères, boldly approached the cordon. As the troops poked him in the stomach with their rifles, he called down the wrath of the United Nations upon them and told them they stood before the eyes of the international press. Puzzled and a little frightened by this brave display of authority, the soldiers backed off and, with some churlish prodding and pushing, allowed the refugees to pass.

When we reached the refugee camp near the Honduran border town of Colomoncagua, they gathered round to tell for the first time their stories of life in the Salvadoran border area of Morazan, an existence of almost incomprehensible brutality. One man, who said his son had been tortured, and then executed with a machete by Salvadoran troops, shook his head with disbelief: 'It is as if they did it for fun,' he said.

Here are brief extracts from a few of the dozens of eyewitness report of incidents on the Salvadoran border, gathered from refugees, doctors, priests and aid organizations last week.

It is not possible fully to verify these stories without the evidence of the Salvadoran and Honduran soldiers who are accused of committing the acts – evidence which could be acquired only in the international court and by extensive cross-checking with other eyewitnesses. Some credibility is added to their stories in that none of the refugees I spoke to would confirm a report printed in the the *Guardian* that 1,500 refugees were killed by the Salvadoran army while they hid in a large cave in the border area. None of them knew or had heard of any atrocity on such a scale.

On March 16, 8,000 Salvadoran refugees attempted for two days to cross the River Lempa, near the Honduran border town of Virtud, while the Salvadoran Air Force dropped bombs and strafed them, and the army fired mortar shells and machine-guns. The Honduran army blocked the refugees' escape route by forming a cordon. It was exactly the same technique used at the River Sumpul massacre last May. Then, on March 18, the Honduran army dispersed. Catholic priests and members of the relief organization Caritas helped refugees, most of them women and children, across the river.

The priests say at least 10 of them drowned and others were hit by bullets. Father Manuel Himenez was swimming with two elderly women when bullets raked across the woman on his right and her body floated downstream. Fr Gallagher saw people killed by mortars.

He and Father Fausto Milla say that at least 20 male Salvadoran refugees were killed by Honduran troops on the Honduran side of the river. Some were shot, some beaten to death with rifle butts. Another Salvadoran was killed by a Honduran soldier with a machete. The number of dead on the Salvadoran side of the river is unknown. The Honduran government denies that anything happened at the River Lempa that day just as it denied, at first, that anything happened at the River Sumpul last May.

On March 22, the French doctor, Bruneau des Ouillerès, was driving on the road a few miles from Colomoncagua and as he passed the River Negro the road was blocked by Honduran troops who turned him back. Bruneau stopped his jeep and walked through the forest towards the river.

He waited for the Honduran troops to leave and found the corpses of 16 recently-killed males, some of whom had Salvadoran identity papers. They had been burned on the arms and legs, some had been staked to the ground, then shot repeatedly in the chest. Two other men were still alive but mortally wounded. He went to get help. When he returned the 18 bodies were gone. He lodged a protest with the Honduran army in Tegucigalpa and with the United Nations in Geneva.

These are the accounts of peasant refugees from the Morazan province, most of them from the canton of Meanguera:

Pedro Hernandez, 57. Three of his cousins were shot by Salvadoran troops when they raided his house and burnt it to the ground. He hid in a cave with his two daughters and about 70 other people. There was room to sit but not to stand up. For days they had water but no food. They were under frequent aerial attack from bombs 'that exploded with flame and burnt everything around.' They escaped during a lull in the bombing.

Porfirio Mejie, 42, from Meanguera: On January 12, Salvadoran soldiers shot his 17-year-old son in the field outside his home. The army launched a full-scale attack on his village with planes and troops. He estimated 80 people were killed. He fled to a cave on the perimeter of the village. For days he counted five planes buzzing the village, firing machineguns and dropping bombs. They burnt the houses and the fields. He spent two months in the mountains before he escaped to Honduras.

Andres Ramirez from Meanguera: Troops came into his house and asked where the guerrillas were hiding. He said he did not know and they shot his wife, Maria, in the head. He fled to the mountains. He stayed in the village of Zapotal – which, he says, was then attacked, leaving 42 dead. 'Some of them were women who had just given birth, some were babies.'

Guadelupe Romero, 71, from the village of Cuacamaya: Troops came into his house on October 16, lined up his 26-year-old daughter and his four grandchildren aged 11, nine, six and two, and shot them.

Catelina Ramierezi, 21, from Meanguera: 40 soldiers came into her house and asked her husband for his identification. They took him into the front garden and shot him. Her mother-in-law was walking towards the house and they shot her too.

Flore Fidaz, 21, from Junquillo: Her mother, two sisters and seven nephews and nieces, aged six, three, seven, two months and five months, were killed by Salvadoran troops. Her sisters were raped and their throats cut. The older children had their throats cut. The babies were strangled. She fled from the house and saw a soldier tying a grenade round the waist of a small child. The soldier exploded the grenade, killing the child in front of his parents.

The most terrible story of all was told to me by Santiago Hernandez, who is only 10. He comes from Torola. He was working in the fields and went home to find his mother, father, four brothers and four sisters all dead on the floor. 'They had blood all over their chests. They were piled up. I ran away to another village, a place called Zapotal. They were bombing with planes. I hid for four nights, then a lady took me with her and we came to Honduras.'

The 450 refugees who plodded into Honduras on Tuesday now share a refugee camp with 4,500 other Salvadorans. They live in orange and green tents and have insufficient medicine or food. Unless the doctors receive more antibiotics some of them may die. The only thing they do not lack is spiritual succour. On Tuesday the 450 new arrivals, exhausted after their weeks of marching, were greeted by Jimmy Swaggart, a US television evangelist, in his spotless safari suit. He had flown into the border area in a fleet of three planes loaded with film equipment for a Swaggart TV Special. As the video cameras rolled, he led the refugees, all of whom are Catholics, in a chorus of Jesus Loves You. He then asked them to bow their heads and pray for forgiveness.

The president of Honduras, General Policarpo Paz Garcia, also resorted to prayer last week at a reception given by the American Association of Christian Businessmen in a Tegucigalpa hotel. It was one of his first public appearances after a lengthy illness. His subjects say irreverently that he had been on a *pata* – a drunken binge – since New Year's Eve, when his 'illness' was clearly visible and he had to be propped upright by the Honduran archbishop.

The president and his American hosts at the reception sat in front of bottles of Coca-Cola and took part in what was described as 'moments of meditation to search for a solution to the problems of Honduras.'

Sunday Times
26 April 1981

Crusaders in the crossfire

Honduras has become the latest victim in the struggle between the Left and Right in Central America. Roman Catholic priests do what they can for their desperately poor parishioners – but they too have become victims of the violence.

Father Earl Gallagher, a country priest, clattered up the road to his parish of Guarita, high in the Honduran mountains close to the border with El Salvador. He drove in starts and jumps, his Toyota jeep locked into four-wheel drive as the road plummeted almost vertically into rivers and up the other side through thick mud and across bedrock.

He remembers glancing in his rear-view mirror at a Jeep that followed closely behind and watching a scene that was like a clip from an old gangster movie. The passenger leant out of the side door of the pursuing Jeep, aimed a handgun at Gallagher and fired. Bullets whined around him. With a presence of mind that would do credit to a stuntman, Gallagher slewed his Toyota off the track, crashed into the undergrowth and rolled out of the driving seat into the cover of a ditch.

His attackers paused for a moment then drove off. Gallagher recognized an officer from the Honduran army based in the camp in Guarita. A bruised but otherwise intact Gallagher walked off to find help.

He is an unpriestly looking man. He was born in Brooklyn, New York, worked for years with young blacks in Harlem and still talks with the fast wit of the New York streets. He is 38, small and wiry with a tousled grey beard. Except for special, ceremonial occasions he always wears a T-shirt and jeans. He is a long-distance runner and can often be seen jogging across the Honduran hills on parochial business.

He amuses and bemuses his flock who cannot understand why someone so young should show such a chronic symptom of old age as grey hair. They call him, affectionately, 'the old billy goat'. But a priest he is, trained in the Capuchin order of the Roman Catholic Church, a group founded in 1525 and noted for its asceticism and charitable work. The assassination attempt last year was not a case of mistaken identity and it came as no surprise. When Gallagher went to complain at the army barracks about the attempt to kill him, he was roughed up and sent away.

The priests have aroused the hostility of the local landlords, the Honduran army and, to a lesser extent, the government, who suspect them of communist sympathies and support for the guerrillas in neighbouring El Salvador. At the very least, the democratic, socialist ideals of the Capuchins are seen by the authorities as a disruptive influence on the Honduran peasant.

Gallagher and five other Capuchins, all Americans, work in an unusual parish. It is vast, covering 170 towns, villages and hamlets in west Honduras, some of them so remote and inaccessible that the priests have to leave their Jeeps and ride on donkeys. The country is spectacularly beautiful. Mountains covered in pine forests soar into the clouds from valleys full of banana trees, corn and coffee plantations. Waterfalls gush out of sheer rock faces and buzzards circle constantly in the thermal currents.

Their parishioners are among the poorest people on earth. More than half the children are under-nourished and the families eke out a subsistence living. Disease is rife and medical treatment is primitive and hard to get.

The priests work with the peasants, attempt to organize farm co-operatives, schools and clinics and aid to the 11,000 Salvadoran refugees who fled across the border away from the war between the guerrillas and the army in their own country. On the whole, they get little credit for it.

Being a priest in Central America is a hazardous profession. In El Salvador, there were the murders of Archbishop Oscar Romero and the four American nuns, but in less publicized assassinations, dozens of priests and their lay workers have been killed in Central America in the past decade. So far, Honduras has avoided such bloody extremes, but these six American priests who work in a remote, extremely tense area near the Salvadoran border face the greatest threat.

All the priests have been threatened with death or expulsion: two church delegates, laymen who represented the priests in the villages and who worked with the Salvadoran refugees, have been found dead. One priest was arrested, claimed he had been tortured and fled the country. In a bold move, the Church threatened in late 1981 to excommunicate the entire Honduran army if the priests were threatened or molested. 'We may have gone a bit far there,' said Gallagher's colleague, Father Joe Gurak.

Although their position has eased since the Pope's visit to Honduras earlier this year, the priests have often been frightened and demoralized. Parishioners would walk out during their sermons, shopkeepers would refuse to serve them especially in San Marcos, a small town near the Salvadoran border and the home of many of the more conservative landowners. Each army roadblock – and there are dozens of them to stop Salvadoran guerillas infiltrating and arms flowing the other way through to Salvador – became a test of nerves.

Gurak, who is 40 and comes from Yonkers, New York, felt 'a rejection of my work and my person. People wouldn't listen to what I said or talk to me. What goes on in Honduras – the hatred, violence and poverty – became almost too real. I had a sense of failure. I felt the work I was doing was like dropping pebbles into the Grand Canyon.'

The Capuchins sent him back to New York for rest and recuperation: 'Going to bed at night I could feel the pain going out of my feet,' said Gurak. Nonetheless, he began to miss the rigours of life in Honduras. 'When I first came here I thought I could be Honduran. I quickly realized I could not. Simply, they have an ability to suffer which I do not possess. But back in the States I missed their warmth, the closeness of their families. I thought there was still something I could do.'

I first met Earl Gallagher in 1981 during a *Sunday Times* investigation into the massacre the year before of between 500 and 800 Salvadoran refugees, mostly women and children. They were killed as they tried to cross the River Sumpul, which marks the border between Salvador and Honduras, in a joint operation against Salvadoran guerillas conducted by the Salvadoran and Honduran armies. The violence was horrific. Children were cut in half by Salvadoran soldiers and mercenaries; the bodies of dead babies turned up in fishermen's nets downstream.

Gallagher had been walking one morning near the Sumpul and noticed the banks of the river looked black. 'They were covered in a carpet of buzzards,' he said. 'I went closer and found the bodies.' He carefully gathered evidence and tape recordings of eyewitness reports and sent them off to Washington. Nothing happened. The Honduran and Salvadoran governments at first denied the killings took place. The world's press paid scant attention. Gallagher's disillusion was so great that he was on the point of leaving for good. It seemed that nobody much cared about this obscure banana republic.

That, at least, has changed. Honduras is firmly on the map in both Washington and Moscow. It has become the land-based carrier for US troops, in their fight against communism in the area, to wage a covert and guerrilla war against the leftwing Sandinista regime in Nicaragua, and to combat the communist guerrillas who threaten the US-backed government of El Salvador. Honduras, which has a fledgling democracy under President Suazo Cordova after years of military rule, describes itself as an 'oasis of peace' in Central America and has become America's firmest ally in the region.

In September, 1,000 US soldiers splashed through the surf on to a beach near the Honduran town of Puerto Cortes as a naval battle group lay offshore. They were the first instalment of 5,000 men in a massive US military manoeuvre called Big Pine

II which will continue into 1984. The point of the operation, as one US officer bluntly put it, is 'to scare the shit out of Nicaragua' and to show US support for its Honduran ally.

News travels fitfully in the remoter areas of Honduras. Three hours away by Jeep, at the priests' house at Ocotepeque, a dusty little town only half a mile away from the border with El Salvador, life went on as normal.

Gallagher was due to go on a month's leave and was rushing from room to room saying goodbye with the eagerness of a small boy at the end of term: his dream of a large, rare sirloin steak with chips in a New York steak house was drawing closer. Father Joe Walsh, who at 69 is the oldest of the six priests, wore a tartan hat and yellow trousers like an elderly Floridian dressed for a round of golf. In fact he was off to see an 82-year-old Honduran who was sick and thought he was going to die. Walsh gave him the last rites while the old man's grand-daughter brought the coffin back from the house on a donkey. It will be stored in the rafters until the old man needs it.

Philip Bowen, a Capuchin from New York on a brief two-month visit, came back from Guarita, the almost inaccessible village up in the mountains, carrying a two-year-old boy called Francisco. The mother had thrust him into Bowen's arms saying the boy was starving and she couldn't afford to feed him. Francisco will now grow up in the church hospital which has become a small orphanage.

Joe Gurak drove off to Santa Lucia to celebrate Corpus Christi. It is a dismal place in a perfect setting. A few huts huddle in front of a stone church where a boy rang the bell as the priest arrived. The visible poverty of Santa Lucia is a sign that, although Honduras may now be at the centre of American geo-political strategy, its fortunes have declined rather than improved. The people are even poorer than they were last year. Malnutrition is increasing and some are actually starving to death.

Superficially, there seems no reason why Honduras should be the second poorest country in Central America next to Haiti. It is lush and big with 43,000 square miles for a population under four million. But the main exports – coffee, bananas and wood – have declined because of depressed world prices and lower US demand. Although half the peasants own some land as a result of an agrarian reform policy dating back to 1962, individual holdings are often too small to be viable and there is no money for development.

The priests help the peasants to organize into larger, more profitable farms; they advise on the best uses of resources; and fight oppression by the landlords, army and government, who see them as a direct challenge to their long-established rule.

According to a Honduran human rights report issued by an organization called Centro de Documentacion de Honduras, 49 people were assassinated for political reasons in the first six months of this year; 22 people have disappeared; others have been tortured and imprisoned without trial.

Father Joe Walsh says: 'The people are fatalistic. You can't tell people to take up arms, they would be killed. Violence is not the only way, although the army is afraid that will happen. The elections in 1981 seemed to be their big chance. They had a democratic government, but nothing happened. If anything their conditions are worse. We have to work against poverty in the small towns by getting the peasants to organize and help themselves. It's slow but we're getting there.'

A group of men standing under a beech tree in Santa Lucia cautiously discussed national events. They had heard of the American military manoeuvres on the radio and one man, a peasant with a tiny piece of land, thought they were a good thing. 'The Americans will protect us from the guerrillas in Salvador and Nicaragua,' he said. 'We don't want to be like that. Things are bad in those countries.' Another man disagreed. He thought it was dangerous and that Honduras did not want a war with anyone. 'The Americans are pushing us into a war with Nicaragua,' he said.

On the whole, conversation fixed on the immediate business of living. Last year's harvest had been a disaster. The villagers had run out of their own corn and beans in February, seven months earlier, and had been buying at high prices ever since. 'Things are critical,' said Theresa Deras, who has six children and is expecting her seventh. 'People are buying salt and sugar in little twists of paper for a few cents. I used to sell sweets and

142

biscuits I bought in El Salvador but now no one can afford to buy them.'

A question about Honduran politics was greeted with silence except for a throat being cleared and phlegm hitting the stones outside the church. The village is riddled with fear and suspicion: about the next meal and the next harvest; about the army, which is based nearby and has raped some of the local girls; about the Salvadoran guerrillas who have raided neighbouring villages; and about war with Nicaragua.

There is suspicion too about the evangelical sects which vie with the Catholic Church for the peasant souls. There are more than 20 of them, including the Reverend Moon's church, working in Honduras. They pose a direct challenge to the Catholic Church. They are better funded, and their grim recipe for salvation – no drinking, no dancing, no singing, no extra-marital sex – seems to have an appeal for the peasants. The priests admit that the evangelicals are eroding their flock in many of the parishes.

It was a relief to find among Gurak's parishioners something rare in any society in the world, a completely happy man. Alehandro Landaverdi lives in a mud hut in a cornfield in an area called Mangos Mochos ('mangoes cut off'), named casually a few years ago after someone cut down a mango tree. He is a grizzled man of 60 who looks after five young children. His wife lives and works as a cleaning lady in a house a few miles up the mountain.

His hut contains no furniture, just some blankets on the floor. There is no electricity, sewerage or running water. He has a fat, black pig that sprawls in the yard, a few chickens and a thin dog. His three daughters are pretty until they smile: all of them have lost their front teeth.

'I am gloriously happy,' he said. 'Life has been good to me.' He is building an extension to his hut so that 'I can have guests visiting me'. They will have a perilous journey. The track to his cornfield runs about three miles from the nearest road and crosses two rivers. The first has a rope bridge which sways and creaks 30 feet above the river. A third of the wooden planks have rotted away. The second rope bridge is lower and shorter, but the handrails are made of barbed wire. Anyone who loses their balance and grabs the rail will get a gash on the hand. 'The mayor said he would fix the bridges,' said Alehandro's son-in-law, 'but there isn't enough money.'

Alehandro grabbed the land with a group of local peasants two years ago from the landowners, two women called Maria and Therese, who live in San Marcos. As it was uncultivated, they could, according to Honduran law, take it over. But Maria and Therese called the army and had them thrown off. They returned – and so did the army. One peasant was arrested and Alehandro went into hiding. But the peasants were persistent and, after a year of army harassment, they settled on the land. Alehandro still carries a large revolver stuffed into his belt.

His plot provides a miserable living. He eats tortillas, rice and beans. 'Meat,' he says, 'is difficult.' He sells his produce to the travelling dealer, called the 'coyote', for knockdown prices because he cannot transport the corn all the way to market. He is still happy: 'I work until I am sleepy and then I read the Bible until the light fades and then I sleep.'

We left Alehandro's hovel, which is flea-ridden and swarming with small, yellow flies, still glowing with his golden vision of the simple life. A few hundred yards down the path towards the barbed wire bridge, the dream was dented. His son-in-law, Hose Enriques, who escorted us, launched a withering attack on poor Alehandro. 'Don't listen to him, he is an old fool who knows nothing,' said Enriques. 'Most of his children don't get education and they don't get enough to eat. And you know what he said about reading the Bible. He is a liar. He can't read.'

This friction within Alehandro's family points to a much broader conflict. Alehandro is the sort of peasant the Honduran Government and the US administration like to see, contented and uncomplaining. It is a rare virtue. The priests see increasing despair and restlessness among many of the poorest families which, if the government continues to ignore it, could produce yet another violent revolution in Central America.

Next morning at the priests' house in Ocotepeque, Francisco, the starving little boy who had been abandoned by his mother and put in the hospital, was sitting listlessly on a bench, his eyes staring, like an old man. The nurse said he had had some food and was doing very well. Earlier that morning he had looked around and even, the nurse thought, given the glimmer of a smile. 'He should be OK in a few months,' she said. On this occasion, at least, Gurak and the priests had dropped something considerably more substantial than a pebble into the Grand Canyon.

Sunday Times Magazine
13 November 1983

Haiti's unholy war

The voodoo drums in the Caribbean island of Haiti will beat with more than their usual frenzy later this month in celebration of a military and political victory by the voodoo priests.

The thousands of priests and priestesses and their followers, believed to form the bulk of Haiti's six million inhabitants, will be able to practise their dark rites legally for the first time since Haiti's independence in 1804. On March 29, Haitians will vote in a referendum on a new constitution which will guarantee freedom of expression for all religions, including voodoo. The vote is expected to be a resounding Yes.

It will be a political triumph for the priests, called Houngans, and follows what they claim as a victory in a vicious, and largely unreported, 'holy war' between the followers of voodoo and Haitian Christians.

Max Beauvoir, who calls himself the 'voodoo pope' of Haiti, says that 1,500 voodoo priests and priestesses were slaughtered last year by 'Christians', both Catholic and Protestant. Beauvoir says they were hunted down and killed with stones and machetes by the Christian mobs. Some were disembowelled, others were mutilated, burnt and tortured. Haitian newspapers report a lower death toll, but the incidents are still terrifying: 30 bodies of voodoo priests found in a temple last April, a dozen priests killed last June, a priest and priestess murdered in the same month.

146

'We have 67 verified deaths, including five priests roasted to death in Gonaives in July,' said Haiti's Ethnology Bureau director, Dr Max Paul, who has tried to monitor the killings. 'Hundreds more have been killed and buried secretly, temples have been destroyed and more than 1,000 priests' homes have been ransacked.'

Although officially illegal, voodoo, an ancient African religion, has always been widely practised in Haiti. The late president, Papa Doc Duvalier, used the priests as spies on the peasants and sometimes wore the traditional clothes – a black top hat and dark glasses – of the malign voodoo god, Baron Samedi.

Many Catholic and Protestant priests in Haiti have denounced voodoo as 'Satanic' and called on the Houngans to renounce their faith. But they deny any involvement in the killings. Father Jean Bertrand Aristide, a Catholic priest whom Beauvoir considers one of his greatest enemies, says that killings have taken place, but that the motive was political, not religious.

The massacres began a year ago when the Haitan dictator, Jean Claude Duvalier, Papa Doc's successor, fled the country, taking an estimated 800 million dollars of State money with him. Many voodoo priests were thought to be close to Duvalier and to be members of his hated militia, the Ton Ton Macoute. As the Catholic Church, and particularly the Pope's visit to Haiti in 1984, sparked the revolution against Duvalier, there was a natural tension between the Catholics and the Houngans.

Beauvoir denies this and has his own strange conspiracy theory: that it was an attempt, by a coalition of the Christian Churches with the blessing of President Reagan, to stamp out voodoo. But why would President Reagan devote even a moment of his time to attacking voodoo priests in Haiti? 'We know he is very concerned,' said Beauvoir. 'He talked about "voodoo economics".' Beauvoir also accuses the United States, which gives the bulk of foreign aid to Haiti, of defoliating the trees and poisoning the people.

Whatever the motive, Beauvoir, whose own temple was attacked and his brother-in-law shot, was not prepared to turn the other cheek. The Houngans returned violence with violence: 'I like to think that we, although not me personally, killed an equal number of the Christians,' he said. The voodoo priests 'caught Christians and cut them up into three parts. They put the bodies in sacks along with 50 gourdes (10 US dollars) and sent them to their families. They quickly got the message,' said Beauvoir. After these reprisals, he says, the killing of voodoo priests reduced to a trickle of two or three a month.

The men at the centre of Haiti's religious tensions are bizarre. Beauvoir sits in his fashionable Peristyle (voodoo temple) just outside Port au Prince at a desk with a computer terminal, two telephones and an Anglepoise lamp. The keys to his new Peugeot hang on a 500-year-old statue of the voodoo god of communication, Legba.

Each morning he logs on to his IBM computer, containing such files as 'voodoo precepts', 'the methodology of voodoo' and lists of murdered priests. 'My IBM is an important weapon against the Christians' said Beauvoir. 'I can analyse their tactics.'

Beauvoir is a cultivated man of 53, educated in biochemical engineering in the US and at the Sorbonne in Paris. He speaks four languages fluently. He became a voodoo priest in 1973 when his grandfather, who was a Houngan, asked him to do so on his deathbed. Beauvoir is now getting a national and even international reputation. He has organized the voodoo priests and their supporters into a national political lobby called the 'Bode National'. He has started a world voodoo organization with its headquarters in the Caribbean Cultural Centre in New York. Last week a Japanese academic went to his Peristyle to discuss 'the correlation between voodoo and Japanese history.'

One of the leaders of the radical Catholics in Haiti is Father Artistide, a small, intense young man who was ordained as a priest five years ago. He describes himself as a 'liberation theologist' and his views seem remote from the Vatican. He believes, for example, that the leaders of the Catholic Church are white supremacists attempting to force their culture and teachings on the blacks of Haiti.

In his office in a Catholic school in Port au Prince Father

Aristide has a full-size effigy of a Ton Ton Macoute with a noose round its neck hanging from a hook in the ceiling. He is very proud of it. 'The uniform is real. It came from the body of a murdered Macoute,' he said.

None of this bodes well for the Haitian people, who are plagued by poverty, illiteracy, malnourishment, government corruption and disease. Malaria and tuberculosis still devastate the population and, in the absence of official statistics, some foreign doctors believe that one in seven Haitians carries the Aids virus.

Foreign doctors blame the 'cures' of voodoo witch-doctors, who are still feared and respected, for many of the country's health problems.

Although the religious war has fizzled out, there is likely to be political violence as the presidential election race hots up this summer. Few Haitians believe that the election will solve their problems. 'There have been many presidents in Haiti,' said Father Aristide. 'But they are all the same. There are some people saying take up weapons, but I say what is the point of that?' Aristide says he will use 'priestly weapons: love and prayer'.

The effigy hanging in his office, however, tells a different story.

Sunday Telegraph
15 March 1987

The
snake-charmer

Among the millions of Salvadorans who voted in the Presidential elections last weekend was a curious figure: a male, elderly Englishman in a neat white shirt and a peaked cap, who would look more at home on the Sussex Downs than on the gusty streets of San Salvador.

John Boursot, a small, rather fragile man with a few strands of grey hair, is known locally as Don Juan. He is 75, was born in Sussex, grew up in South Kensington and has lived in El Salvador since 1944. He has joint British/Salvadoran citizenship and has worked for 19 years as the curator of reptiles at the zoo in San Salvador, the country's capital.

Many Salvadorans are afraid to say how they voted for fear of reprisal from right-wing death squads, the army of the Communist guerrillas. But it takes more than a threat to frighten a man who has survived being bitten by a lethal coral-snake, a viper, and a puff adder.

'I voted for Arena (the Right-wing party which won the election),' said Mr Boursot, who is a virulent anti-Communist. 'These Arena chaps might be tough enough to defeat the guerrillas. The other parties are absolutely hopeless.'

Five days a week Mr Boursot walks two miles from his house to his ramshackle reptile house. In a city racked by civil war, where bombs explode almost every night, where there are kidnappings, rapes, and the bodies of political victims turn up

150

regularly in ditches and rubbish dumps, few Salvadorans have the time or inclination to visit the zoo.

It is a sorry, neglected place, and, according to Mr Boursot a fitting symbol of modern Salvador. 'It is really the zoo of death . . . Everything seems to die here.'

The ground just inside the zoo entrance looked black from a distance and seemed to move. It was a thick carpet of black buzzards. 'They are visitors not residents,' Mr Boursot explained. They were waiting for scraps of meat from the lions' cage at feeding time, or perhaps for the demise of another of the zoo's residents.

The crocodile poked its nose through the green slime of its pond and Mr Boursot prodded the snout with a metal pole. The crocodile sprang to life, brushing its head and snapping at the sprightly Mr Boursot. 'Poor old chap. Thought he might be getting his lunch,' he said.

He leaned over the furious reptile and sang a song in a high voice: 'Dee, dee, dee, dum, dum, dum.' He does this to all the animals, even to his deadly, bad-tempered pet rattlesnake, which spits venom at the glass window of its cage every time Mr Boursot brushes past.

Mr Boursot opened its door and stroked its back with one finger. 'Dee, dee, dee, dum, dum, dum.' The snake rattled and reared its head. Mr Boursot whipped his finger out of the cage. 'Calm down old chap, calm down.'

The list of casualties at San Salvador's zoo is alarming, the result, according to Mr Boursot, of neglect, stupidity and occasional malice. The baby elephant died after it killed its keeper by throwing him to the ground with its trunk and stamping on his chest with his foot. 'Starvation,' Mr Boursot explained. 'They fed it one quart of milk instead of 24 quarts.'

A former zoo director ate the swans for his Christmas dinner. Young king vultures were found dead a few weeks after they emerged from their shells, murdered, Mr Boursot postulated, by a rival of the curator of birds.

The zoo was given a pelican. 'The staff had no idea what it was.' They fed it with tortillas until the pelican, which eats fish, was almost starving to death and collapsed with its bill dragging on the floor.

151

Mr Boursot took it home, gave it minnows to eat, and the pelican seemed to thrive. 'I put it in a taxi and took it to the sea (about 40 miles from San Salvador) . . . It was very lively. We stood on the road by the beach and as cars went past it watched them and swished its head from side to side. Swish, swish.'

Mr Boursot let it go and watched it flap out to sea. Then, suddenly, it dive-bombed into the sea and disappeared. 'I don't know what it was,' said Mr Boursot, 'a heart attack perhaps.' Or the curse of San Salvador's zoo.

The bison died. A mountain goat died and the zoo staff buried it in a hole too small for its body: its rotting head and horns stuck out of the ground.

'There is no interest in the zoo, no enthusiasm; nobody gives a damn, if you will excuse the expression,' said Mr Boursot. A wading bird was moved to a new pool with high concrete sides. The bird tried to wade in, fell 3ft into the water and drowned.

The zoo bought a giraffe, but as they loaded it into a truck it had a heart attack and died. A zebra arrived dead. 'We lost an ostrich, an antelope, a baby tiger, a tapir, parrots and a sloth,' said Mr Boursot. Boys climbed over the zoo's walls and stoned the hippo. It survived. A woman grabbed a goldfish out of the ornamental pond and put it in her handbag. It died before Mr Boursot could get to it.

Mr Boursot has a bungalow near the city-centre where, since the death of his father at the age of 98 and a half, he has lived alone. It is little piece of English suburbia, with chintzy chairs, thick curtains and prints of the Sussex Downs near Arundel. His father was a champagne importer in England and Mr Boursot came to El Salvador really by accident.

He was in the United States in 1939 when his American visa expired. 'There were no ships to England because of the war, so I went to Miss Rose at the Bon Marché Travel Agency in New York and said: "Where should I go?" "Guatemala," she replied.'

After four years in Guatemala his visa expired, and he accepted the hospitality of El Salvador where he has lived ever since.

The job of reptile curator has allowed him to indulge his love of snakes, which dates back to 'when I was the size of a grasshopper'.

He visited Britain on holiday for the first time in 1982 and found that both good and bad things had happened.

He marvelled at the punctuality of trains in modern Britain and the automatic doors that open and close between compartments. 'You go through these doors like a prince,' he said. He went from London to Oxford by train and enjoyed it so much he was reluctant to get off. 'It left at 1.25 pm exactly. The punctuality was alarming.'

There is no such alarm in El Salvador. He has been waiting for a phone, damaged in the earthquake, for two years. His electricity and water is almost always off because of guerrilla attacks on the outskirts of the city. He shares his house with a dog, the bad-tempered rattlesnake, a pair of king-cobras, which lay contented in their cage digesting a pair of rats, and a large tortoise which lives in his dining room. The pickled head of a viper and the corpse of a giant scorpion stand on the table.

Mr Boursot believes that the Communist guerrillas will eventually take over in El Salvador, as they well might, and then he says he will suffer the same fate as most of the animals at the zoo. Meanwhile it is a lonely, precarious life sustained by Mr Boursot's strange passion for the reptiles in the zoo of death.

Last week there was more bad news. One of his tiny cardinal tropical fish seemed poorly and appeared to be floating upside-down. 'I think it has tuberculosis,' said Mr Boursot. 'It is probably doomed.'

Sunday Telegraph
26 March 1989

Noriega's sex trap shackles United States

The US ambassador to Costa Rica, Curtin Winsor, received an intriguing invitation in 1985 from the military chief of neighbouring Panama, General Manuel Noriega. He asked Mr Winsor if he would like to spend a weekend at one of the General's country retreats.

Ambassador Winsor was approached by Gen. Noriega's brother, who explained the delights awaiting him. The villa was on the Azuero Peninsula overlooking the Pacific. There would be good food, deep-water fishing and an opportunity to discuss Central America. There were other, more exotic, pleasures which Gen. Noriega's brother failed to mention.

Mr Winsor was interested, despite Gen. Noriega's growing reputation as a drug dealer, arms smuggler, tyrant and double agent. 'I knew he was a scumball, but not a contagious scumball, if you know what I mean,' he said.

He decided to check it out and rang his friend, Ted Briggs, the US ambassador to Panama. Mr Briggs roared with laughter and told Mr Winsor he was about to spend the weekend in one of the most notorious 'honey traps' in Latin America. 'It was a set-up,' said Mr Winsor. Gen. Noriega lured senior American officials from Congress, the CIA, the Defence Department and the Administration to the villa, which was stocked not only with seafood but also with bevvies of pretty girls or pretty boys for the delectation of his guests.

The bedrooms were wired for sound and equipped with

154

hidden cameras. As the important guests cavorted they were captured on film, which the General would store in his vast film library as an insurance policy for the future.

Mr Winsor turned the invitation down. Many other US officials did not. 'I can't give you names, but look around,' said Mr Winsor. 'Who's soft on Noriega? That's where you should look.'

Gen. Noriega's efforts to entrap US officials were not always so subtle. A colonel based in the Canal Zone was summoned to Gen. Noriega's house in Panama City for 'important discussions'. The colonel arrived in full military dress to find Gen. Noriega naked with a girl or (the colonel is not quite sure) a boy sitting on his lap. Semi-naked, senior members of the Panamanian Defence Force lay around their leader like actors in a Roman orgy. 'I want to show you what I really am, Colonel, so there is complete trust between us,' said Gen. Noriega. The colonel left.

Mr Winsor, who was ambassador to Costa Rica from 1983 to 1985, believes that Gen. Noriega's ability to blackmail US officials is the only logical reason for what he describes as America's 'spectacular inaction' over Noriega and Panama. 'Godammit,' said Mr Winsor. 'The State Department has been saying "Kill the son of a bitch". The CIA, the DoD [Department of Defence] and the other agencies do nothing.'

US inaction during the coup attempt in Panama 10 days ago could indeed be described as 'spectacular' and President George Bush faces growing criticism from Congress, the press and his party for bungling an opportunity to oust Gen. Noriega. Nobody has suggested that Mr Bush stars in one of Noriega's blue movies, but the President's and the US's relationship with the General is curious and raises disturbing questions. It also casts grave doubt on the sincerity of Mr Bush's war on drugs.

A theme heard continually among the Panamanian opposition leaders and US officials who have attempted to investigate Gen. Noriega is that the General 'must have something on the US administration'. Efforts to expose Noriega and uncover his links to the US have been blocked time and time again.

The Miami prosecutor, Dick Gregorie, who indicted Noriega on drug trafficking charges, quit the government earlier this year disgusted by what he regards as the sham nature of the war on drugs.

Jack Blum, former counsel to the Senate Foreign Relations Committee, spent years investigating the US/Panamanian connection. He too has left Congress in disgust at US inaction. He discovered that the US gave Noriega 'all kinds of mixed signals', a mixture of public condemnation and private encouragement.

Mr Blum says that a 1986 policy review by the State Department which recommended strong action against the General was shelved. 'The State Department was told by higher levels to forget it,' said Mr Blum. He describes the US economic sanctions against Panama as a 'farce'. 'The US administration imposed sanctions and the Treasury Department immediately exempted most of the major payments to the Panamanian Government.'

Senator John Kerry wrote to the US General Accounting Office last year to ask every government agency for their information on Noriega. But the National Security Council banned any agency from giving information to the GAO or to Senator Kerry. 'The NSC was putting the lid on the garbage,' said Mr Blum.

Gen. Noriega's involvement with Colombian drug traffickers has been known since the early 1970s, when an investigation by the US Drug Enforcement Agency recommended in the secret Defeo Report that Noriega should be assassinated.

In 1978, the DEA has reports of Noriega's visits to Medellin in Colombia to meet the heads of the drug cartel. Through the Seventies and Eighties Panama became the money-laundering centre and the main drug trans-shipment area for the Medellin bosses. Gen. Noriega was, simultaneously, in the illegal arms business and sent weapons to the anti-American Marxist guerrillas in El Salvador and to the Sandinistas in Nicaragua.

Mr Blum is nagged by worrying questions. Why did Mr Bush meet Gen. Noriega in 1983 and again in 1986? Why did the head of the US National Security Council, John Poindexter, meet the General in 1985 and 1986? Why did Noriega fly to Washington for a series of meetings with the then head of the CIA, William Casey, in the mid-Eighties? One of the reasons –

to judge from secret documents declassified during the Iran/ Contra investigation – appears to be that the US asked Gen. Noriega for his help in shipping arms to the Contra rebels in Nicaragua and for permission to use his secret drug and arms airfields. If drugs came back to the US as a result then, according to Mr Blum, the US administration turned a blind eye.

It must have confused the General to be attacked by the US administration in public then, in 1986, to be invited as an honoured guest to the US War College in Washington DC.

While the US administration lambasted Noriega the drug dealer, Admiral Dan Murphy, Vice-President Bush's former chief of staff, made two trips to see Noriega in Panama. Admiral Murphy said that he went as a private citizen to drum up business. But there is no doubt, says Mr Blum, about the clear signal of US approval and encouragement these visits gave Noriega.

Mr Gregorie, the former Miami prosecutor, believes that many in Washington regarded his indictment of Noriega as an unfortunate accident. They made their feelings clear, after the indictment was handed down in January 1988, by blocking his attempts to investigate the Panama connection further.

Mr Gregorie argues that if Noriega were to come to trial in the US it could precipitate a 'constitutional crisis'.

In his defence, Noriega could call upon all the documents about his past contacts with the American government. Some of these could be highly embarrassing, for example a full transcript of the 1986 meeting between Vice-President Bush and Noriega. Mr Gregorie spent years amassing evidence of Noriega's connection with drugs but found little help or encouragement from the Department of Justice. 'There were a number of people who said: "What the hell is this, who is this Assistant DA making foreign policy?",' said Mr Gregorie.

He attempted to investigate the smuggling of guns and chemicals used in the manufacture of drugs which is rife in the Panamanian free trade zone. But when he approached the Drug Enforcement Agency for help he was referred to the FBI. When he went to the FBI he was referred back to the DEA. The investigation never took place.

Another prosecutor, Robert Merkle, who was investigating the Medellin cartel's use of the Bahamas, says he received a phone call from the Department of Justice warning him that 'We don't want any more Noriegas'. Mr Merkle knew what this meant. It was a warning not to proceed with the indictment of the Bahamian Prime Minister, Sir Lyndon Pindling. For Mr Gregorie the final blow in his attempts to investigate drug trafficking came when a leading drug boss in the Medellin cartel slipped through his fingers.

Last October, he discovered that Jorge Ochoa was on holiday in Venezuela and he got the permission of the Venezuelan government to seize him. When the US ambassador to Venezuela discovered the activities on his turf, he killed the operation. Two months later Mr Gregorie resigned. 'It was obvious to me they didn't want me there.'

Mr Gregorie now specializes in insurance law for a suburban Miami company.

Sunday Correspondent
15 October 1989

MIDDLE EAST

Inside Sinai: settlers head for last stand

Truckloads of Israeli troops, sirens wailing, roared across the salient in north-east Sinai last Thursday at noon. An army helicopter, belching black smoke, thundered low across the sand dunes. It was a sight that has often terrified Israel's foes. On this occasion, the enemy was a small group of young, unarmed Jews who had moved, illegally, into a makeshift settlement in the middle of a tomato field.

The operation quickly took on more the character of a soap opera than an army raid. A soldier discovered he had been sent, accidentally, to arrest his own younger sister, Tami. Another sat down with the settler he was supposed to remove, and wept in sympathy. One settler, a 17-year-old girl called Nurit, shouted at the soldiers barely older than herself: 'You're not in the army to attack Jews.' The soldiers looked shamefaced. After a few scuffles, and a lot of tears, the settlers were hauled off to army cells in Beer Sheba.

'We will be back again and again,' said Nurit. 'It is God's will.'

Indeed, the scene will be repeated for the duration of what few believed could be achieved without a fight – the withdrawal from the Sinai peninsula which Israel captured from the Egyptians during the Six Day War in 1967. Most of the 3,000 settlers will have gone by the end of this month. The Israeli government is determined that the territory will be handed back at the time laid down in the Camp David agreement – at noon on April 25.

Few doubt that it will succeed, although withdrawal is not proving easy. The pressure is building up dangerously, not so much from settlers but from a group of religious zealots who call themselves the Stop The Sinai Withdrawal Campaign. Last week about 1,500 of them barricaded themselves into the Sinai settlement of Yamit. They will wait, one of them said, either for the prime minister, Menachem Begin, to change his mind or for divine intervention. 'God gave us this land,' said one of the Yamit zealots, Menahem Gottlieb, citing Genesis 15, verse 18 as justification. 'To give it up is to spit in God's face.'

If there is a battle for the Sinai, it will be here, a bleak settlement of concrete maisonettes near the Gaza Strip, now fortified with sandbags and barbed wire. The Yamit Motel, once a haven for tourists, looks like an armed camp, with sentries posted day and night. The militants intend to make their last stand in an air raid shelter just outside the motel.

There are ominous rumours, but little evidence, of armed resistance if the army moves in. There has been talk of suicide. A militant rabbi preached the value of sacrifice and one settler, taking this literally, threatened to stick his finger into a light socket.He then stood on a chair with a rope round his neck and threatened to jump if the army came into his house. The army withdrew.

The Sinai withdrawal is full of bitter ironies. It is a sour task for Begin. He has had to order army demolition teams into the village of Neoth Sinai – the very place to which he said in 1977 he dreamed of retiring, and where he was assigned a three-bedroomed cottage. It will now house Egyptian tourists.

The Israeli defence minister, Ariel Sharon, who almost sabotaged the peace talks by sneaking settlements into the Sinai, is now responsible for clearing them out. He is doing so energetically, and is running ahead of schedule. He foiled the militants' plan to send 100,000 supporters into Sinai by putting up a chain of roadblocks.

The settlers, who were once Israeli folk-heroes, building homes in the wilderness and making the desert bloom, are now seen as greedy parasites on the meagre Israeli exchequer, grabbing fat compensation and moving into villas in Tel Aviv and Jerusalem. Begin has sought to salve his conscience and the settlers' anger by handing out huge sums. The total compensation will be in the region of £165 million.

'The price of peace is high,' an Israeli government spokesman pointed out. The government estimates the total cost of withdrawal – including loss of oil revenue from the Sinai wells, which could have made Israel self-sufficient, the removal and relocation of military bases and the loss of roads and settlements – at more than £11,000 million.

Sinai is four times the size of Israel, a barren triangle of desert and mountains inhabited for centuries by Bedouin tribes. Since the Israeli takeover, the clientele has changed dramatically. The east coast has become a kind of St Tropez where young Israelis and Scandinavians frolic, often in the nude.

To the intense delight of 60 reporters on a government tour of Sinai last Tuesday, they found the lissom, naked form of Karen at the settlement of Neviot. Her breasts jutted provocatively towards the mountain peaks of Saudi Arabia only 14 miles away across the Gulf of Eilat. Karen lamented that her all over suntan will be cruelly interrupted when Neviot shuts down for good next week.

More vital for Israel is the loss of Sinai's 'strategic depth', the 130-mile buffer between Israel and the Egyptian border which served it so well during the Yom Kippur war in 1973. The Israelis will lose three Sinai air bases, two of which are considered to be the most modern in the world with underground, bomb-proof hangars. They will also lose their electronic early-warning bases and a naval base at the tip of Sinai.

'The world should not forget we are giving away this land for peace,' said a government official. 'The Egyptians are giving away nothing.' The Egyptians do not see it quite like that. 'The Sinai is ours,' said an Egyptian tourist, hopping on to a coach on the Israeli side of the border. 'We are getting what is ours.'

The Egyptians argue that the Israelis have got a good deal: that they have handed over a demilitarized zone, policed by a multi-national force of 3,000 and off-bounds to the Egyptian military, which will still serve as a defensive buffer. The

Israelis have neutralized their most powerful neighbour, Egypt, and received an assured oil supply for the next 15 years.

Most settlers we talked to echoed the view of Maureen O'Hara from Staffordshire who sat, demurely in a bikini, on the beach at Neviot. She is married to an Israeli and has lived there for four years. 'We hate to leave but I think the Egyptians are sincere,' she said. 'We should give peace a chance.'

Peace is not assured, however. Although President Hosni Mubarak of Egypt has pledged commitment to Camp David, Israelis fear that in a crisis he will ally with the Arabs, not with Israel.

And a crisis over Palestinian autonomy in the Israeli-occupied West Bank and Gaza is looming. The Egyptians have made it clear they want to see the emergence of an independent Palestinian state but every day Israeli control of the West Bank seems to tighten. There is a proposal before the Israeli parliament tomorrow to replace all 18 Sinai settlements with new ones on the West Bank.

Much of the opposition of West Bank religious zealots from the Gush Emunim movement to the ceding of Sinai stems from their fear that it will be their turn next. Guarantees from Ariel Sharon have a hollow ring. 'We will defend the Jewish communities in the West Bank,' Sharon has said. 'I assure you we would never agree to their removal. Half a million Israelis would stream into the region to stop it.'

The Stop the Withdrawal Movement is thought to be merely flexing its muscles in Sinai for the real battle in the West Bank. 'If the government touches those settlements there will be blood,' said a Yamit militant.

Sunday Times
14 March 1982

Iraq rallies after the desert fiasco

An Iraqi officer waved one arm towards the plain of Dwaireege beneath him, across a desert densely packed with the greatest arms bazaar in the Arab world. His gesture encompassed tanks, heavy artillery, recoilless rifles, anti-tank and anti-aircraft missile batteries by the hundred, thousands upon thousands of trucks and tank transporters, and a maze of bunkers so huge and complex that the desert itself seemed hollow.

'Is this the disintegration of the Iraqi army? Is this defeat, like the Persian propaganda says?' the officer asked rhetorically. He had a point. I was standing with two other reporters, the first to be taken to the new Iraqi battlefront, nearly nineteen miles inside occupied Iran and still about four and a half miles from the Iranian army.

From an observation post, the Iraqi army looked as neat and efficient as a model in a Sandhurst war game. Yet we were close to the Iranian town of Dezful, where the Iraqis last month suffered their most humiliating defeat in a war which they had thought to win in days – but which has dragged on, at a cost of tens of thousands of lives, for a gruelling eighteen months.

The Iraqis, after claiming a 'tactical victory', now officially concede defeat at Dezful. They lost 135 square miles of territory and thousands of prisoners. The carnage on the Iranian side was as horrific. Iraq claims that more than 20,000 Iranians died as they swept, oblivious of the danger, into the Iraqi guns.

'It was terrible,' the officer said. 'The ground was littered with bodies, some still holding their rifles. Our reinforcements began firing at them and I said "You are killing dead men."'

The lumbering Iraqi army – which some military experts regard as overburdened with its Soviet equipment, manned by inexperienced troops – was cut off by a daring Iranian pincer attack. The Iraqis withdrew, baffled by the tactics of the dishevelled Iranian revolutionaries – around whom myths have grown up.

'We captured an Iranian officer and he suddenly took a pill,' an Iraqi soldier said. 'I thought it was cyanide. Then he tried to walk away from his guards. When we grabbed him, he was astonished. He thought the pills had made him invisible.'

Iraqi stories of the Iranians' fanatical bravery are mingled in tales of abject cowardice: 'A French photographer pointed his zoom lens at an Iranian trench and two soldiers promptly surrendered.'

The Iraqis, with their allies and paymasters in the Gulf, were stunned by the Dezful fiasco. They were appalled by Iranian propaganda and the ensuing crop of Western reports that their army had disintegrated and that the Baathist regime of President Saddam Hussein was on the verge of collapse.

To judge by my two trips with the Iraqi army into occupied Iran, the former at least is not true. The Dezful front has been reinforced by thousands of fresh troops: day and night, trucks bring in supplies along the newly surfaced roads.

At a forward command post close to the front, the Iraqis seemed secure and relaxed as they dined on chicken and beef. A BBC man, taping his live report from the front, recorded not gunfire but the sound of Arab music from cassettes, the chirp of birds and the burps of replete Iraqis.

We spent the night in the marshes of Howizeh, within range of Iran's heavy artillery. Gleeful Iraqis watched a hardcore pornographic movie on a video machine. 'The. . . . Persians are saying their prayers,' said one soldier.

On the surface, the Iraqi army exuded confidence. The country itself is embroiled in frenetic construction. Baghdad, where more than £1,140 million is being spent on a new infrastruc-

166

ture, has all the charm of a hot, dusty, mudcoloured building site.

President Hussein is trying to modify his blood-curdling image, well deserved after his vicious treatment of any opposition – from, Kurds, communists and members of his own Baath party to the Shi'ite Muslims who make up more than 50 per cent of the population (Saddam and his government being members of the rival Sunni group of Muslims).

Among the reassuring measures he ordered was for his new portrait to be hung everywhere. It showed a plump, moustachioed, smiling man of 46, with a child on his knee, caring, the father of his people.

Beneath the smile, though, Saddam Hussein is still very tough indeed. His ubiquitous Mukharbarat (secret police), who drive steel-blue Mercedes cars, have infiltrated every aspect of Iraqi society. Protest of any kind is punished ferociously. All foreign publications and even typewriters are banned. Asked on foreign TV if the stories about his repression were true, the president answered proudly: 'Naam' (yes).

Diplomats in Baghdad believe that he is secure because the opposition has been emasculated. But appearances are deceptive and realities in Iraq are hard to come by.

Diplomats are allowed no contact with ordinary Iraqis and confess they are ill-informed. The British embassy has been without a telephone for months. The Americans occasionally have a phone but now have no water.

Last week, Iraq suffered a devastating blow when the Syrians, who are supporting Iran, closed the border with Iraq and cut the oil pipeline, which carried 400,000 barrels of oil a day. At a stroke, Iraq lost almost half its revenue. This will stretch even further the generosity of Saudi Arabia, which is already bankrolling Iraq to the astonishing tune of up to £1,700 million a year.

President Hussein now faces an acute economic crisis – and despite diplomats' belief that he is secure, street gossip in Baghdad gives clues to a different story.

There is evidence of a middle-class backlash against the war as students face call-up on June 1. Students in one bar last week were, somewhat recklessly, cursing their president.

167

Government officials complain about rising prices, there are rumours of dissatisfaction within the army and the Baath party, there are signs of underground anti-Saddam groups among the Shi'ites.

For the moment, Iran and Syria wait for the Saddam Hussein regime to topple while the Iraqis wait for the Ayatollah Khomeini's death or overthrow. The only certainty in this long and bloody war is that the *Baghdad Observer* newspaper will continue to print, each day, its sad list of Iraqi 'martyrs' who have died at the front.

Sunday Times
18 April 1982

Battle of Manger Square

A group of tourists on a pilgrimage to one of the holiest Christian shrines, the reputed site of the manger where Jesus was born, had instead a baptism of fire in the modern politics of the Israeli-occupied West Bank.

As their coach parked in Manger Square, a few yards from the Church of the Nativity, they found that the words of the Christmas carol can be decidedly misleading. The Little Town of Bethlehem is rarely still, these days.

The tourists arrived just when 300 or 400 Palestinians from the nearby Dheisheh refugee camp were gathering outside the police station to protest over the death of an 18-year-old boy, shot by Israeli soldiers during a riot. The demonstrators came equipped with stones, carried in bags tied to the back of a donkey. 'It is very difficult demonstrating in Manger Square. There are no stones lying around,' said one of them.

At about 10.30 a.m., the first stones were thrown and the battle of Bethlehem began. Policemen fired pistols, Uzzis and M16s through the windows of the police station. Bullets whined off the shutters of gift shops, the Arab mosque and the Christian monuments. It was an hour before reinforcements of Israeli soldiers arrived and the rioters dispersed, taking their wounded with them.

This incident took place in what is now a town of some 80,000 Palestinians, half Muslims, half Christians. Bethlehem lies a few kilometres from Jerusalem in territory that Israel captured during the 1967 war. It is in beautiful hilly country which Palestinians consider their home, because they have always lived there, and which Israelis believe is the spoils of war and part of the ancient Jewish homeland.

Every year, 750,000 tourists go there. Religion is big business.

For the inhabitants, though, the violence on the West Bank, the affairs of the Palestine Liberation Organisation and arguments over the next round of autonomy talks between Israel, Egypt and the US, are matters of more urgent concern.

According to the Palestinians, 15 of them were killed and 273 injured, mostly by Israeli bullets, during three weeks last month. Official Israeli statistics put the dead at nine and the injured at 90. Bethlehem has seen its share.

The town is run, in a fashion, by the mayor, Elias Freij, a small man of 63 with a Charlie Chaplin-style moustache. His opulent new office, built with a grant from the Kuwaitis, looks out over Manger Square.

Last week, we both watched as a group of Palestinian students tried to take over the Church of the Nativity. The protest was nipped in the bud by Israeli soldiers, who carted people away in the backs of Land Rovers. Such events are common place. Freij's hand barely paused as he signed letters and souvenir books.

Being one of the 26 Palestinian mayors on the West Bank is a precarious profession. Four mayors have been sacked by the Israelis for their support of the PLO. The future of four more is in the balance. Freij, despite his pledges of loyalty to the PLO as the rightful leaders of the Palestinian people, is perceived as a moderate. Some Israelis hope that such leaders will erode extreme PLO support.

He has become the favourite mayor of foreign politicians. He met Alexander Haig, the US secretary of state, and half the governments of Europe have sent representatives to his parlour.

They all come to hear the Freij solution that the PLO and Israel should mutually recognize each other; that this is part of Saudi Arabia's Fahd peace plan – which, he says, will be accepted at the next Arab summit – and that the Americans will then endorse it and start talking to the PLO.

The Israelis will 'try and stamp their feet' but American and European pressure will force them into negotiations from which a Palestinian state on the West Bank will emerge. Thus the world's most critical problem will be solved.

Having advanced this solution, Freij immediately begins to knock down his own scheme. The Syrians, the most important influence on the PLO, will not accept the Fahd plan. Nor will the Israelis. Nor, in their present mood, 'with feelings at boiling point', will the Palestinians. Freij gazes moodily across Manger Square.

All this may go down well with visiting journalists and politicians. It doesn't find much support in his own community. The radical wings of the PLO have condemned him. So have the students of Bethlehem University, where mention of his name brings hoots of derision.

'Freij is more use to the Israelis than their own soldiers,' said Faiez Damiery, 33-year-old head of the students union. 'He is not allowed on the campus.'

Damiery, who spent five years in Israeli jails for PLO activities added: 'If I wear a T-shirt with the PLO colours, I can be arrested. If I write about the PLO, I am censored. Freij is a quisling who meets secretly with the Israelis' civilian administration. Whatever the Israelis do against us, the PLO gets stronger.'

Freij's comment on Damiery is: 'He is a child, mouthing slogans.'

At the Dheisheh refugee camp in the suburbs of Bethlehem, criticisms that Freij is 'an Israeli Palestinian,' 'a nobody,' cannot be so easily dimissed. His modest proposal is seen as treachery. The 10,000 citizens of Dheisheh are the bedrock of PLO support. They refuse to move from their cramped and squalid camp, built by the UN in 1956, because 'that would give legitimacy to the Israeli occupation.'

Among the camp's inhabitants is Khaled, a deaf-and-dumb boy who guides tourist coaches into parking spaces in Manger Square. Last week as a five-man Israeli army patrol lolled against the wall of the Church of the Nativity, he gave a

171

dramatic mime of the battle of Bethlehem. For his finale, he lobbed an imaginary stone at the soldiers – who, without even flinching, just scowled back.

Sunday Times
9 May 1982

What Reagan's envoy ought to know about the Assad family

The new US special envoy in the Middle East, Robert Mc-Farlane, faces an interview in Damascus today that US diplomats have learned to dread. He is meeting Hafez Al Assad, the president of Syria, a tall man with a stoop and a diffident manner, a posture reminiscent of the French comedian Jacques Tati, but with an international reputation closer to that of Caligula.

In the demonology of the US State Department, Assad looms large. It was his refusal to meet the previous envoy, Philip Habib, that led to the latter's premature retirement two weeks ago. Assad is pro-Soviet, pro-Libyan, passionately anti-Israel and anti-American.

His large army, equipped with brand-new Soviet planes, tanks and sophisticated electronic equipment, faces the Israelis in Lebanon's Beka'a valley and refuses to budge. He is stubborn and ruthless, not hesitating to unleash the Syrian army on his own citizens during a Muslim Brotherhood revolt in the northern city of Hama last year, killing between 10,000 and 20,000 of them.

Assad is now the main obstacle to every US policy in the area – from negotiations for withdrawal of all foreign troops from Lebanon to the broad Reagan initiative for Middle East peace, announced by the US president in September 1981.

McFarlane will find Assad slightly melancholic and even more remote than usual. In the past week, the Syrian leader has effectively lost two of his tiny circle of close aides – not from the bullet, which is customary in Syria, but from disease.

His information minister, Ahmad Iskander, has incurable brain cancer. His former prime minister, Mahmud Ayyoubi, is critically ill in hospital with brain fever, after being bitten by a mosquito. To compound Assad's problems, Syria is suffering an outbreak of typhoid and cholera.

The only ray of hope for US policy passed secretly into the presidential palace in Damascus last week. It was a note from one of Assad's close friends who now lives in the US, urging him to give something, however cosmetic, to President Reagan. 'The Jewish lobby in America fears any president in his second term of office,' the message ran. 'It is in Syria's interest to get Reagan re-elected.'

Despite Assad's critical position in the Middle East, and the fact that he is now wooed by the US administration, he remains a shadowy figure, one of the least known world leaders. McFarlane's diplomatic briefing book will contain only the barest details.

Assad is 53, a man of ascetic tastes who neither drinks nor smokes. He has only one wife. Remarkably for a Syrian leader, he is not corrupt. He was born at Qardaha, in the north-western Latakia province, and is a member of the Al-Matawirah tribe of the Alawite sect, a strange schism from the Muslim Shi'ite faith which developed in the remote area of Syria and took on bits and pieces from the Christian and pagan religions.

The Alawites are a once persecuted minority in Syria (they make up less than 10 per cent of the population, which mostly belongs to the Muslim Sunni sect) and the contempt remains. 'I respect the president,' said a Sunni Muslim who is a friend of Assad, 'but I wouldn't let my daughter marry his son Basil because he is an Alawite. I'd rather she married a Christian.'

For Assad, the dangers of coup and assassination from his own population are greater than the threat from Israel. He fears for his life. Since the last known assassination attempt in 1981, when a member of his own bodyguard rolled a live grenade towards him in the guest palace (the would-be assassin was blown up and Assad unhurt), he has rarely been seen in public.

He appears on TV most nights, performing the affairs of state – but, eerily, there are only pictures and no sound.

Yet he has the reputation of being considerate to his friends, bright and with a wry humour. He works hard, though on a strange schedule, going to bed at 4 a.m. and rising at 11 a.m.

Recently, late one night, he phoned his defence minister, Mustafa Tlass. 'The president was puzzled by the derivation of the Arabic word for "listening,"' Tlass said. 'We spent an hour on the phone, going through reference books, tracking the word back through the centuries.'

McFarlane would certainly gain one significant insight into Syrian society if he were to sit of an evening on the cafe terrace in Jahez Gardens, the Bond Street of Damascus, and watch the strange mating ritual of the rich and powerful young Damascenes.

He might see Basil, the president's 19-year-old son, roar round the block in his Porsche, one eye on the road and one on the pretty girls – followed by the foreign minister's son in a BMW, then by the son of a general in the secret police and the president's nieces.

On a good night, more than 100 rich teenagers habitually cruise the block. Their cars are usually bullet-proof, and are always tailed by the white, French-built cars of the Syrian security police. They would prefer to stroll along the streets and chat to the girls, one of the young men explained, but the constant danger of assassination precludes it.

But the primary cause of fear in Damascus lies just round the corner from Jahez Gardens, in an apartment protected by troops and an anti-aircraft gun. It is one of the residences of the president's brother, Rifaat, a handsome 50-year-old who is, by general consensus, the most hated man in Syria. He commands the 15,000-strong defence squadrons, responsible for protecting the regime, thwarting plots and coups, and providing the president's praetorian guard.

Rifaat's excesses are legandary. His men are held responsible for the massacre at Hama and for killing the regime's critics at home and abroad. If a smart foreign car catches their fancy, they take it.

'No one would be so stupid as to ask Rifaat for their car back,' a young Syrian told me.

Rifaat, who has four wives, 11 children and a reputation as a ladies' man runs the family businesses and has accrued extra-ordinary wealth. An American banker from Dallas said that Rifaat deposited $100 million last year, 'and that is just the tip of the iceberg'.

He is in Switzerland this weekend, where his holdings in numbered bank accounts are vast. He owns property in America, Europe and Britain. Rifaat's favourite haunt in Damascus is a night club where pretty Polish and Argentinian girls perform erotic dances on stage in front of a cracked mirror. The prices would bankrupt the average Syian.

Why, Syrians ask, does the president not curb his brother's power and life style? The question was put directly to Assad at a recent meeting with a friend. Assad replied: 'How can I do it? I need the protection of his army. It would be like cutting one of the legs away from under me.'

The armed forces are the key to power and Assad has ensured that his own family, tribe and sect dominate the crucial positions. The extended Assad family permeates Syrian society in a complex of power.

His sister's son, Muhammed, works with Rifaat: his brother was chairman of the National Assembly's security committee and now works as the 'family fixer' in Atakia: his wife's relatives have key positions in the special forces, the air force and the defence ministry; his uncle has a key position in the secret police, investigating senior members of the armed forces.

The family tree, however, is blighted by sudden death: one of Assad's nephews was assassinated in November 1977; a cousin was killed in 1978; another nephew was shot dead at Aleppo in May the same year.

Apart from his tribe and family, Assad relies on a small kitchen cabinet of hand-picked advisers: a few members of the ruling Syrian Baath party; Mohammed al-Khouli, the head of air force intelligence, who is said to be the most frequent visitor to the palace; and the president's political advisor, Dr Rikabi, a man in his 60s.

176

Now that illness has knocked out two key members, his closest friend and aide is Mustafa Tlass, the defence minister. Although Tlass is a Sunni (Syrian cynics call him the token Sunni in the government), their friendship goes back to boyhood, when both attended the military academy in the city of Homs, and plotted together to pull off the coup that brought Assad to power nearly 13 years ago.

Away from the battlefront and party intrigues last week, Tlass was doing one of the things he likes best. He sat in his swimming trunks by the pool of one of the luxury hotels in Damascus, surrounded by a bevy of Damascene beauties. 'I love beautiful women,' he said. 'I love to take their photographs.'

His view of British politics is frankly sensual. He dislikes Mrs Thatcher because she is 'too tough, too manly'. He adores the Princess of Wales: 'I did not meet Thatcher even when she came to Damascus but to meet Princess Di I would ride anywhere on my camel.'

Tlass's other hobby is photographing flowers with his Hasselblad camera, and a book he has produced on the flowers of Damascus is to be published shortly.

'My problem is getting up early in the morning so that the dew is still on the flowers. But then, I can only take pictures of beautiful women in the evening, and to use a flash is desecration.' In appreciation of his love of flowers, the Dutch have named a gladiolus after him.

Back at his sumptuous office in the defence ministry, his smile faded – and so, when they meet, will McFarlane's. Tlass is confident and hardline: 'Syria is not worried about Israel or the American marines,' he said. 'We have a guarantee from the Soviet Union that they will not allow Syria to be defeated, and that guarantee is being translated into action.

'The Israelis may have their guns in range of Damascus. So what? I have missiles in range of Tel Aviv. As long as Lebanon is under Israeli domination, then we stay there. When Lebanon is free of domination, then Syria will withdraw. We have no intention of increasing the Israeli empire. That is my message for McFarlane.'

In face of this intransigence, one US diplomat thought he had discovered a new route to the heart of Tlass and the Syrian

177

regime. 'Instead of sending McFarlane,' he suggested, 'we'll send a cute girl round to Tlass's with a bunch of gladioli. It might get us further.'

Sunday Times
7 August 1983

Prince in the firing line

The celebration of the Queen's birthday at the British Ambassador's residence in Amman was, everyone agreed, 'jolly good'. The sun shone, perhaps a little too fiercely, and the garden was packed with British diplomats and the Jordanian upper-crust. Men glinting with gold medallions and with neatly combed moustaches, women fresh from the hairstylist and *haute-couturist*, paraded on the lawn and played bingo.

The British Ambassador, Alan Urwick, did a roaring trade behind the perfume and chocolate stall; Scots pipers, specially imported from Cyprus for the day, played mournful airs. Jordanian children tumbled on the lawn in the sack race. It was an English church fête successfully exported to the Middle East. One diplomat had spied on the American fête the day before and said: 'It was rotten. They only started having them because we do. It serves them right nobody turned up.' A diplomat's wife dressed in a little cap and apron, serving cups of tea at about £1.50 each, reflected on how well the Jordanians took to British customs: 'The only other place I've noticed it was when I was in Kenya. We all get on together so well.'

For some of the expatriate 'Brits' it showed that despite our waning influence and the fact that these days it is the American Ambassador who calls all the shots, we still have a special relationship with the Desert Kingdom.

After all, Transjordan, as it was then called, was created by the British – without much respect for ethnic or tribal groups – in the dismemberment of the Ottoman Empire after the First World War. The British chose Abdullah, grandfather of the present King and Crown Prince, to be the ruler as a reward for the help his family (called the Hashemites) had given in defeating the Turks. They gave the throne of Iraq to his brother, Feisal. In 1946 Britain gave up its mandate over Transjordan and Abdullah established the independent Hashemite Kingdom of Jordan. The two men now at the top, King Hussein and his brother Prince Hassan, are products of the British public school system. Hassan, said one English lady, is just like Prince Charles.

That same morning, the Prince was in his own garden up at the royal palace and he bore little resemblance to Prince Charles. His Royal Highness Crown Prince Hassan Bin Talal, former Harrovian and graduate of Oxford, more importantly heir to the throne of the Hashemite Kingdom and 39th in descent from the Prophet Mohammed, the founder of the Muslim religion, twisted his lips into a strange and frightening grimace. He grunted. His right foot shot out with snake-like speed and thudded into the paunch of a sandbag. He hurled his Taekwondo master, a sixth dan from Taiwan called Chiou Hwa Chen, over his shoulder. Chen retaliated with a vicious kick to the thigh. With a high-pitched scream, Hassan splintered a piece of wood with his bare knuckles. Then the Prince stalked off to the library 'for a bit of intellectual exercise.'

Despite some cosy similarities, Hassan's world of plots and intrigue, the imminence of death, coup and invasion are absurdly remote from the fives court at Harrow or the Oxford common room. Nevertheless, Charles and Hassan do have things in common. They are both around the same age – Hassan is 36, Charles is 34. They both like sport. Hassan scuba dives deep beneath the Red Sea, he climbs mountains, rides horses, plays squash, flies small planes and helicopters with more verve perhaps than skill. 'Never get into a helicopter with Hassan,' said a diplomat. 'I did and he turned the sodding thing on its side, laughing that deep laugh of his.' They both play polo, although here Hassan has the edge. He plays twice a week with the Jordanian army team in fast, vicious games. He has some advice for Charles: 'I think he falls awkwardly. If he had some training in judo, he might have a softer landing.'

So both men have bitten the dust occasionally, but there the similarities end. Whereas Charles's role is symbolic, Hassan's is not. His brother is absolute ruler of the Kingdom, and sits on one of the world's shakiest thrones. Death stalks the Hashemites. When Hassan was at Harrow he was invited to have tea with an old Harrovian, Winston Churchill. The great man looked at the little Prince and said: 'I know you. Your grandfather was bumped off, wasn't he?' He was. As King Abdullah left his morning prayers at a mosque in Jerusalem in 1951, he was shot dead. The eight-year-old boy at his side, now King Hussein, was hit by a stray bullet, but it bounced off a medal on his chest.

Their cousin, King Feisal II of Iraq, was murdered by revolutionaries. The brothers have survived coups, plots and assassination attempts. Hassan was shot at daily as he went from his home, then in the suburbs of Amman, to the palace during the Palestinian guerrilla uprising of 1970 which was brutally put down – a civil war the PLO has neither forgotten nor forgiven. Amman had become a home from home for revolutionaries. 'We had them all,' said Hassan. 'All the factions of the PLO, the Black Panthers, Chinese guerrillas, even Carlos. A total of 70,000 armed men. The war was not Jordan v the PLO, but order v chaos.'

Hussein's bed exploded after a valet put a bomb under it. His chef tried to poison his food, but experimented first on the palace cats and was exposed. An assassin substituted concentrated acid for his eye drops. In May, I went to a small celebration at the palace. The King, a tiny figure dwarfed by a huge, gaudy picture of himself, took the salute of his massed bands and Jordanian pipers. It was a poignant moment. Nobody had really believed he would survive long enough to celebrate the 30th anniversary of his accession to the throne.

When Hassan went to prep school in England, his guardian was Miss Hills, a prim lady now in her seventies who spent two weeks earlier this year visiting her former ward. Although Hassan might strike fear into the heart of Yasser Arafat, Miss Hills is unmoved. 'He was a handful, oh yes, he was,' she said. 'I tried to treat him like a normal little boy which of course he was. But in Jordan he was treated like a god. I remember taking him on to a plane at Amman airport and he shook hands with more than a hundred people. He did so many naughty things I can't remember them all. He used to push people into lakes.'

'I don't remember pushing people into lakes,' said Hassan. 'Oh, yes you did,' snapped Miss Hills. The Prince went silently into his gymnasium where, among a clutter of weight-lifting machines, he has a full-size picture of the human body with arrows pointing to the 'kill spots' for karate blows.

Miss Hills's strictness must have curbed the rebellious little prince because his behaviour at Harrow, if not impeccable, was good enough for him to become captain of house. He enjoyed Harrow, although he balked somewhat at the British version of history, especially when the curriculum got round to the Middle East and the land of his ancestors.

Hassan took up his job as number two in Jordan as soon as he finished his finals in Oriental Studies at Christ Church, Oxford, in 1967. He got an honours degree 'by the skin of my teeth'. As he swotted for exams his country was embroiled in a war with Israel, losing in the process the West Bank (an area on the west of the Jordan River) and East Jerusalem, the third most holy site in Islam. It was a disaster for Jordan and a personal dishonour for the Hashemite family. Hassan got the first plane allowed back into Amman.

He shares the chores of government, concentrating on domestic issues, economics, development and the problems of the internal security of the Kingdom. Threats come from everywhere: from Israel to the west; another enemy, Syria, to the north. Although Iraq to the east is an ally, it is at war with Iran. And when the Ayatollah Komeini threatens to take his Muslim hordes to the gates of Jerusalem, the path lies straight through Jordan. Jordan shares the common problems of the Arab world, radicalism and religious fundamentalism, but also the threat from its own Palestinians, who are now more than 60 per cent of the population. When Israeli politicians talk of Jordan being the true Palestinian state, the Jordanians do not take the implied threat lightly.

182

The gossip in the *souk* is that the brothers don't get on very well, although Hassan's loyalty to Hussein is not in question. They see each other daily (their aides are in touch hourly) on affairs of state, but socially they do not mix much. They are markedly different characters. The King had a reputation as a playboy with a relish for the Western way of life. He has been married four times, twice to Western women; Hassan is the more overtly serious of the two, earnest, intellectual. The word in Jordan is that Hassan is not as popular as his brother with the people, and, more important, with the armed forces.

He plays an increasing role in foreign policy, making trips abroad on the King's behalf, seeing the stream of diplomats, dignitaries and heads of state who flow into the palace. Few of them have more than the vaguest idea of what to expect. Outside Jordan, Hassan is almost totally unknown. What information does filter out is mostly unfavourable. Whereas the King has charm and a permanent smile, the Prince is brusque, his lips pursed, his moustache seems to bristle. He is small but powerfully built. Both the West and the East see him as a hardliner and fear he lacks his brother's skill at artful compromise. He can be a little arrogant. One British Foreign Office official flew with Hassan on a visit to Britain and listened as he rattled away in his rapid English, slowly enveloping the official in a polysyllabic fog. 'When I came to write down my brief for David Owen [then the Foreign Secretary] I thought what a bright chap the Prince is; but I don't understand a thing he said.'

Hassan and Hussein have twin palaces up on the Royal Mountain in the centre of Amman. Security is unobtrusive but very tight. Hassan's palace is modest by Arab standards, an elegant villa with high, cool, vaulted ceilings. Next door is an office complex manned by sleek, bilingual young men and very pretty women.

He lives with his wife Sarvath, who comes from a distinguished Pakistani family, and three of their four children. Their eldest daughter is at boarding school in England. He met Sarvath in London courtesy of the British popular press. 'I was staying in Claridge's with a bout of measles and a paper ran a story about the lonely and spotty Prince,' said Hassan.

'Sarvath's father was Pakistani High Commissioner and invited me to stay.' Sarvath is willowy, intelligent and sharp. 'What's it like being a Princess?' I asked in an unguarded moment. 'What a banal bloody question,' she said.

At home with Princess Sarvath in the palace, Hassan's image softened. He joked about the bad breath of a prominent Arab leader. Sarvath said she was trying to change the Prince's reading which tends to get bogged down in the legal ramifications of Israeli policy in the occupied West Bank – on which the Prince has written his own tome – or in *Trilogue* magazine. 'I forced him to read Ken Follett [the thriller writer] and he's starting John Le Carré.' A copy of *The Little Drummer Girl* lay on the coffee table. 'He's very good with the kids,' said Sarvath. 'I'm off to London tomorrow and I know he'll make sure that he's home in time to read them a bedtime story.'

Next morning, we left for a village feast about 20 kilometres east of Amman. Even absolute monarchs have to keep an eye on their popular support, and every couple of weeks Hassan makes a trip into the country to press the flesh. He drives himself, with a back-up of three Land-Rovers filled with troops, and carries a ·38 revolver by the ashtray and a submachine gun which clattered around under my feet in the passenger seat.

The feast would have seemed familiar to T. E. Lawrence and indeed to the Prophet Mohammed. Two hundred grizzled tribal elders, chiefs and local big-wigs sat in two lines in a long, thin tent. Although Hassan wore a leisure suit, most of them had headdresses and robes. We feasted on trays of mutton boiled in sour milk, soaked in yoghurt on beds of rice and Arabic bread. The food was gathered in the traditional way, into a gooey little ball with the bare right hand. Then we all sat down and the Majlis (or council) began. I sat opposite an imposing Imam, a holy man, dressed in a black robe and a grey beard who left the tent to say his prayers on the grass outside. On my left was an example of the new Jordanian, a computer expert, who wanted to make Amman the centre for computer-aided design and drafting. He explained that regular prayer after meals was really an ancient form of calisthenics. It aided the digestion and kept you fit. The Imam would probably not have agreed.

At the Majlis the lowliest peasant can say what he likes,

within reason, to the ruler. Farmers and peasants got up and griped to the Prince about artesian wells, the lack of telephones and electricity, government restrictions on the sale of lamb. He listened patiently and his aide took notes. An old man draped himself round the tent pole and told a long, involved bedouin story, then launched into another. Everyone listened. 'It's not that what he is saying is interesting, which it is not,' said a guest. 'We are listening because we respect age.'

'That was an example of the democracy of articulation,' said the Prince as we drove back to Amman. In Jordan, where there are no elections and the cabinet and members of the National Consultative Council are appointed by the King, it is the only sort of democracy the people have. On the whole they seem content. Despite chronic problems in the economy, Jordanians seem to live well. The population has a per capita income of only 1800 US dollars a year, more than Egypt and Syria but a lot less than their oil-rich Arab neighbours. Jordan has only potash, minerals and some agricultural produce to export and a large, well-equipped army to support. But parts of Amman, especially around the Marble Mile where ambassadors have their residences, are as chic as Bond Street. Blonde Scandinavian air hostesses decorate the bar of the Intercontinental Hotel wearing clothes from the local boutiques. There are restaurants, plush hotels, well-stocked shops, an Uncle Sam hamburger restaurant. There are traffic jams composed mainly of Mercedes and Chevrolets. The paradox was summed up by the Prince's former press aide, who now runs a travel agency. His office is palatial, glittering with gilt and polished wood – but it was empty. 'Business is very, very bad,' he said.

In fact, Jordan lives on the dole. It gains most of its wealth from the remittances of citizens working abroad and from direct aid from the Arab world which agreed at the Baghdad Conference in 1978 to support Jordan to the tune of $1,250 million a year. Because of war between Iran and Iraq, Iraq has not paid up this year and the grant has fallen to just over 500 million dollars.

Hassan has used the aid well, ploughing it into agriculture, technology and science. Modern advances have even intruded into the Islamic faith, and the call to prayer which booms out from the ancient minarets of Amman is not the live voice of the muezzin but a taped prayer beamed out from the central mosque to receivers across the city.

Although political parties are banned, the regime is liberal and enlightened compared with its Arab neighbours, Iraq, Syria and Saudi Arabia. Yet there are glimmers of discontent. The authorities keep a wary eye on a new extremist Palestinian group called Moab, which is believed to have Syrian backing and recently placed a series of small bombs in Amman. There is a constant fear of the spread of the kind of Islamic Fundamentalism which deposed the Shah in Iran.

One day, the Prince went to a Youth Forum in Amman, where young Jordanians are encouraged to state their views to their elders and rulers. Smartly dressed, polite, articulate young men and women, like a meeting of Young Conservatives, addressed the Prince on the problems of youth employment and their 'involvement' in the development of Jordan. 'We are lucky,' said the Prince. 'Our young people are more concerned with passing exams than with religion and politics.' But during a recess a girl from the University of Jordan said that the campus organizations were 'dominated by Fundamentalists. The rest of us feel out of place. There are radical political groups, of course, but they are underground.'

On the surface everything seems content, secure and cohesive in the Hashemite Kingdom. But Hassan knows that things have rarely been worse. It has been a rotten year which has left both Hassan and Hussein exhausted and depressed. Jordan, which had preserved a shaky equilibrium for 10 years, was thrust into centre stage by President Reagan's Peace Initiative for the Middle East, which proposed a 'Palestinian entity' on the West Bank in federation with Jordan.

The two brothers were asked to deliver the PLO, while the US would turn the screws on its client state, Israel. Hassan was pessimistic, but saw it as the only chance for peace. 'The clock was ticking,' he said. 'Time was running out.'

They began a dizzying round of negotiations, encouraging the moderate Arab states, trying to placate the radicals, soothing the Russians. Hassan even lobbied the Japanese. The strain was so bad that Hussein woke up with nightmares about the initiative and once was rushed to hospital with a suspected heart attack. Arafat was a constant visitor to the palace and, to Hassan's concern, the town began to fill up again with PLO guerrilla leaders.

Then the clock stopped and it all ended in disaster. Hussein felt betrayed by the US, by Arafat and the PLO and even by his Arab brothers. A private letter from Hussein to Reagan dated April 10, 1983, is chilling in its hopelessness. 'Confronted with these developments,' the King writes, 'I have reached a dead-end after striving with all my heart and ability to surmount countless obstacles. I am unable to identify a single ray of hope I have not pursued over the past several months.'

Hassan's forecast is bleak: 'The PLO has become zionized. It works as a conscience for the Palestinian people but it doesn't offer a solution. Its politics have become polarized between the right and the left, who are vilifying the centre.'

He believes the Israelis will now annex the West Bank and make it part of Israel. He fears they will try to force the 1,200,000 West Bank Palestinians across the river into Jordan. 'We cannot absorb them,' he says. He predicts the partition of Lebanon between Israel and Syria, and that the Iraq-Iran war will continue to tear the region apart.

In the words of the old Harrovian Winston Churchill, the Middle East provides 'a melancholy and alarming picture'. Sometimes Hassan pines for the 'alpine remoteness of Harrow' or the cloistered calm of Oxford. 'The one big problem of being a Crown Prince is that you can't take a year's sabbatical.'

Sunday Times Magazine
10 July 1983

'A shell blows out
the taxi window'

The Bedawi refugee camp in the northern suburbs of Tripoli is a short and normally rather pleasant drive from the city centre. The coastal highway passes through orange and bamboo groves along the sea shore, then turns sharp right, winding through small cinder-block houses to the camp which stands on top of a hill with a fine view of the Mediterranean.

Last week, as the camp became the site of Yasser Arafat's last stand against the forces of the Syrian army and rebels from the Palestine Liberation Organization, it was not an easy place to get to.

I set out from Arafat's headquarters in the centre of Tripoli with a colleague, Patrick Cockburn from the *Financial Times*. There was, officially, a ceasefire last Wednesday, and the PLO had insisted there would be 'no problems'.

The coastal highway looked ominously quiet and empty. It is now peppered with shell holes and the Arafat loyalists have built earth chicanes across the road. A PLO machine-gunner on the back of a pick-up truck had set up a position in one of the orange groves. A few fighters could be seen moving through the bamboo.

As we turned up the hill towards Bedawi the taxi stuck in the mud and the shelling began. The first rounds whistled past and landed 150 yards away in the orange groves. Then they began to move towards us across the highway. We escaped with a CBS

TV crew who were fleeing the camp – just as a shell blew in the taxi's back window.

It seemed better to try at night. Kassim Mohammed, a PLO ambulance driver who makes the journey several times a day, ferrying the wounded back to a Palestinian Red Crescent hospital in Tripoli, said the fighting usually quietens down after dark. He offered to give me a lift.

The casualty rate among the ambulance drivers is appalling. Three of his colleagues were shot on Monday and have now joined their patients in the hospital. After the earth chicane Kassim turned the lights off and drove up the hill in pitch black.

'If you turn on the lights they shoot at you,' he said. He crawled along using the buildings as cover and accelerated over exposed ground.

We arrived at the small bungalow that serves as PLO head-quarters at about 10 p.m. Two of Arafat's fighters were drinking sweet Arabic tea from a tin kettle by candlelight. It was late for them to be up, they said. The battle, which usually stopped at around 7 p.m., began again at 5.30 a.m. They didn't fight at night because it was cold and their position was so exposed the enemy could see the flash of their guns.

Their colleagues and the PLO commander in Bedawi were asleep and snoring on camp-beds, their Kalashnikovs by their sides and the RPG-7 rocket-launchers stacked neatly, like umbrellas, in the hall.

The atmosphere was eerie and frightening. The camp was built after the Palestinian exodus from Israel in 1948 and had a population between 10,000 and 15,000 refugees. The small, cinder-block houses are packed into tiny, winding streets that can barely take the width of a car. It may have been squalid but for the residents it was safe.

Life has been very different for the past 10 days. On Wednesday night the camp was dark and still. There was a faint flicker of pencil torches from the PLO positions and from Arafat's number two – the military leader, Abu Jihad – who was making an inspection tour before the next day's battle.

Under our feet, deep below the ground in large air-raid shelters, the remaining civilian population of Bedawi – a few thousand women, children and old men – were asleep, packed tightly together. A few shells thumped into the camp but the two fighters at headquarters barely noticed and none of the others woke up. 'It is nothing,' said one of them. 'They are just saying "we are here".'

The view from Bedawi was apocalyptic. The oil refinery to the north had been hit by shells a few days before and then rekindled by the shooting. Huge spouts of flame shot into the sky. Two pillars of smoke rose thousands of feet in the air and formed a massive, black cloud.

More terrifying was what we could not see. On the ridge of Tourbol Mountain, a short distance to the north, and to the east and west of us lay Syrian tank, rocket and infantry battalions, a few hundred Libyans and the ranks of the PLO dissidents led by Sandhurst-trained Abu Musa. Their guns were trained mostly at us.

One of the two fighters in Bedawi said he had been expelled from Jordan in the 'Black September' war between the Jordanian army and the PLO in 1970, and again from southern Lebanon by the Israelis last year, then travelled by boat to Tunisia with Arafat, back to Damascus and into the Syrian-controlled Bekaa Valley area of Lebanon from where he was expelled by the Syrians two months before. 'I am staying in Bedawi,' he said. 'I will not leave. I will fight and die.'

Many of his colleagues have already died. A silver refrigerated truck with a blue stripe along the side stands humming in the car park opposite the Islamic hospital in Tripoli. It is a mortuary for some of the dead from this short war. About 40 bodies lie inside, wrapped in transparent plastic sheets.

Arafat's headquarters is in a house down a cul-de-sac in the Zariyeh district of Tripoli. His fighters are everywhere in the town centre, careering through the streets in jeeps and hanging around the amusement arcade playing the 'Wizard of War' video game. They don't act like people whose final days have come.

And, in a long interview last week, nor did Arafat. He is a small man, almost bald, and his stubble has turned grey. He was courteous, witty and almost cheerful. Although Tripoli is his last remaining base anywhere within striking distance of Israel, he denied it was essential. 'I have a military base in Yemen. My headquarters are in Tunis. I am only in Tripoli because my men are in danger,' he said.

This weekend the Syrian forces and the PLO dissidents are poised for a final attack on Bedawi. They are being restrained partly by Arab mediators and partly by the Soviet Union which does not wish to see its old ally, Arafat, wiped out.

Syria would like him to retreat into political and military oblivion. But they might be underestimating him. 'You don't know what has happened in the past seven days,' he said. 'The Palestinian people, the Arab nations, Europe, the Soviet Union, the United Nations, the Pope, Eastern Europe have condemned Syria. They are rallying to our support. We are a volcano that is still erupting under that bankrupt nation, Israel. I tell you,' said Arafat, jabbing his finger, his eyes bright: 'I am a man of history. This is my vision.' He handed me a biscuit and went upstairs to a military meeting.

The two fighters in Bedawi camp last Wednesday passionately respect Arafat. But their vision of the future is not so clear. Kassim, the ambulance driver, said to the fighters. 'Sometimes I am not sure what direction our revolution is going to take. What is the future for us?' The fighters shrugged as one of them disconsolately poked an olive out of a bottle with a live heavy machine gun bullet.

Sunday Times
13 November 1983

'Israel has never faced an enemy like this'

The Phoenicia restaurant on the quayside of the city of Tyre in southern Lebanon would not win a star from Michelin but serves a good *Coquilles St Jacques*, crisp fried Sultan Ibrahim fish and chateau-bottled Lebanese wine. It commands a fine view of the port and the Mediterranean. The only snag is that in the evening diners have to enter and leave the restaurant running, at a crouch, to avoid the rifle and machine-gun fire that rakes the harbour area.

When the firing starts, which it does every night at about 6.30, the waiters politely suggest that guests move inside to tables behind a stone wall. The restaurant still stays open until 10 p.m. The owner is proud that so far all his clients have survived and only one of his staff has been slightly injured by a ricochet.

The evening pyrotechnics that send white and red tracer bullets buzzing round the harbour come from a block house at the port entrance commanded by two South Lebanon Army militiamen who are armed and funded by the Israelis. 'They are madmen,' said the waiter. 'They fire at dogs, cats, and bats because they are scared.' Their fear is understandable. The post is attacked several times a week by Shi'ite guerrillas who seem to regard the militiamen and their firepower with contempt.

After three years of Israeli occupation, life in Tyre and the nearby villages is almost unbearable. The city's only hotel, the

192

Elisa Beach, has been bombed twice because the former owner was suspected of being an Israeli collaborator. Explosions and gunfire erupt every night as the Israelis and their surrogates fight it out with the Shi'ite gunmen from the Amal militia. As Israel slowly withdraws from the territory it invaded in June, 1982, the fighting has grown more vicious and the death toll spirals.

Last week there was a terrible cycle of attacks and reprisals. On Sunday a truck carrying 100 kilograms of TNT was detonated by its driver as an Israeli troop-carrier passed by about a mile inside the Lebanese border near the Israeli town of Metullah. Twelve Israeli soldiers were killed. According to local reports, the driver will go down in the Shi'ite annals of martyrdom as the first woman suicide bomber.

The next day Israeli armour attacked the village of Zrariye north of the Litani river, a staging post for arms and men which fuel the Amal guerrillas in the south. Thirty-four people were killed, 10 of them civilians, in a 17-hour battle. One driver was crushed to death when a tank rolled over his car.

On Tuesday a Shi'ite suicide bomber aimed at, and just missed, an Israeli convoy outside Tyre. It exploded killing the driver and injuring one soldier. Two more Israeli soldiers were killed at a checkpoint by the Litani river. And so it went on all week.

The 'iron fist' policy that Israel has imposed on the south should be enough to crush any resistance. Hundreds of local Shi'ites have been arrested, hooded and interrogated. Villages and towns are surrounded and searched meticulously every day. The penalty for being even the relative of a suspected resistance fighter is severe. Your house is blown up or demolished by bulldozers. Every road has checkpoints where, as a defence against suicide bombers, the soldiers will fire at any car that contains only one person.

In Hallousiye, a village near Tyre, Israeli soldiers last week dealt with a suspicious looking car by firing two rounds at it from an M60 tank. After dark any car travelling outside the towns or villages is shot at.

The intelligence network built up by Shin Beth, the Israeli equivalent of the British special branch, is daunting. A cafe owner who offered use of his telephone to journalists, who are officially banned from southern Lebanon by the Israelis, was arrested. His phone line was cut.

But the Israeli strategy simply hasn't worked. The resistance has increased leaving the government in Jerusalem bewildered and the soldiers shocked and afraid. 'Get me out of here,' said a young Israeli officer in Hallousiye. The defence minister, Yitzhak Rabin, who visited Tyre under massive security last Tuesday, has said: 'Israel has never encountered an enemy like this before who is prepared to blow himself up like a human bomb. Their fanaticism knows no bounds.'

The image of the Shi'ite guerrillas in Israel is of bearded fanatics with pictures of the Ayatollah Khomeini round their necks, gripping the steering wheels of suicide cars. The foreign minister, Yitzhak Shamir, says they are controlled by Syria. Rabin has blamed the Iranians. The head of Israel's northern command has given a cruder definition: 'They are vermin, snakes and scorpions,' he said. The prime minister, Shimon Peres, is puzzled by the fact that the attacks have increased as Israel withdraws. 'Why the hell are they shooting at the backs of our soldiers?' he said.

Part of the answer can be found in Borj Rahhal, the village about 10 kilometres from Tyre that was raided by Israeli troops yesterday. We visited it earlier last week. The 1,500 inhabitants are Shi'ite Muslims, like 80% of the population of southern Lebanon. There is a simple mosque but the village is too small to warrant a permanent *sheikh* (religious leader).

The people were friendly and the wizened *inukhtar*, village mayor, invited us to lunch with the local doctor and the headmaster. There were only a few signs that morning that Borj Rahhal is in the front line of the fight against Israel and one of the seven hill villages called the 'chain of Shi'ite resistance'. There was the rubble of 10 houses bulldozed by the Israelis during a raid, the remains of the doctor's clinic that was also levelled, and the wreckage of his Volkswagen car. One villager carried a two-way radio, part of the intelligence network that informs the resistance of the approach of the Israeli army. One had a revolver tucked under his shirt. A week ago the body of a man who was suspected of collaborating with the Israelis was found in a ditch in the village, shot in the back with a machine gun.

The doctor, Ali Jaber, a vigorous, articulate man who speaks fluent English, gave a passionate account of Shi'ite feelings. He studied medicine in Cairo and in 1976 returned to his village where he opened a clinic.

Now at 39, Jaber is a member of the political wing of Amal which leads the resistance in the south. When we spoke he had already been arrested by the Israelis once, shot at three times and his clinic was bulldozed because, the Israelis say, they found a box of bullets in it.

Last year Jaber found a bomb wrapped in paper under a chair in his other clinic in Tyre and he suspects an Israeli agent planted it. He keeps constantly on the move, dodging the Israeli patrols. He travels to his patients and to injured guerrillas by foot at night. 'I know the secret paths through the valleys and over the mountains,' he said.

Over lunch of kebab and humus, the doctor said he was willing to do more for the cause and would be perfectly prepared to carry out a suicide mission. 'Everyone in this room would be willing to die in the fight against Israel,' he said. 'I know this sounds strange to people in the west, perhaps you think we are crazy fanatics. You do not know when you are going to die, but you will die, maybe in an hour, a day a month, a few years. But to know the exact moment of your death is a marvellous thing,' said Jaber.

'Why are we doing this? We are not fighting for the sake of fighting, but with the aim of getting the Israelis off every millimetre of our land. I have no right to kill an innocent Israeli and I would not attack him in his own land. But I have the right to protect myself in my own land. If I do that and I am killed I will go to heaven. God will be on my side. If the situation can be changed by an explosion, there are many here in this village who would ask whether they could carry that bomb,' said Jaber.

The conversation turned to a local hero. Hassan Qassir, a 19-year-old student of electrical engineering. On February 4 he drove a car packed with explosives into an Israeli convoy, killing himself and, the villagers say, 10 Israeli soldiers. The Israeli estimates of the toll are lower.

The headmaster said that Hassan was a handsome boy with blue eyes and a bright future who always came top of his class. He was a devout Muslim who prayed and fasted but not fanatically so. He volunteered for the suicide mission after the Israeli army fired bullets and tear gas into his technical college. A girl was killed in the raid. But, according to the headmaster, what outraged Hassan was that the soldiers cursed the Koran and the prophet Mohammed.

Jaber explained how Hassan's mission was arranged. First he volunteered to do the job. Then it had to be approved and blessed by a senior Shi'ite *sheikh*. 'Sometimes it is Sheikh Fadlallah in Beirut (a Shi'ite leader with strong links to Iran) or a sheikh in Najaf in Iraq or in Qom in Iran,' said Jaber. 'They said OK to Hassan's mission. When he got into the car that morning he was smiling and laughing,' said the headmaster.

Hassan was following in a long Shi'ite tradition. His namesake, Hassan, the younger son of Ali, the son-in-law of the prophet Mohammed, was called 'the lord of all martyrs'. (He was also called 'the great divorcer' because he married and divorced 100 women and the manner of his death was more appropriate to the latter title: he was poisoned after a harem intrigue. The spirit of martyrdom is now so strong in Borj Rahhal, said Jaber, that women, the old and the sick were eager to get on the list.

Throughout our interview, Jaber spoke freely to us and had no objection to his name being used or his picture being taken. Judging by the reports of yesterday's Israeli raid on his village, he may have been reckless to do so. The report, from United Nations sources, said that the Israelis had arrested five villagers – among them a doctor.

Yet the militancy among the Shi'ites of southern Lebanon is relatively recent. For centuries villages like Borj Rahhal remained calm and uneventful.

In 1974 Imam Musa Sadr, who studied theology with Khomeini in Iran and went missing, believed dead, in Libya in 1978, began a movement called Amal, Arabic for hope, to help the poor and underprivileged Shi'ites. He started the military wing in 1975 with help from Yasser Arafat, the chairman of the PLO.

In the late 1970s Amal and the PLO fell out and the first battles in Borj Rahhal were fought against the Palestinians who tried to take over the village. 'We fought them sometimes every week,' Jaber had told us. 'We understand they deserve a homeland – just so long as it isn't ours.'

The Israelis were welcomed by south Lebanon Shi'ites in 1982 because they forced the PLO out of the area. Relations between Israelis and Shi'ites would have remained cordial had the Israelis left within a few months. But they didn't.

They tried to get villagers to join pro-Israeli militias. When they were resisted, the Israelis went on the offensive. Villagers were arrested and imprisoned, their houses searched, and the fury that now plagues the Israelis began to take shape. In 1983 the villagers decided to resist Israeli soldiers when they tried to enter their communities. In 1984 they went further and aimed at expelling them altogether from southern Lebanon.

In Borj Rahhal – even before yesterday's raid – there have been enough incidents to fuel the villagers' anger. Some 120 men have been arrested and sent to a prison camp. Three villagers, including a 16-year-old girl, were killed resisting the Israelis army and black flags of mourning still hang in the village.

Resistance went hand in hand with religious fervour. Jaber told us that the young people began to reject 'foreign ideas' like communism and come back to God. The last straw for Jaber was when the Israelis broke into the village mosque looking for arms. 'They smashed the glass. And I saw an Israeli soldier pissing on a copy of the Koran,' he said.

The desire for martyrdom intensified but suicide is not the villagers' only form of resistance. They have learned lessons in guerrilla warfare from the PLO.

By intensifying their attacks on the Israeli troops as they withdraw from Lebanon, the Shi'ites hope to accelerate the process to such an extent that they can claim to have achieved something that none of the Arab nations – Jordan, Syria, Egypt – could: to get the Israeli army on the run.

Jaber was furious that other groups – Hizbullah, the party of God, which is Iranian backed, the communists, the National Syria Social Party and the Sunni Muslim Nasserites – have jumped on the bandwagon.

At 4 p.m. last Wednesday we left the village. The doctor rushed off to see a patient with a colonic inflammation. The Amal fighters prepared for their next missions. 'The Israelis may control the country during the day, but at night Lebanon is ours,' said Jaber.

Yesterday – in daylight – the Israelis raided the village and Jaber was almost certainly arrested.

Sunday Times
17 March 1985

Palestinians face more carnage in fight to the finish

Fierce battles raged between Palestinians and Shi'ites in three Palestinian camps south of Beirut last week despite the attempts of the Syrian and the Lebanese presidents to negotiate a ceasefire.

Although there was a lull in the fighting on Friday, the Red Cross, which had only been able to evacuate a handful of wounded during the past two weeks, was unable to enter the camps.

Many fear that the fighting will go on until the Palestinians are defeated by the Shi'ite militia, Amal. There is a danger that the fighting could spread to the Bekaa valley and to the south, where the Palestinians have large camps in Amal-controlled areas.

The toll of dead and wounded is heavy. Amal, despite support from the Shi'ite sixth brigade of the Lebanese Army, with its superior weapons and armoured cars, has failed to win a decisive victory, and is reported to have suffered more than 400 dead with more than 1,000 wounded. There are no accurate figures for Palestinian casualties.

Eyewitnesses last week said two camps – Sabra and Chatila – were wastelands. The tightly packed houses had been destroyed by artillery bombardments. Whole areas had been razed to the ground by bulldozers and dynamite. The Palestinians are believed to the using vast networks of tunnels to hide their men and equipment. The stench of rotting bodies permeates the camps.

Sabra and Chatila, where more than 800 Palestinians were slaughtered by Christian Phalangist militiamen in 1982, have been the scene of new atrocities. Injured fighters in hospitals, prisoners and civilians have been murdered.

The *Sunday Times* and the BBC last week reported killings at the camps. The BBC's Arabic language report of the atrocities was monitored by the Amal fighters, so the BBC immediately withdrew its three reporters because it feared attempts would be made on their lives. After these reports, Islamic Jihad, which has claimed responsibility for kidnapping foreigners in Beirut, threatened the foreign press for their 'false' reporting. The Amal leader, Nabih Berri, complained to the British Ambassador in Beirut, David Meirs, about 'biased and inaccurate reporting' in the British media.

The *Sunday Times* can confirm the truth of last week's report. In fact, many reports of killings were not included in the report because eyewitnesses were afraid for their own safety. Our best estimate now is that between 100 and 200 unarmed Palestinians were killed, but it is impossible to be certain of the number.

Accurate reporting of the battles in the camps is almost impossible, not least because Amal has banned the press from them. One reporter who went to Sabra camp last week was told by an Amal militiaman: 'If you come here again you will be knifed until you are dead.'

There has been scant reference to the atrocities in the Beirut press, although most reporters and thousands of people have heard the stories. 'If we print them we will get a bomb through our window,' said a local reporter. On the whole, people in Beirut are indifferent. Massacres have been carried out by the fighters of most groups – Christians, Palestinians, Shi'ites, Druzes – in most major conflicts over the past ten years of civil war. Massacre has become almost a ritual of war in Lebanon. 'What's new about all this?' asked a leading Christian politician last week. 'Of course it happened. There is a lot of bad blood between Shi'ites and Palestinians.'

Normally, atrocities are widely reported by the international press. However, fear and intimidation are now so great that even these sources of information are drying up.

Many reporters have been withdrawn because of the risk of being kidnapped or killed. Those that remain find it increasingly difficult and dangerous to work. It was possible, if risky, to report the killings and the brutality of Israel's 'iron fist' policy in southern Lebanon. Reporters were then welcomed by Amal leaders and encouraged to witness and report on the Israeli actions. Now that Amal is under scrutiny for its actions in the camps, it is attempting to suppress the news. Television cameras have been banned from filming; one crew that attempted to film was shot at.

Journalists who are normally in fierce competition have joined in a strange alliance. They have shared their sources and information and agreed to release stories simultaneously so that one newspaper or agency does not find itself isolated and the target for threats and attacks.

Last week the system broke down.

The BBC and the *Sunday Times* found themselves first with the news. One news agency ran their story of the massacres a day later and quoted, not its own sources, but the *Sunday Times* and the BBC. Another reported the incidents only to its clients in the west. The news was deliberately held back from Middle East clients because of the real danger to staff in Beirut. Some newspapers either ignored or played down the story.

'You've got to be realistic in Beirut, and many other countries in the Middle East,' said an experienced Beirut reporter. 'For example, if President Reagan made a stupid mistake in a speech we would all report it. If Saddam Hussein [the President of Iraq] did the same thing I would not report it. If I did I would be on the next plane out of Baghdad. You have to impose a degree of self-censorship.'

Being 'realistic' in Beirut means facing up to the facts about the atrocities that have occurred. Cases such as that of the young, wounded Palestinian and his sister, aged about 13, who were on the ground floor of the hospital at Sabra. A soldier, a member of the sixth brigade, told the girl to pick up her brother. She refused and they were both shot dead.

Then a group of six Palestinians were brought out of a ward and ordered to strip. The soldiers and militiamen examined them for powder burns and marks of gun straps on their shoulders to see if they were fighters. The six were taken to a ditch dug just outside the hospital and shot.

Another boy had been wounded by shrapnel. A militiaman said; 'You got this fighting.' The boy claimed: 'By the Imam, I was wounded in an accident.' The militiaman said: 'You bastard! You got this fighting!' The boy was shot.

One eyewitness said soldiers and militiamen then threw grenades and explosives into the basement of the hospital, where, it is believed, Palestinian fighters and their families were hiding. There is no figure for how many were killed; there was only a terrible stench from the rubble.

Soldiers also ran into the building where the medical staff were hiding. There was shooting and an explosion. Then silence.

In an area just north of the entrance to the Sabra camp, six Palestinian prisoners were lined up and a bulldozer ran over them and killed them.

A group of 15 Palestinians wearing white shorts and T-shirts, patients from a hospital, some of them with saline drips still in their arms, were gathered together by Amal militiamen and shot with machine guns. 'The bodies were dancing', said an eyewitness.

A Palestinian nurse came out of Sabra with a wounded man. The man was shot by Amal militiamen, and the nurse was stabbed with a bayonet. The bodies were taken away in a lorry.

There are many other reports. Palestinians were shot at the American University Hospital in Beirut. A refrigerated truck outside the hospital contained the bodies of 55 men. An eyewitness who examined the bodies said 20 of them had been shot at close range and appeared to have been executed. Three had their throats cut.

Hundreds of Palestinians are still missing. They may be prisoners or they may have suffered the fate of so many of their fellow fighters.

Sunday Times
2 June 1985

The pursuit of happiness in a city of grief

The scene this hot July day could have been taken from a travel brochure advertising a seaside holiday in a Mediterranean city. Twin 17-year-old sisters, Roula and Randa Nehme, arrange their tanned bodies, clothed in tiny bikinis, on the sea wall which juts out into the Mediterranean. They will stay there until 7 p.m. Around them in the Summerland resort, under a sky which remains almost entirely blue every day from May through to October, are a couple of thousand perfectly-cooked bodies, lying on sunbeds, eating, drinking or swimming in the three pools.

At the If Boutique in the city centre, ladies are crammed into the little shop on the first floor trying on the latest fashions, complicated creations with belts, zips, buckles, pleats and bulges which will set them back several hundred pounds (sterling).

Families stroll along the Corniche by the sea eating salted almonds and roasted corn on the cob from the dozens of food stalls. The narrow streets are crammed with stalls selling vegetables, fruit, shirts, jeans and perfumes. On Hamra Street, police sergeant Mohammed Ali is on the prowl for illegally parked cars. He has already handed out five tickets, and a tow truck stands by. His colleague is on point duty at the Hamra crossroads and with a lot of whistle blowing and cursing he keeps the heavy traffic inching forward.

There are only the vaguest hints that this is taking place in

203

the world's most dangerous and war-torn city, Beirut, Lebanon, which is now in the eleventh year of civil war.

If you walk past the basking twins to the end of the sea wall in Summerland in West Beirut you can just hear a muffled booming. It is tank or rocket fire from the 'Green Line', the demarcation that splits the city between Christian East and Muslim West, or heavy artillery from the mountains above Beirut. There is, occasionally, a sharper crackle of automatic fire from the southern suburbs close to Summerland. It causes no more than a lull in the conversation.

On Hamra, the 'Oxford Street' of West Beirut, the stern face of the Ayatollah Khomeini glares down from walls and banners as a reminder that this is Muslim West Beirut. There is a poster of a smart young man with neat hair and a small moustache, smiling into the camera like a student at his graduation. Underneath, in Arabic, the poster explains that he is a martyr, a suicide bomber who drove a car laden with explosives into an Israeli army patrol.

One of the stallholders on a street off Hamra has more interesting things than shirts to sell. Under the layers of Cellophane-wrapped shirts are revolvers wrapped in greased paper.

At the Hamra crossroads people have stopped to have coffee at the Modca café and a Lebanese television crew is filming the policeman on point duty. After a year and a half when militiamen controlled the streets the police have, this day, been told to resume their duties under a complicated security plan worked out by Syria and the various Muslim militias. The item is the lead on the local television news that evening.

The images we have of Beirut through the years of civil war, and the Israeli invasion in 1982, are almost exclusively of death and destruction. They are true. There are no accurate figures for the number of people who have died violently during the past 11 years but it could be as high as a hundred thousand. There are few buildings left in the city which are not pockmarked by bullets, and few days when shots are not heard. Hundreds of thousands have had to leave their homes.

It is a city accustomed to extreme violence, and it must have been a relief for Beirutis to read the news in the respected

Middle East Reporter on Monday, July 22: 'Newspaper reports spoke of general calm prevailing in Muslim West Beirut.'

So what happened on this day of prevailing calm? A rocket was fired at the Beirut radio transmitter. A bomb went off at the office of Kuwait Airways on Hamra (one injured). Groups of rival Druze militiamen were fighting (eight dead) and Muslim Amal and Palestinians fought in the Palestinian refugee camps in Beirut (one dead, several injured). A gunman opened fire from his car in the city centre and two rocket-propelled grenades were fired at an army barracks. Fighting continued along the Green Line and shells landed in eight different residential areas of Beirut.

Normal life in the city has a surreal tinge to it, which becomes almost addictive to the foreigners who choose to live there. At a cocktail party for an Australian teacher in a flat overlooking the Corniche, we watched glowing red tracer bullets from a heavy machine gun somewhere behind us in the city bouncing like flat stones off the sea until they fizzled out.

Liz Sly, who is English and has lived in Beirut for three years, says that conversations at Beirut parties turn sometimes into a macabre Monty Python sketch. One person will say: 'A shell hit my apartment building last week.' 'That's nothing,' another guest will say. 'My dining room was wrecked by a rocket-propelled grenade.' 'You're lucky,' says another, 'I was kidnapped, locked in the boot of a car, blindfolded and interrogated for three days.'

A nurse was chatted up in the lobby of a hotel by a bearded man who boasted that he was one of the hijackers of the TWA jet in June. She declined his overtures; but there is evidence that he is indeed one of the original hijackers, wandering freely in West Beirut and boasting of his exploits.

Outside the Commodore Hotel in West Beirut, where most of the foreign journalists stay, two militias, one Druze and one Sh'ite, confronted each other and fought for two or three hours with rifles, machine guns, and rockets. Then, on Hamra, the two militia leaders approached each other and embraced. The little tiff was over. The bodies of three dead militiamen were carried off. The shops re-opened and life returned quickly to normal.

205

Beirut is in anarchy. There is no central government. The President, Amin Gemayel, a Christian, has no control in West Beirut and does not dare set foot in it. He receives scant respect in Christian East Beirut. His cabinet has not met for months. Half the Lebanese army, the Muslim half, mutinied in 1984. Policemen spend most of their time at home or in their police stations.

The country is ruled from Damascus, the capital of Syria. Local power is in the hands of the militias. In the East it is the Lebanese forces who collect taxes, run their own illegal port and police the Christian enclave. West Beirut is a mess. The main militia is Amal, which is Shi'ite, followed by the PSP, which is Druze. There are also Hizbullah, the Party of God, Islamic Amal, the Sunni Muslim Mourabitoun, two pro-Syrian militias who mainly carry out suicide operations, the Communists and two rival Palestinian factions, plus pro-Iranian extremists.

Each of them controls a network of street, demands 'taxes' or protection money from the residents and businessmen and spends much of its time at the throats of the others. They all fight the Christians, Amal fights the Palestinians and sometimes the Druze, the Druze and the Palestinians fight each other, Amal fights Hizbullah. They kidnap Westerners, a dozen of whom are still held somewhere in Lebanon, but mainly each other. A great many Lebanese are kidnapped each week. Fifteen hundred Palestinians are still missing after battles in the camps in Beirut in May.

How can life for the million and a half inhabitants go on?

The man who struggles to see that it does and to bring some order to the chaos is Chafiq Sardouk, the mayor of Beirut. Sardouk is a small, dapper man who has been the mayor for three years and remains remarkably good-humoured. The problems of Ken Livingstone, head of the GLC, or Mayor Ed Koch of New York pale against the things that Sardouk faces daily.

In his wood-panelled office in Barbir, dangerously close to the Green Line, he said that he 'seemed to have annoyed somebody'. He had ventured a mild criticism of Syrian intentions towards the Palestinians in Beirut, and that morning he was attacked in the whole Arab press, from Tunis to Kuwait.

The night before someone had fired a heavy calibre round through the mayor's window and it had smashed the onyx pencil holder on his desk and embedded itself in the wall. 'Good shooting, eh?' said the mayor, holding up the pieces.

If ever there was a local hero in Beirut, it is the mayor.

He is proud of his title. 'I am the president of Beirut, the mayor, the amir, the prince of the city,' he said. He heads a municipal council of 24, half of whom come from the East and half from the West. Because of the fighting on the Green Line they cannot meet. Half his 7,000 municipal employees never turn up for work (although they are still paid), either because they have fled Beirut, or because they have joined militias.

The city pulls in about US$400,000 a year through direct and indirect taxes, but this is only a quarter of its proper revenue. People simply don't pay taxes and it takes a brave tax collector even to enter the southern suburbs.

His entire fleet of ambulances was commandeered by the militias who took the city name off the sides and painted on their own. The electricity supply does not work well because the fighting often knocks out the supply from one of the two Beirut power stations, and only a quarter of the city streets are lit at night.

His main worry is public health. Only half the 2,500 garbage collectors turn up for work. Nevertheless most days about 70 trucks tour the city picking up rubbish and the streets are remarkably clean. That week Sardouk was concentrating on cleaning up Hamra Street and the city centre to boost Beirut's morale.

'I am a friend to all the different militias,' he said. 'I am very well liked by Christian, Shi'ite, Druze and Sunni, they all like me.' Not quite all. His office has lines of holes stitched neatly across the walls and ceilings by some automatic weapon. Last year the phone rang in his flat, three floors above his office, and his daughter answered it. A man said that the family had better get down to the basement because in five minutes they would be shelled. They went downstairs. A few minutes later a shell destroyed his flat. He rebuilt it. A month afterwards it was destroyed. He now squats in an opulent apartment owned by King Fahd of Saudi Arabia who, wisely, has not visited Beirut since the troubles began. The king still keeps a penthouse flat, a car and a driver on standby in case he ever returns.

The mayor has never been to the police about any of the shootings or shellings. 'What could they do, why should I bother them?' he asks.

In King Fahd's flat, under the coffee table, he keeps a personal armoury: a Kalashnikov rifle with a clip of bullets in the breech and another taped to the side, an M16 rifle, and a cluster of pistols.

He has tried to bring peace to his city, but in vain. In 1984, he says, he called on all the people of Beirut, whatever their religion, to march for peace on May 6. The leaders of some of the city's militias pointed out that the time was not ripe, but undeterred the mayor went ahead with his plans for a massive peace march with 300,000 people. On Saturday, May 5, he gathered his organizers together in his office for a final meeting.

It was interrupted by machine-gun fire which smashed through the window and added a line of holes to his wall. The mayor and the organizers went into the basement and listened to the radio. 'I heard that five people had been killed that night, then 20, 30 and 75. That night in four hours 145 people were killed and more than 300 wounded. I said to my organizers: "My dears, we cannot do this march for peace."' He called it off.

Although Sardouk is left with the mere vestiges of his mayoral authority, he is hopeful that times will change. 'I am the mayor,' he says. 'I am powerless, but at least I have that title between my hands.'

Many Beirutis remember the good old days when Beirut was called 'the Paris of the Middle East' and the late President Nasser of Egypt called it, contemptuously, 'that big night club'.

At the government press office, in West Beirut, which runs well despite the lack of a government, Eliane Gebara, the press officer, and a French journalist, Gabriel Dardaud, who is in his eighties and has lived in Beirut almost all his life, were reminiscing. They remembered the heady days when Kim Philby, the British spy, was in Beirut drunk and indiscreet before he fled to Moscow, and how his father St John Philby died drink in hand in the bar of the Vendôme Hotel.

For the wealthy in those days a night out in Beirut began with a drink on the roof of the Vendôme, followed by dinner in the Panache room of the Phoenicia, Arabic dancing at the Red Peacock, and disco at the Caves du Roy. Then to St Simone for a swim in the moonlight, and up to the mountains for breakfast. All these places have been destroyed. Few people go out at night any more: they sit at home watching videos.

The mayor can still take some pride in his city, however, and it still functions despite the odds. These are some of the normal things people do on what the *Middle East Reporter* described as a quiet day in Beirut.

At 6.30 a.m. Rabih Suki, a medical student, is jogging along the Corniche before the sun becomes unbearably hot, garbage trucks are touring the city and at the old American Embassy, which was blown up by a suicide bomb in 1983 killing 63 people, the day is beginning. The Americans have moved out (their new embassy annexe was also suicide-bombed, in 1984) and now, on the ground floor, local mechanics fix cars, and Shi'ite refugees from southern Lebanon live in the upper floors.

It is not a good day for a sheep, lying panting on the pavement in the southern suburb of Bourj El Barajneh, its feet tied as it waits for slaughter. The carcasses of sheep and cows are already hanging from hooks having strips torn off them for the first customers.

There has been fierce overnight fighting along the Green Line and that morning only one of the crossing points is open. The line, which runs through rows of devastated, deserted buildings and streets where Christian and Muslim armies confront each other across a few yards of rubble, is quiet but ominous. After a complicated piece of local diplomacy between the warring factions they have agreed to let the Haddath crossing open, a quarter of a mile of exposed no-man's-land between earth barricades.

Firing might erupt at any time: people have been killed in the area the night before and snipers are always present, secreted behind sandbags, looking for a victim in the cross-hairs of their sights. Despite the appalling risks, hundreds of people cross the city every day. That morning there is a quarter of a mile of traffic waiting to go through: trucks, oil tankers, vans and private cars. The newspaper delivery van driven by Ibrahim Achmad goes through from east to west just before seven. Two of his predecessors making the same trip have been shot dead by snipers.

At the Sabra and Chartila Palestinian refugee camps west of the city people are making breakfast and starting work in a scene of utter destruction. More than 800 Palestinians were killed there in 1982 by Christian militiamen, and recently, in May, more than 600 were killed by Shi'ite Amal militiamen who bombarded the camps for three weeks. In Sabra hardly a building stands. Syrian workmen with bulldozers are levelling the rubble. Dead bodies still turn up. Twenty-one were found down a well, and bits and pieces are picked up by the bulldozers. Soldiers stand by to wrap them in cloth and carry them away for burial.

Between three and five thousand people still live in the ruins. Women and children pick up pieces of metal and sell them to a scrap metal merchant who is in the camp with his truck. He pays cash and then takes a load down to a salvage ship in the port. It is then taken to Japan or Europe, where it may turn up in a new Toyota or Mercedes. Since the civil war began this is a boom industry. A boy rides a donkey-cart with a water tank on the back, shops open and carts stand in the rubble selling cakes for breakfast. The commercial spirit in Lebanon has been dulled by war and the collapsing Lebanese pound, but it has not disappeared and it is still possible to buy almost anything in Beirut. Two shops in the southern suburbs make the point. One of them, called From A to Z, sells second-hand radiators, chandeliers and Roman, Greek and Phoenician artefacts, pillaged from the ruins of Byblos, Tyre and Baalbek. The owner, Mohammed Daha Nassar, says he has some very nice Greek stone rollers, which were used to smooth patches of earth, for only 200 Lebanese pounds (about £10) and a 2,000-year-old incense burner. 'It would make a lovely champagne cooler,' he says. 'Only 500 Lebanese [about £25]. It is a conversation piece.'

Across the road is a shop with a large hatstand outside

210

festooned with army uniforms, ammunition belts, caps and holsters. It is a militiaman's boutique. Full military uniform for a man is £Leb250 and for a boy £Leb75. An ammunition belt is £Leb30, and militia-designer T-shirts saying, in English, 'Kill 'em All, Let God Sort Them Out', are only £Leb35. Inside, the shop sells guns. The owner says he is out of Kalashnikovs (a Russian automatic rifle, at only £Leb2500), because four people had come in to buy one each that morning. He does have Czech 9mm pistols for £Leb700, a Spanish 9mm pistol for £Leb850, and a very nice ·38 Smith & Wesson pistol for £Leb2500. He says trade has been very good during the civil war.

The upmarket businesses are also doing well. Goody's supermarket in West Beirut looks as chic as Fortnum & Mason in London. The owner complains that since foreign airlines stopped coming to Beirut, because of frequent shelling at the airport and the danger of hijacking, he cannot get lobster, mussels and oysters from Morocco or fresh *choux de Bruxelles* from France. His customers have to make do with *champignons parfumés, soupe vietnamienne* and *miel de montagne*.

At the Academie de Beauté off Hamra Street women are having face packs, hair removal and pimple treatment. Business is good, says the owner, Dr Georges Dfouni, although there is little call for his services as a cosmetic surgeon. These days 90 per cent of his customers are Muslim women, he says. 'Muslim women are afraid that their husbands might find someone else more beautiful and divorce them, so they take good care of themselves.'

On the East side of the city Serge Hochar and his brother Ronald are at their winery in Ghazir, near Jounieh, blending and sipping the 1983 vintage of their wine, Château Musar, which is accepted as one of the great wines of the world. The wine also deserves some sort of medal for courage. The Hochars have brought the grapes through sniping, shelling, bombing, and through Israeli, Christian, Druze and Muslim checkpoints to get it to their caves.

At midday they go up to a new village, Belhorizon, on the hillside overlooking Jounieh Harbour, where Lebanese, confident of their country's future, are buying new villas for

US$250,000 a time. The Hochar family has 25 per cent of the stock, and there is no shortage of customers or investors.

Pierre El Khoury, the architect who used to be the Lebanese Minister of Public Works, says he is surprised that so much private building is still going on in Lebanon. 'It is a sign of hope. Many people feel that Beirut will once again become the Arab capital.'

Back at Summerland, where the American hostages from the TWA jet were taken for their last supper before their release by their Shi'ite captors, the beautiful people of West Beirut are taking the private bus down to the beach. The resort is in the southern suburbs, surrounded by a poor Shi'ite Muslim area where many are religious fundamentalists and women wear the veil. Inside there are no veils, in fact very few clothes at all.

Summerland seems above confessional or political dispute. Christians, Muslims, Druzes and foreigners relax and play in the sun together. Sadly, Summerland is not normal. The people are rich and sophisticated, above the street battles that rage outside. It is an oasis in Beirut, a reminder of the lazy, luxurious days that some Beirutis enjoyed before this war. A very beautiful girl, daughter of a general in the Lebanese army, refused to be photographed. 'In a way it's obscene,' she says. 'There are a lot of people getting killed out there.'

At the end of the sea wall, just beyond where the twins are still lying, the boom of the Green Line guns can be heard above the roar of the surf.

Sunday Times Magazine
22 September 1985

Egypt on the brink

On a sweltering afternoon in Cairo, near the pyramids of Giza, the obviously irritated voice of Margaret Thatcher cut through the heavy air. 'You must keep a firm grip on public expenditure,' she said. 'If you don't have any incentives you won't have people working flat out.' A peasant and his donkey plodded past the mosque where the late President Sadat used to pray, oblivious of this good advice in an unknown language. Dogs sprawled panting in the shade of a bush.

Ismail Osman, the nephew of Osman Ahmed Osman, chairman of Arab Contractors Ltd and reputedly the richest man in Egypt, is a great admirer of Mrs Thatcher: on a visit to London he videoed her being interviewed by Brian Walden and has played the tape so frequently that he knows his favourite bits off by heart.

We sat in the bedroom of Ismail's weekend cottage, a small bungalow by the pyramids, as he lay on the bed and slid Mrs Thatcher into his video machine. 'This is a good bit coming up,' he said. 'What I really want to put to you is this, do you really in your guts feel a certain conscience about those who fall to the bottom of the pile?' said Ismail, imitating Walden. He leant forward and wagged his finger: 'How in the world can you produce the resources to help those who fall to the bottom unless you encourage your wealth-creators?'

'That's it,' said Ismail. 'That is the solution to Egypt's problems.' Ismail's family is a member of that small but powerful layer of Egyptian society, the very rich, who are nicknamed by their many critics 'the fat cats'. Ismail's uncle Osman is believed to be the fattest cat of all. Ismail, as a director of Arab Contractors Ltd, is deemed to be merely plump. It is a label he energetically denies. 'I am not a rich man,' he said. 'I am very humble and modest. Please take off your shoes: I will carry them for you. That is why I am liked in Egypt.'

His uncle founded Arab Contractors Ltd and continued to be the chairman after the company was nationalized by the late President Nasser in 1961. He also started 125 private companies in Egypt. Driving through Cairo in Ismail's battered BMW was a study in the power of the Osmans. A cement lorry roared past us. 'It is carrying cement from an Arab Contractors factory to an Arab Contractors construction site,' said Ismail. We crossed a flyover built by Arab Contractors, past an office block built by Arab Contractors. The company has built all the major factories in Egypt, office and apartment blocks, bridges, schools, hospitals and hotels. It is building the new Cairo metro system and the new terminal at the airport. Egyptians tell a joke about Osman. A school teacher asks a boy: 'Who built the Ottoman Empire?' 'Osman Ahmed Osman,' says the boy.

The family has created enormous wealth. Its critics say that most of the wealth is for itself at the expense of the public sector of the Egyptian economy. One charge laid by the Egyptian author and former adviser to both Presidents Nasser and Sadat, Mohammed Heikal, is that the public company Arab Contractors, run by Osman Ahmed Osman, subcontracts to private companies also run by Osman. The left wing maintain that the rich in Egypt have grown richer while the poor, the vast majority, grow poorer. The debate, to which Mrs Thatcher is an unwitting contributor, is bitter. 'My critics are lying,' said Ismail. 'Osman is a big liar,' said Heikal.

Egyptians may disagree about the solution. But all agree about the problem: their country stands on the edge of disaster. People predict that unless the government of President Hosni Mubarak finds some way out of the economic mess then civil disorder and even revolution could swiftly follow. Some believe that if the government cuts subsidies on a whole range of basic products and replaces them with cash payments to the very poor, as the World Bank and the International Monetary Fund are urging it to do, it could push Egypt over the brink. It would cause rioting and the army would have to intervene. There would be bloodshed followed by fiercer riots which could set the scene for revolution or an army coup.

Egypt is the most powerful Arab country in the Middle East, the closest ally of the United States, and partner with Israel in the Camp David peace agreement. Its collapse would cause unimaginable turmoil throughout the Middle East.

The statistics on the state of Egypt are horrifying. Foreign debt is more than US$30 billion and last year an emergency US grant of $500 million only just averted default in the repayment of official debt to the US. The World Bank and the IMF warned Mubarak that its budget deficit and export/import gap had reached perilous levels.

The population of Egypt is 50 million and is rising at a staggering 1 million every ten months. The housing shortage is desperate. Cairo alone has a population of 7 million and needs a million new homes immediately: by the end of the century it will need 3·5 million. Its streets are clogged with more than a million vehicles, the air is foul: Cairenes live for most of the year in a kind of yellow fog composed of car exhaust, industrial pollution, burning refuse and dust from the desert. The state of its sanitary arrangements can be judged by an item in the newspaper *Al Ahram*, in which a columnist 'deplored the falling of children into uncovered cesspools and losing their lives in consequence'.

On top of all that, the four pillars of the Egyptian economy – oil, worker remittances, tourism and fees from the Suez canal – are crumbling. Mubarak and his prime minister, the economist Ali Lutfi, have brought in some reforms and plan more, but even their modest proposals run the danger of triggering social upheaval.

The growing poverty and social tension has been a key element in the rise of religious fervour in Egypt, which raises the spectre that the country might become an Islamic theocracy like Iran.

Islamic extremists from the Al Jihad group murdered Sadat in October 1981 and tried to cause an insurrection in the city of

Assyut. Many of its leaders and supporters were imprisoned; others went underground and are believed still to be active. In July Mubarak began a fresh crackdown on the extremists with the arrest of 37 people, all members of Al Jihad, on charges of sabotage.

But the greatest blow to the government came in February this year when the young conscripts of the Central Security Services – the Egyptian riot police – rioted. They burnt hotels, clubs and bars in Giza and the Pyramids roads until they were put down, belatedly and viciously, by the regular army.

More than 100 people died in the battles. At first the government looked for deeper motives, religious fundamentalism or even the hand of a foreign enemy in the uprising. None emerged. The facts were simple and chilling. The conscripts earned £6 (Egyptian) a month (about £2) plus lodging and one meal a day. The rumour that they would have to serve an extra year living in these miserable conditions was too much to take.

It is the gap between the haves and the have-nots which all Egyptians believe poses the gravest threat to Egypt. Every society has inequalities, its rich and poor, but in Egypt, according to the journalist Michel Oude, the gap is 'obscene'. 'The poor live in conditions which are criminal. It is an outrage.'

For the tourist staying in its high-rise modern hotels, Cairo seems a fairly opulent city. And for a minority of Egyptians it still is. At the end of Ramadan, the Muslim month of fasting, the grand hotels were full of Arab tourists and every evening the foyers and staircases were buried under a carpet of pink tulle as wealthy Egyptians held lavish wedding receptions which went on until the early hours. Guests at the most prestigious weddings were entertained by Egypt's best known belly-dancer, the 42-year-old Najwa Fouad, who is said to command several thousand Egyptian pounds for a single performance. Najwa, who has been dancing since 1952 and was Henry Kissinger's favourite during his shuttle diplomacy in the 1970s, has not noticed any economic decline: 'There are more rich people around these days.' Indeed at the Gezira club on the Island of Zemalek, where the wealthy go to ride, swim, play squash and sip lemonade, there is no sign of impending crisis.

216

Bare statistics paint a different picture of the economy; but they cannot even hint at the misery in which millions of ordinary Egyptians eke out an existence.

Abdul Azim Ramadan Imbabi has a secure job as a clerk in a Cairo tractor factory. Every morning just before 8 a.m. he leaves to go to his office and returns in the afternoon to his home, a tomb in the City of the Dead, a huge sprawling graveyard between the Nile and the airport. He lives with his wife and four children in a wooden hut built over the graves of his ancestors. Two wooden trapdoors in the floor lead to the vaults where these forebears lie. As Muslims they are sexually segregated even in death: the women lie beneath the left-hand trapdoor, the men beneath the one on the right. Imbabi's iron bed, where he sleeps with his wife and two of the children, with the other two sleeping on the floor by the trapdoors, is hard against the tombstone of his grandfather. He has made the best of this macabre abode. On the walls there are some posters and a photograph of his mother-in-law – her body lies two metres beneath his feet. In the corner is a large refrigerator. He is lucky, he says, to have electricity. His ancestors, a good deal wealthier than he is, built this hut for funeral services and equipped it with electric light.

His children look healthy. His 12-year-old daughter, Jihan, is pretty, bright and doing well at school. Her father proudly asked her to read some poetry to me. Then her mother sat her outside, between the tombs, and combed her hair with petrol to get rid of the lice.

Imbabi moved to the City of the Dead six months ago after his house in the Bulaq area of Cairo collapsed. This is a common affair: dozens of dwellings collapse every year, often with heavy loss of life, because they are old and decaying or because people add new floors to them without surveys or planning permission.

He is waiting until he saves enough money to have his house repaired, although on a salary of £E45 a month (about £15) this could take a long time. For the foreseeable future, he will live with the dead.

One stratum of Cairo society lives in tombs, another lives on roofs. Two families, totalling 15 people, live on the roof of a

10-storey building in the sprawling slum called Bulaq, a warren of narrow streets and crumbling buildings near the city centre.

The members of the Mourcy family – mother, father and five grown-up children – live in a makeshift hut constructed partly out of Panasonic cartons and Lipton Richbru tea boxes. Immediately in front is an open lift-shaft and a drop of 30m or more to the ground. They have a panoramic view of thousands of roofs which look like the scene after a major earthquake – littered with junk and debris, and with small huts where people live and wash and sleep and work and tend small flocks of chickens.

The father, Mohammed Mourcy, employed by an engineering company, has lived here for 30 years and has never been able to afford to move out. His hut is baking hot in summer and leaks in winter. He has chickens and ducks which run loose on the roof and a dog called Roy chained to the wall.

The Mourcy family has more professional qualifications than most families in Britain. One son, Zakariah, who is 28, is an engineer; Salah is 23 and in his final year at the engineering faculty of Helwan university; and Ghada, another son, is an accountant. Zenab, a daughter, is studying mathematics at university and Yehyah, another son, is an army officer.

Zakariah is longing to move out and start a family in a house of his own. But he simply cannot afford to do so. He earns £E35 (about £12) a month from his job as a junior engineer in the public sector. On that he could not manage, alone, even the rent of the hut on the roof.

From the hut he can see the huge apartment blocks on the island of Zamalek, where the foreigners and rich Egyptians live: it would take four times his annual salary to pay the rent for one of these apartments for a month.

This is a side of Cairo society that the government would prefer foreigners not to see. Ten storeys below, a police van waited to take us to the Bulaq police headquarters for questioning. We were held for five hours while our passports and press credentials were checked by the security services, and then released.

The police chief at Bulaq was very friendly. But the information ministry official who phoned the police station was furious. 'Why were you on a roof in Bulaq? Why not go to the roof of the Ramsos Hilton hotel? Why do you want to look at the slums? Aren't there nicer things to see?'

There are, indeed, more pleasant sights in Egypt. There are also living conditions so dreadful that life on the roof in Bulaq seems pleasant by comparison.

Batn El Bakara ('the stomach of the cow') must be a strong contender for the title of the most unpleasant place to live on earth. It lies at the bottom of a valley carved into a mountain of Cairo's garbage. There are hills of compacted refuse rising on either side, smoking as it rots and ferments in the sun, and the houses are constructed of garbage, corrugated iron sheeting, boxes, cartons and pieces of plastic. At one end of the village is a fetid lake half full of rubbish.

Between 1,200 and 1,300 people live in Batn El Bakara. They are all Muslims. Other colonies of Coptic Christian garbage-collectors live in other parts of the vast dump.

The inhabitants collect the rubbish from the streets of Cairo on carts pulled by donkeys and bring it back to the village, where whole families, including the youngest children, sort through stinking heaps of it by hand. Among other horrors, they will pick through a carpet of flies to strip the rotting flesh from pieces of fish so that the bones can be sold to the factory up the road.

The temperature deep in the rubbish reaches over 40°C, and there is no breeze. The air is strong. Flies form a thin haze and cover everything. A small boy lies on a bed, his nose, mouth and eyes covered so thickly by flies that he seems dead. He is fine, says his mother. Just sleeping.

Sayed Bahaget Hassan is 44 and a second generation rubbish-collector. His father worked in Batn El Bakara and he was born there. Of his seven children the eldest, Maghdi, works with him on his donkey-cart collecting the rubbish: the others, all except the babies, work sifting through the cart when he comes home. They do not go to school.

The children in the village are all filthy. Many of them look sick and suffer from coughs, watering eyes and sores. Most of them have constant stomach illnesses. Sayed said that the most common illness was infection after the children cut themselves on glass and metal in the garbage. A girl had a long cut on her forearm. It was festering and covered with dirt. She brushed it with her other hand every few seconds to get rid of the flies that settled in the wound. Sayed said that doctors do not come to Batn El Bakara and the hospital is a long way by donkey and cart.

When he gets back from his round in the afternoon the sorting begins. The most valuable items are empty bottles (sold to a bottling plant) and animal bones for glue-making. He resells the plastic pots and dishes but says they are often broken. The food waste is thrown to the herd of pigs which snuffle around the village or fed to the packs of dogs.

Sayed looks surprisingly well for someone living in a rubbish dump. He has a digital watch, a gold ring and metal teeth. He says he makes about £E45 (£15) a month – as much as the engineer who lives in Bulaq, but not enough, he says, to get him out of the rubbish dump. Neither he nor his children will be qualified for any other job and Maghdi, his son, is already the third generation of his family to work there.

'I would like a house out of the rubbish,' he said. 'In summer it is hot like this. In winter it is cold and it rains.' Dreadful as the smell and heat can be in the summer it is preferable, the villagers say, to the winter when rain cascades through the garbage and the landscape looks like the battlefields of the Somme.

The government, says Sayed, does nothing for the villagers: there is neither running water nor electricity. They are like a lost tribe in the rubbish.

Yet Sayed's family, like the rooftop hut dwellers and the people in the City of the Dead, carry on working, aspiring, hoping for better times. And it is in this fact that the best, or only, hope for Egyptian society lies – in what Mohammed Heikal, one of its sternest critics, describes as the 'astonishing resilience' of Egyptians in adversity. None of the people we spoke to showed anger against the government or Hosni Mubarak. Their energies and emotions seemed channelled exclusively into finding a better job, or a second job, a new apartment, the assurance of an education for their children.

Yet there is certainly a limit to the distracting power of these economic concerns. The government was taken by surprise when its riot police went on the rampage over the prospect of another year of impoverishment. If their hopes of better times are endlessly deferred, will the desperate men of Bulaq, of the City of the Dead and of Batn El Bakara likewise spontaneously ignite like the garbage among which they live? No one can be sure that the Egyptian state could survive that blaze of anger.

Sunday Times Magazine
10 August 1986

AFRICA

Zimbabwe bleeds
again

It was at about 37,000 feet as the Air Zimbabwe flight from London to Harare was passing over Chad that the deputy minister for rural development in the Zimbabwe government launched his attack.

Mark Dube is a huge, bearded man, a former general in the guerrilla army during the liberation struggle, who does not mince his words: 'You are a big liar and a hypocrite,' he said, 'You journalists, you all write lies about the killings in Zimbabwe and about civil war. What killings? Everything is fine. Go home and write about how the British kill the Irish, hypocrite.'

It is a sign of the times in the new Zimbabwe that the mainly white passengers, tough-looking farmers with ruddy complexions and their exquisitely pale wives, made not a murmur of protest.

Dube's outrage was echoed often last week in Harare. An elderly senator, a member of the Upper House, said: 'You openly attack us because we are black and a small country.' And one evening in the Quill Club in Harare, the watering hole of local journalists, an official press spokesman, nicknamed 'The Chef', hurled a copy of *The Economist* onto the table. 'Lies, lies,' he said, 'they ought to be thrown out.'

The point was taken up later in Harare by Major General Colin Shortis, head of the British army contingent which is training army units here. As we sipped tea and admired the lovingly tended garden outside, it was difficult to see much wrong in the state of Zimbabwe. A servant brought toast and anchovy paste. 'Bit hard to get, but tuck in,' said the general.

He feels the country is misunderstood abroad. Life is marvellous, he says, the people are friendly, prime minister Robert Mugabe is trying his best against considerable odds. The army is coming along 'jolly well'.

And life for many, both black and white, *is* marvellous: gin and tonics sparkle in the exclusive atmosphere of the Harare Club (formerly the Salisbury Club), beer flows in the Quill, the black and white elite dine sumptuously at La Fontaine, ladies in white dresses can be seen playing bowls and send their children to private school, the rich still have their pools and their servants – at a new minimum wage under Mugabe's socialist rule.

A couple of miles from the general's suburban mansion, at Harare's high court, justice was taking its solemn – and independent – course. Seven former leaders of Joshua Nkomo's guerrilla army, Zipra, charged with high treason and possession of arms of war, sat in the dock dressed in dark business suits looking like a row of chartered accountants. The man sitting in judgment upon them, Mr Justice Squires, white, and perspiring gently under his wig and crimson robes, was the former minister of defence under the Ian Smith government and the man responsible for hunting down Zipra guerrillas – a perfect recipe, it would seem, for a miscarriage of justice.

But Judge Squires dismissed the treason charges against six of the seven. A marvellous example, as the general pointed out, of how the law works freely and dispassionately in the new Zimbabwe.

The visitor who wishes to sustain this cosy view should not, however, dig too deep or go to Bulawayo in Matabeleland, an hour's flight from Harare. In Bulawayo a government official advised me not to drive on the Victoria Falls road, through the area where killings took place last month. 'I most strongly warn you not to go up there,' he said. 'The police have said they will at best arrest, or at worst shoot journalists. The soldiers are a bit trigger-happy. I know it sounds like a giggle, but they are pretty unruly.'

226

In fact at the only checkpoint I came across the police were courteous, but it seemed odd to be warned first about the behaviour of the security forces rather than the dissidents they were there to control.

The main victims of the 'unruliness' are members of the Ndebele tribe which forms 20 per cent of the population but is the majority in Matabeleland, and the main support for the newly-exiled Joshua Nkomo.

A doctor in a Bulawayo clinic told me some appalling stories of ill-treatment suffered by Ndebele subjects picked up by government troops. One woman, he said, had been beaten on the head with chains and clubs. A man had been forced to eat raw sewerage. Another had been beaten then forced to walk naked in front of women prisoners.

'I don't get the bad cases, just the minor ones,' said the doctor. 'But what turns my stomach is the deliberate humiliation. And these people are guilty of nothing, they were all released.'

The tragedy is that the age-old divisions between Shona and Ndebele are, to some extent, being bridged. The head of Zapu, for example, now that Nkomo has gone, is a member of the Shona tribe. The minister Mark Dube, whom I met on the plane, is an Ndebele and yet has government rank. Apparently there is little employment discrimination against the Ndebele, though they do get less than their share of jobs in the government and high-ranking positions in the army. However, in the army itself there are far more Ndebele than there should be on a strict percentage basis.

What is happening in Matabeleland is the ugly face of Zimbabwe. Despite government denials, evidence of the army's brutality has been building up. There have been eye-witness reports, body counts, TV film, photographs, testimony from doctors, missionaries and diplomats.

But this violence is matched by that of the guerrillas whose actions provoked it in the first place. White farmers in Matabeleland live in constant fear of attack by these 'dissidents' – former members of Nkomo's Zipra guerrillas, many of them deserters from the Zimbabwe army who roam the bush imposing a reign of terror. Local people speak of horrendous brutality – men buried alive, stoned to death or thrown into huts and burnt. Bodies have been found mutilated, often with lips cut off.

The killings are directed as much against the hated Shona tribe at Mugabe as against the whites, and the actions of the dissidents have become increasingly political. The shooting near Bulawayo last weekend of Eric and Christine Stratford and their two young granddaughters bore the clear stamp of dissident terror. The killers asked workers on the Stratfords' farm whether they were good employers or not, then executed the whole family. Their point was simple and brutal: the dissidents can protect you from the white land-owner, but Mugabe cannot.

Both British and Zimbabwean officers accept that Mugabe had to do something about the situation in Matabeleland. With the number of dissidents estimated at between two and four thousand, the farmers had begun to arm themselves with automatic rifles and form their own vigilante squads as the only form of self-protection.

But by sending in the Zimbabwe army's Fifth Brigade, composed entirely of members of the Shona tribe, Mugabe was increasing the chances that violence – fed by tribal hostility – would increase. Evidence of the kind cited above, some of it handed personally to Mugabe, suggests that since the arrival of the Brigade, a minimum of 500 men, women and children have been slaughtered.

The killings have decreased in the last few weeks, but the Fifth Brigade is still in the area, and the dissidents, according to reports last week, are back in greater numbers with new weapons, including heavy machine-guns.

All this is provoking accusations that Mugabe is becoming a sanguinary dictator.

There are two interpretations of what is happening. The first is that the image of Mugabe as a man of peace and reconciliation, established after the Lancaster House conference, was a false one. He was in fact always ruthless, and, since independence, has been planning single-mindedly to get rid of his only real rival, Nkomo, and destroy his party, Zapu.

The second version says that Mugabe's hand is being forced

by the hard men in his cabinet, but that he himself opposed the tribal violence that has been unleashed.

It is the raising of the Fifth and Sixth Brigades which has really fuelled the suspicions of his critics.

Their nickname is 'Gukurahundi', which means 'the winds that blow away the dirt'. But they are more widely known in Zimbabwe as 'Mugabe's Muscle' or 'the Shona hit men'. Some of the soldiers themselves brag: 'We are the party army.'

Both brigades are trained in great secrecy by the North Koreans. The Fifth has been used, since January, in Matabeleland and the Sixth will be based in Harare, providing protection for Mugabe. The North Koreans have also trained 'local militias' and the first batch, dressed in sandy uniforms and wearing red stars, were seen driving through Harare recently en route to a rural area, singing revolutionary songs.

This leaves Zimbabwe with two armies: one trained by North Korea, and one, by far the biggest, trained by the 165 members of the British Military and Administrative Training Team with Nato equipment, tactics, administration and traditional spit and polish.

Mugabe's links with North Korea go back a long way. The president, Kim Il Sung, supported Mugabe's Zanu party during the liberation struggle, arming and training his troops. The North Koreans opened a mission here in May 1980 and began to support the military again in April 1981, when they invited Zimbabwean pilots to North Korea for training.

In August that year they sent the first batch of 100 military advisers and gave modest aid in tanks and artillery. They concentrated, according to a South Korean diplomatic source, on 'unconventional training. They have taken revolutionary cadres from Mexico and Sri Lanka and trained them to establish revolutionary bases. It is Kim Il Sung's way of exporting his revolution.'

The training of the Fifth, which has about 5,000 men, ended last July. It is equipped with East bloc armour, rather ancient T-34 and T-55 tanks and with AK-47 rifles. At the Independence Day celebrations the troops gave exotic displays of karate, judo and mass PT. 'Quite smart, quite good,' said a British adviser.

The Koreans themselves have been spotted several times in public – men in white, knee-length shirts, white sandals and Kim Il Sung lapel badges, strolling around the manicured golf courses of local hotels. But there were early forebodings of the future when the budding Fifth Brigaders came into contact with local tourists. Twice groups of tourists were beaten up. The deaths of three British tourists are still linked to the Fifth.

Nkomo, with prescience, attacked the Fifth from their inception. He charged that 'It is obviously a separate army' and would be used to impose a one-party state.

Their behaviour in Matabeleland is based partly on their tribal hatred of the Ndebeles, which is a century old, but also on bad discipline and orders from some officers who told them, according to military sources in Harare, to hit the dissidents hard and 'crack a few skulls'.

The methods of the Fifth were clearly not the solution. They even led Ian Smith, the former Rhodesian prime minister, to turn towards the government's benches during a recent parliamentary debate and say: 'You are making the same mistake we did. You're trying to solve a political problem through military means.'

Mugabe himself is determined to stamp out dissident violence. Speaking in Harare in January, he said: 'Zanu won the country through the barrel of the gun and it will use the gun to destroy dissidents and safeguard the country's independence.' He added: 'The government will hammer dissidents until they realize that Zimbabwe is one and can never be ruled on tribal lines.'

He has, since independence, talked often of establishing a one-party state in Zimbabwe. His idea is a sort of national government, under Zanu.

Mugabe's critics say, however, that he has taken on board some of the most hated legislation from the Smith regime. The emergency regulations, for example, are used to arrest and detain for indefinite periods. It is not unusual for people to be arrested, released on appeal, and promptly re-arrested.

His rigid censorship of the government-controlled press, and his recent virulent attacks on the foreign press are pungent reminders also of the Smith era. Last Thursday night the *Guardian* and *Sunday Times* reporter, Nick Worrall, heard he had been named 'an enemy of the people', and was ordered to leave Zimbabwe in a week.

[Blundy himself was questioned after filing this report.]

There is evidence that Mugabe may have learnt a lesson from the slaughters perpetrated by the Fifth Brigade. Last week, he publicly praised them for their tank manoeuvres, but when the cameras switched off, he launched a full-scale attack on their lack of discipline. There are signs that they are being integrated with the rest of the army, and British advisers will be training some of the Fifth's senior officers. 'A lot of rotten things have been said about the Fifth,' said a British officer. 'I think they could be licked into shape given time.'

The alternative to a military solution to the country's problem – a political accommodation – cannot ignore the man the Zimbabweans call 'the fat man', Joshua Nkomo. 'If they want a political settlement to the dissidents, then I don't think they stand a chance without Nkomo's blessing,' said a senior diplomat in Harare. 'But Mugabe doesn't trust him, he thinks he's a snake in the grass, a devious double dealer.'

So, with Nkomo out of the country, and the soldiers of the Fifth Brigade apparently writing their own rules in Matabeleland, a round of terror has begun which even Mugabe may find hard to stop.

Sunday Times
27 March 1983

How Operation Moses became a human tragedy

Abebe, his wife Mulu and their three young children are one of the hundreds of Falasha families, black Ethiopian Jews, stranded in Sudan after the airlift to Israel stopped on January 6. They live in a straw hut in a refugee camp near Gedaref in eastern Sudan where drought and famine threaten the lives of hundreds of thousands of Sudanese and of those Ethiopians who fled across the border seeking food.

Abebe is a frail gaunt man in his 50s, dressed in a tattered robe. He is so weak he speaks only in a whisper. He and his family are starving.

When I met him on Tuesday morning they had had nothing to eat for two days. He and his three-year-old son, Guadi, who held an empty tin mug, were queueing for a ration card which might enable them to get food. Guadi is emaciated and has a streaming cold. He did not speak or cry and could not even muster the effort to brush away the layer of flies on his face.

When I left them on Tuesday afternoon they still did not have a ration card and even if they had one their chance of getting food would be slim. According to the relief organization, Sudan Aid, supplies are so low that only one tenth of the 20,000 people in the camp could be fed last week.

Abebe's wife and six-year old daughter, Tadela, had been sick with diarrhoea and stomach illnesses. Tadela could not eat or drink even the meagre rations provided for sick children, and that ration has now been stopped. Only Abebe's 10-year-old daughter, Sharje, smiled and seemed lively and free of disease.

Although the Israel prime minister, Shimon Peres, has promised to bring all the Falashas to Israel, Abebe has almost lost hope. His only concern on Tuesday was finding enough food to last him for the next few days.

According to Abebe, the exodus of Falashas from their home, the Gondar province of Ethiopia, became a catastrophe. Whereas many Ethiopians left because of famine, most of the Falashas were not starving in the areas where they lived.

Aid workers and diplomats in Sudan say that they were urged to leave Ethiopia by Jewish organizations which sent workers into their areas, and by Falashas who had returned to the towns and villages to tell people that they, too, could live in the promised land. Aid workers who had visited Gondar say that conditions were not as bad as in the areas to which the Falashas trekked.

Abebe spent eight months in one refugee camp. Umma Raquba, about 50 miles inside the Sudanese border, with 7,000 other Falashas. More than a quarter of them, 1,800 people, died in the camp which went entirely without food for three weeks between July and August last year.

According to aid workers, the death rate among Falashas was also extraordinarily high in the other camps. A member of the Save the Children Fund, who worked in the Docha camp in eastern Sudan, said they died at a far higher rate than the other refugees: 'They were unprepared for the terrible heat of the Sudanese desert. They did not understand elementary hygiene and did not take precautions against disease. They died at a rate of 15 a day.'

There is no accurate figure for how many Falashas are still in Sudan. Seven thousand were airlifted to Israel by the Belgian charter company, Trans European Airlines, which made almost daily flights from Khartoum. The planes were supposed to fly to European airports, as part of an agreement with Sudan, then back to Israel. But according to diplomatic sources in Khartoum, many flights went direct to Tel Aviv.

The Egyptian foreign ministry complained to the Belgian ambassador in Cairo last month that Belgian aircraft, believed to belong to TEA, were flying secretly, without giving their flight plans to Egyptian authorities, across Egyptian airspace in the Sinai, en route to Israel.

The TEA flights stopped on January 6 after the Operation Moses airlift was made public in Tel Aviv and in response to protests by the Sudanese, Israelis estimate that there are between 2,000 and 4,000 Falashas left in Sudan. In addition to Gedaref, camps between Khartoum and Kassala are believed to have Falashas. Some 2,000 are thought to be on the Ethiopian border, prevented from entering Sudan by the army. The Sudanese closed the border to refugees in this area at the start of December.

The Falashas stranded on the Ethiopian side of the border are constantly harassed by bandits and most seem certain to die by starvation. They are not in camps and have no provisions in the rugged territory where they are now trapped.

Those in the Sudan share the plight of the estimated 500,000 Ethiopian refugees and have not suffered any discrimination. There is simply not enough food to go round and the famine has reached the proportions of a major disaster.

At the Wad Kowli camp in eastern Sudan there were 70,000 refugees last week and no food. On Monday at the Tekulbab camp near Kassala there were 25,000 people with only 15 sacks of grain between them. Twenty six people had died the day before. Some 200, mostly children, died of measles in 10 days.

Abebe said he left his home to the north of Lake Tana in Ethiopia about nine months ago. Two of his daughters aged 20 and 15, and a son, aged 22, had already left and they are now in Israel. For Abebe, a weaver and farmer with two small plots of land, Israel must have sounded from his children's reports like the land of milk and honey. His family subsisted, with great hardship, from food saved from the year before.

He paid the equivalent of £60, a small fortune for a peasant, to a leader, an Ethiopian, but not a Falasha, who took about 70 villagers to the Sudanese border. Many families were robbed on the way. On the border they were picked up in lorries and taken to Umma Raquba camp, a group of straw huts and tents which became by last summer the main Falasha camp.

Abebe says conditions there were appalling. There was not

enough food, only a little dura (grain used for cattle feed in Britain) and cooking oil. They suffered from dysentery, diarrhoea, dehydration, malaria and malnutrition. The deaths mounted. A nurse said the Falashas were very poor. They sold any items of furniture or jewellery they possessed to buy coffee, which they drank with almost religious fervour three times a day.

A refugee from Ethiopia, Naod Merani, took me last week up the hillside near the Umma Raquba camp to the Falasha graveyard which has hundreds of stone cairns. 'Often they were too weak to carry the bodies,' he said. 'For six would help carry one corpse. They struggled to build these little monuments which barely covered the bodies.'

The next exodus of Falashas began in great secrecy last November, when they went 'in droves and without warning' according to a nurse. She and other aid workers believe there was a well organized system among the refugees about who would leave and when. Buses arrived at night and flashed their lights in a sort of code from the desert. The refugees were organized into the buses, then driven off into the night.

Abebe says his family missed these buses because they were sick and could not travel. He also said that he did not have the five Sudanese pounds, about £2, necessary for the trip.

These departures continued through November and December and the nurses say the refugees became less secretive and would tell them: 'I'm leaving on Thursday for Israel.' Most of those who left, it seems, went to the camp at Gedaref and then by bus to a holding camp on the outskirts of Khartoum – and eventually at night to the airport. In December Abebe found enough money and took the bus to Gedaref through a desert littered with the skeletons of camels and goats. But he got no further.

Even in January, the least hot month of the year, the temperature is around 100F at midday. The future for Abebe and all the refugees is grim. The aid agencies say the famine is beyond control. The death rate in all the camps is rising at a terrible rate. The refugees face the summer when temperatures go up to 130F.

The camp at Gedaref is now home for Abebe and the other

Falasha families, perhaps 1,000 people in all. 'We never get food here,' he said. 'There is only a little drinking water. I don't have any idea how I will get to Israel. I can't find the way to get out.'

Sunday Times
20 January 1985

Charity unlimited
– but it doesn't
reach the victims

On October 19 last year Michael Buerk, a BBC reporter, arrived in Ethiopia on a worthy but somewhat routine assignment. He was there to cover the famine. It was a story that, despite the hundreds of newspaper articles and films describing and showing its horror and the official reports predicting catastrophe, had caused more indifference than official concern in the West.

Buerk's visit proved to be different. Few four-minute television films can ever have pricked the conscience of the world quite so sharply. It would affect the lives of many hundreds of thousands of starving people right across Africa from Ethiopia to Mauritania.

Buerk went to two feeding centres, at Korem and Makele. There was so little food and there were so many starving people that the camp organizers were forced to pick those who would live and those who would die. They build a low fence around the centre. Those on the inside got subsistence rations. Those on the outside got nothing. Buerk filmed the crowds of people gazing in over the fence who had, effectively, been condemned to death.

It was not a new story. The Ethiopian government's relief and rehabilitation commission had warned of disaster for two years. Its figures are considered to be reliable, even conservative. In 1984 the commission reported that the early rains, called the Belg rains, had failed totally and prospects for a harvest in 1984 were poor. It said that a drop of 30 per cent in food production would put 7·5 million people in danger. Keith Griffin, the president of Magdalen College, Oxford, headed a team of economists in Ethiopia and it had warned of terrible consequences if agriculture declined any further. 'Clearly this cannot be allowed to continue,' he had written in 1982. It did, and the famine and the encroaching desert spread across Africa.

The warnings were not totally ignored, but there was often a disparity between what was promised in aid and what was actually delivered. An Ethiopian government report shows that in one period the United States had promised 50,000 tons of food, but that not one grain had arrived in Ethiopia. Bulgaria had promised 17,000 tons, and by the time the report was written, had delivered nothing. The only country that had kept its pledge was Russia, Ethiopia's closest ally. It had promised nothing, and delivered exactly that.

How many died in Ethiopia and the Sudan, where up to 500,000 Ethiopians fled seeking food, is unknown. Leon Davico from the United Nations High Commission for Refugees thinks the figure is probably in the hundreds of thousands but that no one will ever know. In one UNHCR camp in Sudan the death rate was 100 people a day. In one camp in Somalia 1,000 people died in 10 days. In a camp I visited in February in southern Sudan close to the Ethiopian border, 1,700 Ethiopian Jews, Falashas, died in the first half of 1984. Then, in the summer, the camp officials stopped counting. As a measure of the mortality rate they show you a sprawling graveyard outside the camp. Burials take place each morning. Davico says that the majority of the deaths are not in camps, where at least a rough count can be kept, but in the villages, or in the mountains and the deserts.

The Ethiopian government acknowledges that Buerk's short film, shown in Britain on October 23, then in America and around the world, opened a reservoir of aid for Ethiopia. Before the film, for example, the British Disaster Emergency Committee had raised a record £10 million for their Famine in Africa campaign. After the film, and without any further public appeals, it raised £50 million.

The public concern in Britain moved the government to

238

quadruple its aid to Ethiopia. The US government pledged a staggering £180 million in food aid, enough to feed a third of the 8 million people affected by hunger in Ethiopia for a year. The Ethiopian government official, Dawit Giorgis, wrote in a report of the 'wonderful testimony of the depth of people's feeling towards their fellow men'. He paid tribute to a Scottish couple who had sold their house to live in a trailer and donated the proceeds to famine relief, and to Bob Geldof, the pop singer, whose Band Aid record raised £8 million for Ethiopia and Sudan.

Given that Marxist Ethiopia is extremely unpopular in both Britain and America, which cut off direct aid shortly after President Mengistu came to power, the amount of aid from the West, and the warm thanks from Ethiopia, is remarkable. That Ethiopia's ideological friends in Moscow have made it clear it will get very little from them is also remarkable.

Going on the statistics alone, this is a rare and historic success story. People and governments throughout the world have given enough money – although the exact figure is still being computed – to be pretty sure that no one starves to death in Ethiopia and Sudan, or in other countries in Africa, this year. America and the 10 countries of the European Community alone have provided two-thirds of the food needed by Ethiopia.

The reality is different. Reports produced in April by Oxfam and Save the Children US, which is based in America, say that no aid food or medicine is reaching almost two-thirds of the 7·9 million hungry people in Ethiopia. Almost 5 million people are still starving. Two million of them are trapped in the provinces of Tigré and Eritrea in Ethiopia, where rebels are waging a civil war against the central government. The trickle of aid which got through to Tigré from southern Sudan is drying up. It was carried by the Tigré relief agency, REST, on lorries which travelled at night through Ethiopia to avoid the daytime bombing raids by government planes. Because of a new military offensive by the Ethiopian government, and a new rapprochement with its old enemy, the government of Sudan, these routes may close permanently.

So what has gone wrong?

The relief agencies say the main problem is not food but

transport to take it to the people, often in remote areas, who need it. The 7·9 million people in need of food should get about 120,000 tonnes a month to survive. The trucks available to the Ethiopian government can transport only 40 per cent of that. Oxfam said in May that 'if the job is to be successfully completed, the international community must help to double the transport capacity within Ethiopia'.

It is not as simple as that. According to a Save the Children report, the US government does not believe the figures about trucks provided by the Ethiopians. The US maintains it has enough trucks but that hundreds are being diverted for military use, and more transport would merely fuel the civil war.

Ethiopia is racked by the politics of famine, and millions are suffering for it. Two million of the people not receiving food aid are in the rebel-controlled territory of Tigré. As Save the Children says: 'There are major reasons for not becoming involved in a cross-border feeding operation at this time. [It means taking food covertly into Tigré from southern Sudan.] Such activity would jeopardize our ability to work with the majority of the population by politically tainting us.'

George Galloway, from the charity War on Want, said in a report he sent to the *Sunday Times* in May: 'The famine in Tigré is already far advanced and there are still seven months before harvest. The Ethiopian refusal . . . to allow relief aid into the rural areas of Tigré has led to the death and displacement of hundreds of thousands.'

Tigrean peasants have never been in a worse position. Their land produced no harvest. What goods there are in the markets have increased in price more than 100 per cent in the past few months. Few of them can afford to buy even basic commodities. They are getting only a trickle of foreign aid along the corridor from southern Sudan, and they are not being fed by the Ethiopian government. Three thousand Tigreans a day were, in April, walking for up to six weeks down the mountains and through the desert, in temperatures which reach more than 120°F, to refugee camps in Sudan. Many die along the way, and they reach the camps so weakened by fatigue and hunger that they fall victim to disease, especially malaria which does not exist in their mountain homeland. If this were not enough, they are bombed and strafed by Ethiopian government planes along the way.

The refugee centre of Zila-Zilah, with a floating population of 8,000 to 9,000 refugees, was bombed in early April, according to James Firebrace from War on Want who returned to Britain that month. Four people were killed, and buildings, including the camp pharmacy, were destroyed. Another refugee centre, Terkawa Workemba, was bombed in April.

Food, rather than bombs, can only be airlifted to the people of Tigré with Ethiopian government permission, and so far this has been refused. Only Christian Aid and War on Want are openly sending aid to Tigré through the Sudan, although other charities and some governments are secretly funding them.

Dr Joseph Collins, from the Institute for Food and Development Policy, a private and well respected aid and development agency in California, returned from Ethiopia in March after a two-month fact finding mission. He wrote an angry report. 'In Ethiopia government policies have created the conditions that have made it possible for a natural disaster to become a human calamity of grotesque proportions. The Derg, Ethiopia's military dictatorship, makes relief for most victims impossible and indeed uses famine as a weapon in a war of repression against a large part of the population.'

Government tactics in dealing with the worst areas of famine seem to be founded more on political than compassionate considerations. The government progress report of famine relief published in April in Addis Ababa devotes a section to the resettlement of 1·5 million peasants from the drought areas of Wollo and Tigré in the north and Sidamo in the south. The government has some good arguments. The land is so eroded and abused after centuries of primitive farming that it will no longer produce crops. When it rains the water shoots straight off the high ground into the desert. The building of terraces to hold the rain would take years. 'Contrary to unfounded allegations, [resettlement is] voluntary,' says the report. 'Despite rumours to the contrary [refugees] are settled with their immediate families or whoever they claim to be their dependants.'

Experts on weather agree that instead of taking food to the people, it might make more sense to move the people to land where they might be able to grow food and not be perpetually dependent on aid.

There is evidence, however, that the government has used the resettlement plan to move people out of rebel-controlled areas; and some of its methods are far from voluntary. It withholds grain from refugee camps but provides two cooked meals a day at resettlement transit camps half a mile away. If that does not work the soldiers move the men at gun point. At the Ibnet camp in Gondar province at the end of April, the army forced 50,000 people to move out. Soldiers herded the people out of the camp, then set fire to huts. Two refugees were killed in the camp and 17 bodies were seen by aid workers on the road outside the camp. The government said that the people had been given the choice of resettlement or returning to their homes. In reality, thousands are now wandering in the highlands of Ethiopia. Many of them are likely to die of exposure, hunger or disease.

If the future looks grim for Ethiopia it is not much better for the other countries in the Sahel, sub-Saharan Africa. Five million people are at risk from drought and famine in Sudan, according to the UN office for emergency operations in Africa. And 500,000 are in critical need in Chad, where a total of 1·5 million are at risk. Some 1·2 million people are at risk in Mali, 1·1 million in Mauritania, 2·5 million in Niger, 3 million in Rwanda, 2·5 million in Mozambique.

The area of land reduced to desert-like conditions, lack of rain and bad farming is continuing to spread all over Africa, according to the United Nations, at the rate of 6 million hectares every year. Although governments are aware of the problem and have made efforts to improve agriculture and conserve land, the UN says that 'there is greater awareness of the problem and large increases in donor investment, yet the situation does not improve'.

But there *is* some good news. The drought has broken across much of central and southern Africa. In Zambia and Malawi there have been magnificent harvests. In Zimbabwe it was so good that they can send some of their surplus grain as aid to Ethiopia. But there is little respite for the Sahelian countries, where 33·5 million people are at risk from drought.

242

It has rained in Ethiopia, although the Belg rains in March were too short and too late. There is only a slight hope of a harvest at all. Apart from the erratic rain, there was not enough seed to plant – and not enough people to plant it because they had left their land in search of food in the camps. Even if the rain poured down this summer and Ethiopia through some natural miracle got a bumper harvest, it would still only provide about 20 per cent of the people's needs. Ethiopia must have massive assistance for at least 18 months.

When Buerk went back to the two refugee camps in December, two months after his film, he saw a desert airstrip which had hardly ever, perhaps never, seen a plane. There were two RAF transport planes on the strip unloading food supplies. Davico from the UNHCR says that in camps in Ethiopia and Sudan the death rate has fallen by half. But in some of them 40 people are still dying every day. 'We are still facing the world's worst natural disaster,' he said. 'But the efforts of the past six months have saved hundreds of thousands of lives.'

The aid agencies are now concentrating on the political and logistical problems of getting food to the victims, while agricultural experts are analysing the long term solutions. A British agriculturalist, who has just returned from the Ethiopian highlands, is experimenting with sweet and Irish potato seeds which might survive with limited rainfall.

There is a fear that the world's sense of pity and outrage, which has provided so much money since October for food, transport and medicine, might once again slump into indifference.

'Our fund raising goes in bursts,' said the British Disaster Emergency Committee. 'If there are press and television reports it goes up, if there aren't it tends to fall.'

George Galloway fears that interest is declining. After his trip to Tigré in March he wrote a long article about the disaster and offered it around the British newspapers. 'Nobody was interested,' he said. 'I was a bit shocked and disappointed.'

Sunday Times Magazine
9 August 1985

110 deg: Geldof
fumes as the
protocol rises

As Bob Geldof toured Africa last week, through remote rural areas infested with malaria and amoebic dysentery, his main fear, which has become almost an obsession, was of falling victim to a disease he has called PCS, the Prince Charles Syndrome.

Geldof and the Band Aid director, Kevin Jenden, travelled through the Sahel region, those countries on the southern fringes of the Sahara desert. They are looking at long-term aid projects and intend to spend $1m in each of the four Sahel countries. They go on this week to Sudan and Ethiopia, where the bulk of the $50m raised in the Live Aid concert will be spent on emergency and long-term aid. Last week the trip took on some of the trappings of a royal tour, and Geldof has come down with a chronic case of the PCS, the results of celebrity treatment.

When the Band Aid plane landed at Ouagadougou airport in the desperately poor country of Burkina Faso a reception committee stretched along the tarmac. The Little Singers of the Clenched Fist, the local equivalent of the Boy Scouts, and the Doves of the Revolution, a female singing group, delivered a song of welcome and chanted, 'Geldof, Geldof.' Although a local diplomat pointed out that this was rock-bottom protocol by the hospitable standards of Burkina Faso, Geldof left the airport scowling.

In Timbuktu in Mali he was asked to plant a ceremonial rice

shoot and in Burkina Faso a tree. In presidential style in Burkina Faso he had been allocated his own bodyguard who stayed next to him all day and stood outside his room at the Independence Hotel all night.

In both countries Geldof has sat through long meetings and greetings in small hot rooms. All this is, of course, a sign of how famous and beloved Geldof has become, but Bob detests it. 'It's the PCS. I'm not here as royalty or as head of state. I want to talk to normal people and get some work done,' said Geldof. 'This protocol is driving me mad. These official meetings are terminally boring.'

His image has become a heady mixture of James Dean and Mother Teresa. His fame has spread to villages where the name Prince Charles would bring a blank stare and Geldof is finding it hard to handle. He has discussed the problem with the prince himself over breakfast at Kensington Palace and Charles was, Geldof says, sympathetic.

Geldof is also sick of the press he has been getting. 'It's either vilification, saying Band Aid hasn't got the money to the people quick enough, or it's sanctification, calling me Saint Bob and all that crap. Both piss me off.'

The PCS came to a head on Thursday night in Ouagadougou when Geldof was guest of honour at an interminable concert. Local Wenega dancers shimmied through clouds of mosquitoes to prostrate themselves at his feet. He was dragged to the microphone and asked to sing along with the Little Singers of the Clenched Fist. Geldof shook a castanet and sat down. 'That's it,' he said later at the bar of the hotel. 'No more protocol, no more PCS.' Telexes were sent ahead to Niger and Chad, the next Sahel countries on the itinerary, cutting down official receptions.

Geldof is doing himself a disservice. He does not look or act like Prince Charles. His hair is lank and shoulder length. During official receptions he begins to chew it irritably. His eyes are half closed with fatigue and he has a heavy growth of stubble. Four-letter words trip lightly and frequently off his tongue.

He cross-examines officials in a style which would not come easy to Charles: 'Minister, do you mind if we cut the crap?'; 'Is it true that food aid is going to corrupt officials?'; 'Why don't you get your act together?'

The professional aid workers who have met Geldof on this trip feel this alone is a vital service. 'Geldof can say things that aid workers are dying to say but cannot,' said a United Nations worker. 'He can be rude and brutal. If we did that we would be thrown out of the country.'

Geldof's fame and power have taken both him and Jenden by surprise. Band Aid has expanded massively since the Christmas record which raised $8m. After Live Aid's concert, there are plans for spin-offs, Fashion Aid and Sport Aid. When Geldof gets back to Britain he will go to appeal for funds at the European parliament in Strasbourg, then to the UN in New York.

The trip through the Sahel is mainly to draw attention to the plight of these countries and also to bring famine into the headlines again because people are suffering, Geldof says, from 'compassion fatigue'.

Geldof and Jenden are working 18 hours a day. Although they often disagree, they complement each other in style and content. Geldof likes the messianic approach. On the plane to Mali he talked of 'moral imperatives' of 'mobilizing the world against famine'. In Bamako, the capital of Mali, on Tuesday he lectured a bevy of aid workers in a tent: 'You people represent the most powerful countries in the world. You must look beyond the problem of displaced persons. You have got to think of large-scale plantations of forest to stop desertification.'

This kind of talk is dismissed as well-meaning but naive by most of the aid workers. Even Jenden disagrees, gently deflating Geldof by saying: 'Here you go, Bob, solving the problems of the world again.' Jenden lacks rhetorical flair but likes the detailed business.

They are both defiant amateurs. 'I can say what I want so long as it is an ill-informed pop singer saying it,' says Geldof.

The aid workers in Mali and Burkina Faso were impressed, however, by their professional approach. Geldof and Jenden ask the agencies how the Band Aid money should be spent rather than tell them. 'I disliked Geldof at first,' said an aid worker in Bamako. 'I resented his arrogance, his punk style.

Then he began talking sense and if he can bully the agencies into working together it will be a big success.'

Despite the amateur image, the Band Aid organization, with its experts on intermediate technology and health, its academic advisers at universities, *is* professional. It has shipped grain faster and cheaper than other agencies. In the market in Bamako Geldof spent half an hour haggling in 110 degrees with a merchant for a $3 piece of cloth that he wanted as a souvenir. Jenden says he applies the same principle haggling on a $5m grain deal.

This trip has been a sharp lesson in the problems of aid. The Sahel region has proved a graveyard for the dozens of well meaning aid agencies that work there. When Geldof first arrived he was shocked, not by the scale of the suffering, but by the optimism of the government and the aid organizations. People are still dying of malnutrition in the south. The main problem is not, however, emergency aid for the starving, but long-term development to stop the next famine happening and to cope with the hundreds of thousands who have been displaced.

The irony is that the agencies still distributing food aid sometimes do more harm than good. Peasants are trying to cultivate crops to be self-sufficient and sell produce on the local market. Thousands of tonnes of free grain, about to be distributed in Gao in northen Mali, are threatening to destroy the local market. People will not be able to sell their own crops and there will be no incentive to cultivate the land.

Geldof accepts the principle that you don't solve the problems of long-term famine relief by throwing money at it, 'The problem is that people can lose heart,' says Geldof. 'If you dig a well it makes the land around it arable and people go there, then everyone brings their cattle in, the water gets polluted, the land is over-grazed. It's a vicious circle and people give up.'

In Timbuktu last Wednesday lunchtime even Geldof's moral fervour began to wilt. He slumped in a chair in the L'azalai Hotel, his head swathed in a local turban, sipping warm Coca-Cola. He signed the visitors' book: 'Good luck. You need it. Bob Geldof.'

This could be his last Band Aid trip to Africa. Geldof realizes that a voluntary charity cannot go on for ever. He says that if

Band Aid became an institution with its own paid bureaucracy it would lose much of its power.

'You can't keep on getting on your horse and charging,' Geldof said. 'The built-in obsolescence of Band Aid is that Geldof will become in the end like anyone else.' Jenden intends to leave at Christmas for his architecture firm. Geldof says he intends to go back to being a fulltime Boomtown Rat next year.

Cover-up

The Catholic priest had no doubt that resettlement was a good thing. Father Jack Finucane, the head of Concern, an Irish aid organization, told a group of 60 foreign aid workers, including the honoured guest, Bob Geldof of Band Aid, that the policy was right. International aid groups and Western governments should stop being squeamish and channel money into the programme.

Father Finucane was speaking on October 19 in the offices of the Ethiopian government's Relief and Rehabilitation Commission (RRC) in the capital, Addis Ababa. The commission's officials nodded vigorously. As members of the Marxist-Leninist government of Comrade Mengistu Haile Mariam, their relationship with Western agencies and governments is wary, often downright hostile. This was a rare moment of total accord.

Finucane was angry with the media. He said that they distorted the truth. Geldof had a copy of a Wall Street Journal report of an investigation by the American group, Cultural Survival Inc. On the basis of 230 interviews with Ethiopian refugees, the investigation concluded that between 50,000 and 100,000 people had died as a direct result of the resettlement programme. 'I've read it and I don't believe it,' said Finucane. There had been problems, but nothing on that scale, he said. He had visited the areas – his own group worked in some of them – and he had seen no sign of the horrors the report described.

249

One member of the audience, Michel Fiszbin, from the French medical group, Médecins sans Frontières, listened to Finucane with what he described as disbelief and outrage. Fiszbin had been at another meeting exactly one month before where Finucane had addressed Western ambassadors about resettlement. The story he told at this private meeting, at the Hilton Hotel in Addis, where no press were present, was very different. Fiszbin's notes of Finucane's statement have been corroborated by Concern's head office in Dublin.

Finucane said that half a million people had been displaced in the first phase of the resettlement programme in 'horrible conditions'. He said that out of 77 resettled areas, only two or three had succeeded. As a result, said Finucane, 100,000 people had died. Concern's head office in Dublin said that Finucane's investigation of villages in the resettlement area showed that in some cases 25% of the people died. So which version is true?

Kotebie is a transit camp for the resettlement programme on the southern outskirts of Addis Ababa. The setting is beautiful, with a background of trees and mountains in the thin, pure air of the plateau some 8,000ft above sea level. It is a model camp, and last week the private doubts of Father Finucane and the horrific secret reports of the agencies seemed absurd among these neat, clean tents and huts. Everyone in this camp wanted to be resettled.

For example, Mrs Aregash Yassin, 35, whose husband died in the drought a year ago, walked 270 miles with her two young children to this camp. It took her two months over terrain that a commando would find inhibiting. In her home in Wollo province she was starving to death, she said. Her close relatives had died.

All the 640 people in the camp looked well fed and healthy: 130 children, orphaned by the drought, sat in the sun and had porridge for breakfast. Over the next few days they will all be taken in trucks and buses to resettlement areas in the south and southwest of the country.

Resettlement began in earnest late last year. Some 542,000 people were moved, mostly from Wollo and Tigré, between November 1984 and August this year. The official reason for

250

this vast displacement is simple: the land in Wollo and Tigré has been ruined by drought, overpopulation and bad farming for years. The people cannot live on it. They either move or slowly starve to death. The government plans to move 200,000 people by next June, and another half a million by the end of 1986.

The RRC paints an idyllic picture of resettlement in its promotional literature and films. Each family gets a plot of land, a tukel or hut, and a large backyard. Farm implements, seed and medical facilities are provided free of charge. For a peasant from Wollo this is a pastoral paradise.

This image is not entirely untrue for some resettled peasants. Finucane says, in public at least, that the settlements his agency works in are excellent.

But the operation has not always worked out smoothly. There is no doubt that the international agencies and Western governments have attempted to cover up the horrors that occurred during resettlement earlier this year. They have two fears: that the Ethiopian government, which is extremely sensitive to criticism, will stop co-operating with them and even expel them; and that stories which reflect badly on the Ethiopian government will help to dry up the donations from the West.

Publicly, aid officials refuse to discuss the issue. Brother Augustus O'Keefe, who is now chairman of the Band Aid co-ordinating committee in Addis and was present at the Hilton meeting, walked off in a huff when asked about Finucane's first statement. 'That was a private meeting. I won't talk about it. The press have done a lot of damage here,' he said. 'I have never heard about any problems with resettlement.'

But in private conversations with other aid workers the dark side of resettlement begins to emerge. A senior member of a British agency said that, according to his statistics from transit camps and resettlement areas, about 50,000 people died earlier this year. The Red Cross League conducted a secret survey of the resettlement areas in July and August. It sent its findings to the RRC but did not make them public.

In fact the report was devastating. It said that people were resettled in appalling conditions, without medical facilities, sufficient food or any infrastructure when they arrived at their destinations. Thousands of people from the highlands of Ethiopia succumbed to malaria when they moved to the mosquito-ridden swamps of the lowlands of southern Ethiopia. Red Cross field workers say they estimate that there was a 10% death toll, which means 50,000 people died.

This figure is accepted as accurate by some Western governments although none of them would discuss it on the record. The only agency which is willing to speak out about the terrible death toll and the conditions of resettlement is Médecins sans Frontières which now faces expulsion by the Ethiopian government. As the head of the RRC said: 'Médicins sans Frontières have the biggest mouths and they do the least. I am showing them the door and they can go straight through it.

The deaths among refugees might be attributed to incompetence and bad planning, but the Addis regime also faces serious political charges.

First, it is accused of being motivated by politics rather than the best interest of the people. The government faces civil war in Tigré and Wollo and, the critics say, it is trying to denude the areas of people, starving the rebels of support and recruits.

The government says the fact that the Tigrean People's Liberation Front is fighting for autonomy in these areas is coincidental. They are the very places worst hit by famine. Some independent experts agree with this last point. For instance, Goran Hanson, a hydrogeologist, has studied the area for 17 years with the help of Landsat satellite pictures. He says that the land in northern Wollo and parts of Tigré has been destroyed by overgrazing and drought. The average landholdings are too small and farmers have been forced to cultivate land on slopes so steep they have to attach safety ropes to their oxen to stop themselves plummeting down the mountainside.

But Hanson is not a supporter of resettlement. He believes that there is fertile land in Wollo and that people should be moved there, a comparatively easy task, rather than sent hundreds of miles to the south.

The second – and perhaps most crucial – accusation against

252

the government is that people are not moved voluntarily but that they are forced. It happens in two ways and in the past couple of weeks there were examples of both methods.

The first is simple and brutal. People are rounded up in their villages or at feeding centres by militiamen and soldiers and pushed, at the point of a gun or stick, into trucks. They are taken to transit camps, then to the south.

Korem is a feeding centre in the Wollo highlands, in land that was once lush and fertile and now, even after the meagre rains this year, is parched. People who live in the mountains and valleys up to 30km away come there once a month for dry rations and then stagger under bags of grain on a two-day trek back to their villages. About 23,000 people still live in the camp in huge tent villages because there is no harvest at home. Others are still undernourished or sick from famine and lie, crowded together in huts, all dressed in the same ochre-coloured robes. It is a hot, fly-blown and pitiful place.

Ten days ago, at night, trucks and buses arrived at Korem and more than 600 people were herded into them by militiamen armed with sticks and whips. It is during such enforced removals that families are split up.

Word quickly spread through the camp and by next day more than 10,000 people had fled, fearing that the militiamen would return and cart them away.

Médecins sans Frontières and other agencies say, privately, that this was not an isolated incident. Such forced resettlement still occurs in feeding centres in Wollo and Tigré.

The government's other method of forcing people to move is more subtle but hardly less brutal. Médecins sans Frontières says that a week ago the government banned the distribution of dry rations to 12,000 people who live near Korem camp. No reason was given. The agency has been prevented from giving intensive feeding to 5,000 children at the Kelala feeding camp in Wollo. Two thousand of these children are in desperate need, the agency says, and hundreds are dying.

Médecins sans Frontières can see only one reason why the government does not allow it to give humanitarian aid: the aim is to persuade people to resettle by depriving them of proper care in the areas in which they live. 'The attitude is resettle and you will be given food and assistance. Stay where you are and the government will not help you,' said a senior British aid official who did not want to be named.

The press works under inhibitions similar to those of the aid agencies. I arrived in Addis with Paul Vallely of *The Times* who has written, sometimes critically, about the Ethiopian government. Security officials at Addis airport threatened to lock Vallely up overnight and put him on the first plane in the morning, until Bob Geldof of Band Aid interceded. Reluctantly the officials allowed him to stay until Geldof left. I asked an RRC official, Getaneh Argaw, what Vallely had done to arouse the wrath of the government. 'A year ago he wrote that there was cholera in some feeding camps,' said Argaw. Was that untrue? 'No, there was cholera but we asked the international press not to print it because it might have affected Ethiopian exports. They all agreed except Vallely,' he said.

Fiszbin of Médecins sans Frontiers believes this reluctance to tell the truth is damaging. He says that the international community is pouring millions and dollars of aid into the country but cannot make the correct decisions about how it should be spent.

Next year the Ethiopian government will need massive emergency aid to help the 5m people who, despite some rain in some areas of Ethiopia, will still need food. The emphasis has, however, moved away from immediate relief to long-term assistance for redevelopment in an attempt to insure against the droughts that will inevitably occur in the future. Its main aim is to swing international aid organizations and Western governments behind the resettlement programme.

It is having some success. The Concern organization is working in resettlement areas. Gus O'Keefe believes that some of Band Aid's money should go to these areas. World Vision, Save the Children UK and the United Nations are about to work there. Although most Western governments are still opposed, Canada and Italy are about to lift their ban.

None of the agencies agree with resettlement, at least in private, or like the way it has been carried out but, as one official put it: 'We must face the fact that the government is going ahead, it is a *fait accompli* and we are here to help people in need. If they are in resettlement areas then so be it.'

Sunday Times
3 November 1985

Playing the heavy father

Hundreds of teenagers poured out of coaches and dashed for the entrance to the conference hall. A crowd of 3,000 stretched back through the car park and across the dual carriageway. Most of them were girls and they giggled, screamed and pushed against a wedge of bouncers who used their fists and shoulders to keep them back from the door. From inside the hall came the rhythmic chanting of another 3,000 teenagers. In the west it would take Bruce Springsteen to pull in a crowd like that. But this was Tripoli, the capital of Libya, and the teenage tumult was for the equivalent, in Britain, of the Conservative party conference. The leader, or 'guide' as he prefers to be called, of the Socialist People's Libyan Arab Jamahiriya, Colonel Muammar al-Gadaffi, was topping the bill with a speech to commemorate the late Egyptian president, Gamal Abdel Nasser. He would speak for two hours on Arab unity and the Palestinian struggle.

His arrival on the stage of the General People's Congress Hall caused a wave of chanting and fist waving which swept out of the auditorium across the street and down the dual carriage-way. 'We are Gadaffi,' they shouted. 'Death, death to America. Shit, shit and shit on the US Sixth Fleet.' Despite the fiery rhetoric the crowd was good-humoured, more polite per-haps than their counterparts in Britain. One young man, in a fit of revolutionary zeal, brandished his fist and accident-ally hit me on the head. 'I am very sorry,' he said. 'Did I hurt you?' – and went back to chanting 'death, death to Reagan.'

It was revolutionary theatre. Gadaffi milked the crowd, his head tilted back, swaying slightly on his feet. Six television cameras focussed on his face, which appeared in monstrous proportions on a huge screen at the front of the hall. Every few minutes he glanced down at two television monitors in front of the podium, adjusted his collar and fluffed up the hair over his ears. His smile slipped only once, when he moved to the front of the stage to press the flesh in American style and one of his security guards (trained by East Germans) stepped between him and the crowd. Gadaffi shouted and shoved him roughly out of the way, then the smile flashed back.

This was the real Gadaffi constituency: young people who have been brought up with and known no alternative to the 'Green Revolution', their minds moulded by the slogans, speeches and barrage of propaganda which dominate television, radio and the press. It is almost impossible to avoid. In the El Khebir hotel in Tripoli, where only foreigners stay, revolutionary Muzak, chanting, slogans and speeches boom out of the loudspeakers in the lifts, the dining room and the corridors. Television carries hours of live reporting from the 'basic people's congresses', the foundation stones upon which Libyan democracy is allegedly built. These are more like evangelical services than political debates: speeches are begun, then drowned out by slogan shouting and fist-waving: 'We are Gadaffi! We will die for Gadaffi! Those who are against the Jamahiriya, we will explode them!'

Gadaffi's cult has been carefully nurtured by an East German who has taken Libyan nationality and the Arab name Al Hammish. He is the Libyan equivalent of Sir Gordon Reece, the British prime minister's image maker. Al Hammish has done a good job. The Colonel's picture is everywhere, hanging above streets, in shop windows, on the walls of offices, the faces of watches and the satchels of school children. Someone who had tea with Gadaffi remembers the shock as she looked down and saw the Colonel's smiling face shimmering up from the bottom of the cup. Gadaffi says he has exhorted the Libyan people not to put up his picture, but: 'There is nothing I can do to stop them, they insist.'

He is a vain man. He dresses flamboyantly and sometimes changes his outfit three times a day, from the uniform to the robe and Arab headdress to the powder blue jump suit tucked into his boots. 'Whatever I wear becomes a fad,' he said one evening in Tripoli. 'Suddenly everyone is wearing it.'

Al Hammish needs to spend more time on Gadaffi's image abroad, which is not good. He is seen by many westerners as an oil-rich psychopath whose country is a vast, arid training ground for terrorists. He is unpopular with most of his Arab neighbours and in the past 16 years of his rule has done little to advance his ideal of Arab unity. There have been doubts cast on his sanity by Arab leaders; and a US Central Intelligence Agency report, leaked in Washington, said that Gadaffi was suffering from chronic mental and physical stress. He was supposed to be an epileptic and, according to Israeli intelligence, suffered acutely from haemorrhoids. Unable to sleep, he was to be found wandering the corridors of the Aziziya barracks muttering incoherently.

If all this is true he has made a remarkable recovery.

In January he faced crises that would make most leaders lose sleep. After the terrorist attacks in Rome and Vienna which killed 20 civilians, and which Gadaffi is suspected of funding if not ordering directly, the US Sixth Fleet steamed towards the Libyan coast. There was also the probability of military reprisal from Israel. But these threats did not seem to bother them unduly.

The Israelis, who are Gadaffi's great enemy although he does little to strike at them directly, take him seriously, and some admire his skill in crisis management. With Chad, Egypt, Tunisia and now the US he can take events to the very brink, and then pull back. He turned the massacre in Rome and Vienna to his diplomatic advantage, uniting the members of the Islamic conference organization behind him against the threat of military retaliation from Israel and the US. He almost drove a wedge between the Europeans and the Americans over the question of sanctions against Libya.

Most Western diplomats in Tripoli believe Gadaffi is guilty:

that the Abu Nidal terrorist group carried out the killings and that Gadaffi has given them a safe haven, funds and arms. They also believe that he handled the subsequent crisis with more skill than the Americans.

Gadaffi's public relations *coup* took place on a Saturday night in Tripoli. He invited five women from the press corps to meet Mr and Mrs Gadaffi and their children at home. The ideological reason for this was, Gadaffi said, because he wanted to promote women's rights. Gadaffi also likes women. When only four of them arrived he realized immediately that one was missing. 'Where is the other one, with the long dark hair?' he asked. A car was dispatched immediately to the El Khebir hotel and rushed her back.

Gadaffi lives, some of the time at least, in a tent in the compound of the massively defended Aziziya barracks, next to a large, steel radio antenna. It is an odd compromise between his Bedouin roots and 20th-century technology. Olive green on the outside but brightly coloured inside, with embroidered quotations from his *Green Book* sewn into the fabric, the tent is simply furnished, with mats on the floor. A baby camel and its mother are tethered outside.

All this is to remind him of the tent in the Sirtic desert where he was born. However, a cable snakes from a building nearby, under the canvas walls, to power a television, a video recorder and a bank of green telephones. Gadaffi kept the television on because, he said, he 'liked to keep contact with the masses'. In the background the masses could be heard chanting their hymns to Gadaffi: 'We are Gadaffi! We will die for Gadaffi!'

Safiya Gadaffi, 32, his second wife and mother of six of his seven children, is pretty and aloof. She quickly grew bored with our interview, perhaps because her English is not very good, and left the tent. Gadaffi stroked the hair of his 8-year old daughter Aysha and talked of how he had been misunderstood by the West: 'Reagan should come and see that I don't live in the trenches wearing hand grenades in my belt. The lies that I don't smile or have no family or that I am full of hate would be proved false.' Gadaffi, who has had little practice at the cosy fireside chat so popular with American politicians, carried it off beautifully. He mentioned the books he likes reading (*Uncle*

Tom's Cabin, and *The Outsider* by Colin Wilson) and the music he enjoys (Beethoven). He said he wanted his six sons to grow up to be doctors helping the poor in Africa; that he thought his daughter might have political potential; and that he wanted another baby girl. He talked of meeting his wife for the first time just after he had seized power and was in hospital having his appendix out. She was a nurse and, Safiya agreed, it was love at first sight. If Libya gave out knighthoods Al Hammish should get one.

Gadaffi was curious about America. He asked the *New York Times* correspondent whether the American people really like Reagan, and was amazed to hear that some of them actually love him. 'They love him?' said Gadaffi. 'Love him?' He was shocked to hear that the correspondent was half Jewish: 'But your father is not a zionist?' 'Yes,' said the correspondent, 'he is a passionate zionist,' Gadaffi looked perplexed. His own attitude to Jews is crude, almost Hitlerian, 'They believe they are the master race, that they will conquer the world,' he said. 'This is written in their religion. The only way the zionists will be stopped is by continuous war.'

The pictures taken that night of the family in the tent and the cosy chat with the colonel went round the world. They revealed very little. Libya is, with the exception of Albania, the most closed society in the world. Direct questions to Libyan officials bring no direct answers. Ordinary Libyans are forbidden to talk to foreigners. Press and television are censored, totally. Telephones and telexes are bugged with the latest West German equipment installed by the East German advisors. Revolutionary guards, the young Turks of Gadaffi's revolution, are everywhere in shops, factories and the streets looking for the ideologically impure.

Conversation with intelligent and government-approved Libyans gets nowhere. Ahmed Ibrahim al Fagih, a Libyan writer and author of the play *The Gazelles* (which has been performed in London), asked us over lunch about the problems in Britain. We mentioned unemployment, poverty, the inner cities, privatization. And what, we asked are the problems in Libya? Al Fagih looked blank. 'What problems?' he said.

Colonel Edward Lough, a British officer (now retired) who

ran the British military mission in Libya in the early 1960s, has a different view of Gadaffi, the family man. 'I didn't like him and he made life for my officers very difficult. He was probably not as stupid as I thought, though.' He remembers that Gadaffi was 'inherently cruel'. Once Gadaffi, as the senior officer, ordered the execution of a Libyan soldier by making him run across the firing range. 'They shot at him until he was killed,' said Lough. 'I think he had committed some religious offence.'

Lough watched Gadaffi carefully because he appeared to be drawing around him a group of zealously religious young officers; and he mentioned him frequently in his reports to the Foreign Office. Lough's suspicions were aroused when Gadaffi was posted to a signals unit in Benghazi and indented for the most elaborate radio equipment, far beyond the unit's requirement. Lough reported this, and is still resentful that his cables went unanswered. If the British government had passed the information on to King Idris of Libya then the country might have taken a very different course.

Gadaffi's resentment of the West and his British military instructors is understandable in a young man following in the footsteps of Nasser, the great Arab nationalist. His flimsy knowledge of what life is like outside the Aziziya barracks is less excusable. Gadaffi says that he has created a 'concrete utopia' in Libya. 'Not the Utopia of the Greek philosophers which was only an idea. This is real.' That does not seem a fair description of a country in which three people died in a riot of shoppers trying to buy imported bananas.

Jamahiriya Street in Tripoli used to be one of the busiest shopping areas in Libya. We found it almost deserted. More than half the shops were closed permanently and those that were open had hardly anything in the windows – a single digital watch in one, a few shoes in another, a *Green Book* and an empty film-carton in a third. 'It is almost a miracle,' said a westerner in Tripoli. 'To reduce one of the richest countries in the world to this takes real skill.'

The shops are closed partly because there are no goods to sell and partly for revolutionary reasons. Gadaffi has ruled that people should be 'partners not wage slaves' and small businesses, no longer allowed to hire staff, have closed down. The old city of Tripoli, with its Italian architecture and delightful arcades where the bazaar merchants had their shops, is now empty and decaying. Libyans must shop in huge modern (and empty-shelved) stores called by such imaginative names as 'Supermarket 103'.

Tripoli is a dismal city. Alcohol, and therefore bars, are banned and the few restaurants that remain run out of food and shut just after 8pm. There is no night life, and the streets are deserted except for the occasional prowling police car. The expatriate community works mostly in the oil industry for high salaries with generous holidays and conditions, but complains about the barrenness of life in Libya. The authorities turn a blind eye to the alcohol which the foreigners make themselves – a poisonous concoction called 'flash' which is potent and the colour of urine. Alcoholism, surprisingly in so zealously Muslim a country, is a major problem among the foreigners.

The austerity measures are only partly Gadaffi's fault. The price of a gallon of Libyan oil has fallen from $40 in 1980 to less than $20 this month. Oil income has fallen from $22 billion to about $10 billion a year and, although imports have been cut from $10 billion in 1980 to $7·5 billion last year, Libya is still overspending by almost $2 billion a year. Gadaffi continues, however, to spend billions of dollars on sophisticated military hardware from the Soviet Union, the Argentine and Brazil and to launch grandiose development schemes. The Great Man-Made River, which will pump water from underground reservoirs to irrigate large tracts of the desert, will cost him $20 billion. His steel plants are costly and unnecessary for so small a population (3·5 million); but wages and raw materials costs are too high to compete on international markets.

The Libyans are still well off, and earn more per capita than the British. Everyone owns a house or flat; but nobody is allowed to have more than one, and renting a flat is forbidden unless carried out through the government. Medical care and education are free, pensions are generous. Al Fagih, the writer, lives well on a salary paid by the state and on royalties from his books. He built his own house, took a holiday last year in the Canary Islands and has modern comforts: a car, a video camera. In fact Al Fagih's life style is in danger of becoming ideologically impure.

It is a tribute to Gadaffi's control of Libya, or perhaps his popularity, that his austerity measures, severe enough to cause riots and revolution in other Arab capitals, have been accepted with only minor grumbling by the Libyans. They have learnt, however, to put up with a lot during the past 16 years.

Gadaffi's 'Green Revolution' has a surreal air about it, with elements of Marx, Plato, Rousseau and the Prophet Muhammad – and just a touch of Lewis Carroll. At Fatah university in Tripoli, a large modern campus, I was forbidden to speak to students and could only talk to members of the revolutionary committee, the proselytisers of Gadaffi's revolution. One of the committee members was Mustafa Abukhder, 24, in his final year of medical studies. Was Mustafa a student leader? 'No,' he said. 'There are no leaders.' Could we talk to other students? 'No,' said Mustafa. 'I am a member of the revolutionary committee.' Are other students members of the committee? 'Yes, they all are.' Well, can we talk to them? 'No,' said Mustafa. He had a broad and permanent smile: why was he smiling? 'I am not smiling,' said Mustafa. 'I always look like this. It is good for the muscles of the face.'

One month ago, he told us, the workers at the university had all been sacked and moved to factories. The students now 'happily' carried out the cleaning and gardening and ran the canteen on a work rota.

Quite how Libya works at all is a mystery even to seasoned observers. Theoretically the people themselves control every aspect of government through 1433 'basic people's congresses' which meet all over the country, along with 360 'people's committees' and 48 'people's professional congresses'. They appoint members to the two 'general people's congresses' which meet in Tripoli and Benghazi and they send instructions to the executive committee of the 'general congress', the 20 secretariats making up the cabinet of Libya.

In practice Gadaffi and a small group of close aides, of whom Major Abdul Salem Jalloud is the most important, run the country. One of the most effective weapons they use is fear. Two students were hanged in public next to a portrait of Gadaffi at

263

the entrance of Fatah university during our visit. Other opponents of the regime are executed in secret or simply disappear.

Jalloud works in the centre of Tripoli in a magnificent palace which used to belong to King Idris. He is an odd ally for Gadaffi – a man of Western tastes who used to be seen in Cairo nightspots with an Egyptian belly-dancer. (His lifestyle is more austere these days.)

He controls the revolutionary committees which are moving into every aspect of Libyan life and are now a key element in the Libyan army. For the main fear of both Gadaffi and Jalloud over the past year has not been the threat of attack from the US or Israel, but of a *coup* within. Jalloud has been in charge of hunting down and murdering the 'stray dogs', Libyan dissidents abroad. When I asked him if he still had a policy of getting rid of the 'stray dogs' he said: 'That policy is over; they are all dead.'

In the heady revolutionary days of the Seventies Gadaffi and his wife used to drive around Tripoli in a battered Volkswagen mingling with the masses. Today when Gadaffi leaves the Aziziya barracks he does so in a convoy of armour-plated cars with a decoy convoy of identical cars going in the opposite direction. These convoys were attacked twice last year. When he flies, two identical jets take off. He has good reason to be cautious. There were two revolts among army officers last year, one in the navy and another in the army on the Tunisian border. It is believed that many army officers have been executed.

One of them is certainly dead. Hassan Ishkal, the head of the army in Sirte, number three in the army hierarchy and a close friend of Jalloud, was found with six bullet holes in his body last November. The official explanation was first that he had been involved in a car crash; then that he had committed suicide.

One theory in Tripoli is that Ishkal attempted to kill Jalloud in two bombing attacks and that Jalloud himself ordered his execution. However it happened, his death reveals a crisis in the Libyan army. Ishkal was thought to oppose Jalloud's revolutionary committees' attempt to gain control of the army. He also believed that Gadaffi's adventure in Chad, where

264

the Libyan army controls half the country, was costly and pointless.

If Gadaffi loses any sleep it is probably not over the loss of such men but over the thought that, somewhere in the Libyan army, there is a young, troublesome officer with an ambition one day to live in a tent in the Aziziya barracks.

Sunday Times Magazine
2 March 1986

U S A
1986–1989

Where there's life
there's soap

Joan Collins, the grande dame of American soap opera and at 53 still a sex symbol of international potency, stuck her tongue out at the cameraman and in a flurry of white silky fur coat and raven hair, with glimpses of bosom and thigh, flounced off the set. 'Miss Collins is a little fraught today,' said the woman from the studio public relations department, with a hushed voice.

On the set of Dynasty the producer, Nancy Malone, who has bright red hair and wears jogging shoes, paced up and down with her arms round Miss Collins's shoulders. A studio aide tried to drape a large, white fur coat around Miss Collins but she shrugged it off. 'I'm sick of that coat,' she said. A studio hairdresser kept pulling at the back of her hair, fluffing up the ends, while a make-up man added another level of powder to a face which lay somewhere beneath layers of cosmetic mud.

Then Miss Collins sat on her canvas chair, which has Joan Collins written on the back, and committed a sin so heinous it is one of the few that Dynasty has banned: she smoked a cigarette. There are few episodes in Dynasty's five-year history in which Collins has not either committed adultery or thought about it, coveted someone's husband or, on a really quiet day in Denver, merely lied, cheated and lusted. Dynasty's cast, as a matter of weekly routine, attempt murder, kidnap and rape, they have homosexual relationships and try to steal each other's money. In the strange morality of network television there are a few things they cannot do: smoke, swear or drink too much. Joan Collins, it is true, was allowed to smoke the occasional cigarette on camera, but the networks have now stopped even this.

As Alexis Colby in Dynasty she is paid an enormous salary to play a beautiful, conniving bitch, which she does to perfection. Off stage she has to be Joan Collins, which is a major drama in itself. Privately she is very nice, funny and, even without the Dynasty make-up, extremely beautiful. Few, if any other, women in their fifties could pose for the centre-fold in *Playboy* without looking ridiculous.

She is also very rich. She controls a commercial empire which if not quite as large as Alexis's (worth $20 million) is getting on that way. Collins is said to command about $8 million a year – from Dynasty, commercials, personal appearances, her autobiography, *Past Imperfect*, and other acting roles.

Her personal life, which is a good deal more interesting than Alexis's, is a matter of fevered concern for the American popular press. That evening she made the local television headlines with her fourth, and her messiest, divorce, from her Swedish business manager. The television anchorman sniggered as he said: 'And Joan Collins still says she believes in the institution of marriage.'

Collins is fair game for the media, but it was difficult among her friends on the set of Dynasty not to feel sorry for her. 'She really is very sweet and the newspapers treat her so badly,' said Nancy Malone. 'She gets terribly hurt, poor thing.'

Collins had been on the set in the Hollywood studios since 7 that morning completing the sixth and final day of filming for an episode that will be shown to the world sometime in February. A tiny scene, one of the eighty vignettes that make up a single hour of Dynasty, had taken most of the morning and afternoon.

Collins/Alexis has to flounce into the apartment of Sammy Jo Dean, who used to be married to Alexis's son Stephen and has her eyes on Alexis's fortune. Alexis glares at Sammy Jo and accuses her of spending the night with Stephen. 'What I do with my nights is my business,' says Sammy Jo. 'You have a reputation for, as you would say, screwing up people's lives,' says Alexis. But wait a minute, isn't Alexis's son Stephen a homosexual? 'Yeah, but don't nit-pick,' said Malone. 'He goes both ways. This is Dynasty.'

This is not the stuff of great drama and the lines are so turgid they are difficult to say, a problem which confronts all the Dynasty actors. Collins has trouble with hers. She tried saying 'screwing people's lives up' then reverted to 'screwing up people's lives'.

Collins's consolation is that she stars in one of the two most successful television programmes ever made. The other one, Dallas, is filmed 25 minutes away across Los Angeles in the former studios of MGM. They are now owned by Lorimar productions and lie in an area cluttered with Fatburger hamburger joints, the Martial Arts Suppliers, adult motels and evangelical churches, all of which give a more precise image of modern America than anything Dallas has ever portrayed.

Leonard Katzman, the executive producer and the man they call the 'consciousness of Dallas' sits, a rumpled figure, in a dingy office at the back of the studios, wearing a bright, knitted cardigan and hammering at an old electric typewriter. It is in such surroundings, too lowly even for JR's cattle, that the Dallas myth is created each week by Katzman and his team of four writers.

Katzman says he 'zips away' at the typewriter and can get a Dallas script finished in a day. He rarely rewrites. In this room, on this typewriter, Katzman wrote the most famous cliffhanger in the history of fiction, and kept an entire world in suspense for three months one summer until they discovered 'who shot JR'.

Alexis's little tiff with Sammy Jo, and the words that Katzman zipped off his typewriter that afternoon, will be seen and heard by more than 100 million people in more than 70 countries around the world. Dallas and Dynasty have fans in Zimbabwe and Bangladesh, Israel and South Africa. They are not sold in Eastern Europe and the Soviet Union, but Russians in Estonia, who can receive the series from the Finnish TV transmitters, are addicted. They have been sold to Libya and to Lebanon, where militiamen in Beirut have followed the vicissitudes of JR and Ewing Oil.

Katzman cannot understand it. Dallas was made for an American audience. 'I don't see why people in poor countries would want to see rich Americans pissing their money down the drain,' he said.

In the language of American networks, the two series have 'great demographics'. Advertisers can reach the whole range of American consumers, from black to white, poor to rich, old to young, men to women, heterosexuals to homosexuals by buying time on Dallas or Dynasty. They have become the General Motors of United States television, bringing in about $12 million for each episode, and they have spawned an empire of businesses selling Dynasty scent, JR beer, clothes, boutiques and glossy books.

The stars have become stupendously rich and internationally famous. The British actor Christopher Cazenove, who joined Dynasty in December, 1985, to play Ben, Blake Carrington's unpleasant brother, is now stopped on the street in London, Paris, New York and Los Angeles. During breakfast at a Hollywood hotel, where TV stars are 10 a penny, five people asked him for his autograph. The waiter whisked his eggs benedict away before he had finished them and, when Cazenove protested, said, 'I'm just screwing you like you screw everybody else in Dynasty, Ben.'

Fans in Bangladesh, Gabon and Estonia must have a strange view of the United States. Dynasty and Dallas depict worlds of vast wealth and deep passions where the men are tanned and handsome, or in Cazenove's case, look like a 1940 Spitfire pilot. The women wear exotic dresses like the contestants in a 'Come Dancing' competition and have cleavages as deep as canyons. The characters are motivated mostly by lust, greed and envy, and they speak a strange soap opera language of creaking cliché.

In one recent episode of Dallas, for example, in a scene squeezed between advertisements for Snuggle Fabric Softener and half-price Christmas decorations, the following sentences zipped off Katzman's typewriter onto the screen: 'I'm easy, what you get is what you see,' 'rub salt in my wounds' and 'there's a time to talk and a time to stop talking'. In one eloquent speech JR said, 'Daddy said you can shake leaves off a tree but the trunk is still standing.'

Dynasty attempts to address some of the issues of the day: homosexuality and race, for example. It has the only black leading lady in prime-time television. In the world of Dallas, blacks and minorities barely exist, there are no social issues and the only sort of current affairs discussed around the dining table at Southfolk ranch are the ones JR is having with his bevy of local beauties. Neither series will mention Aids.

Both Dallas and Dynasty have been attacked for spreading cultural pollution, like acid rain, across the world. At a conference in Paris in 1983 for 300 French and foreign intellectuals, chaired by French Minister of Culture, Jack Lang, Dallas came in for mighty condemnation. Speaker after speaker attacked it as an example of the power of the United States to project what they saw as some of the worst products of American culture into almost every home in the non-Communist world. The Latin American and African intellectuals attacked 'US cultural imperialism'. The American novelist William Styron was the only one to offer a word of defence: 'No one forces anybody at gunpoint in this country to watch Dallas,' he said.

The producers and authors of Dallas and Dynasty are unashamed. 'If we were in the business of sending people messages we would have called our company Western Union,' said Katzman. The truth is that they only have the haziest idea why their shows are so successful. 'Beats me,' said Katzman.

Dallas was created in 1977 in a casual way by the television writer David Jacobs. Network executives, who had seen the success of *Roots* and other long-running television dramas, asked him to produce 'a modern saga'. '"Modern saga." I liked that,' said Jacobs. 'We gave it a shot.' He thought the best place for the saga to evolve was Texas because it was 'bigger, brasher, richer, newer than the Northeast and not as trendy as California.' After he started writing the first treatment of a series he called Dallas, he had another bright idea. 'I had a sudden inspiration: maybe I should actually go to Dallas.' The CBS network talked him out of it. They thought he ought to go after he finished writing.

*
273

He has now visited Dallas two or three times and is surprised by his own accidental accuracy. He created a rich, self-made millionaire called Jock Ewing and a corporate history. Jock founded Ewing Oil in 1930 and ran it until 1977 when he retired as Chief Executive Officer. Although it is a multi-million dollar operation, it is nowhere near the size of the oil majors, so Ewing Oil joined other independent companies to form the IOA, the Independent Oilman's Association. The shares of the company are distributed among the family, and the saga's only real link to reality is that it is forced to follow the world oil prices.

The basic idea of Dallas is, however, a lie. Jock Ewing found oil under his land in Dallas county. There is not, and never has been, any oil there.

Dynasty is a rip-off of Dallas. It has a similar rich, self-made man, Blake Carrington, who also made money out of oil. The Carrington fortune, which is estimated at $200 million, gushes from the Denver-Carrington oil company which has wells in the American South West, the Middle East and Southeast Asia. Its expanding interests include refineries, tankers and a new oil-shale extraction process.

The executives go to great lengths to create such superficial reality. The glossy book on Dynasty, *Dynasty, the Authorised Biography of the Carringtons*, even describes Blake Carrington's library in loving detail. The library is a favourite spot for after-dinner brandy. Hundreds of leather-bound first editions line the walls. 'Of special note is the handcarved mahogany statue of a member of the Vatican's Swiss Guard, circa 1750.'

This is not true. I spent 10 minutes in Blake's library on stage 4 and can reveal that Blake has no first editions, and one of the dullest collections of books in any library in the world: *Corpus Juris Secundum, Federal Tax Regulations 1964, The American Federal Tax Reports, Harold the Last of the Saxon Kings* and *The Penal Code of California*. The hand-carved mahogany statue is made of plaster.

Both series have honest, good people as their anchor (Jock and Miss Ellie in Dallas, Blake and Krystle in Dynasty) and a leading bad character whom people love to hate (JR in Dallas

274

and Alexis in Dynasty). Both revolve around the family and the family homes: the dining room in Dallas and Blake's library in Dynasty. Ludicrously, the wealthy Ewing clan all choose to live in the same farmhouse in Dallas. There is no explanation for this. 'I guess if they didn't there would be no television series,' said Katzman.

The characters in both series have something else in common: they indulge in a lot of extra-marital sex, although as Katzman says, 'it is good, clean sex, nothing nasty,' and it is strictly, almost puritanically controlled by the network censor.

As much of Nancy Malone's job involves filming people in bed and in the shower, these moral laws can cause problems. No one can be naked, even under the sheets, and the camera has to avoid, artfully, the glimpse of underwear and leotard in the torrid love scenes. There is a network rule that not only must actors and actresses wear clothing in the shower, but if a man and woman are showering together they must not face each other. 'It's something to do with the proximity of the genitals,' said Malone. 'So we have to have one facing the other's back, which is pretty weird.'

There is also a ban on swearing. No more than three mild curses are allowed per episode.

If the writers and executives are not sure what they are doing right to make their shows the most popular in the world, they are keenly aware of what they do wrong. There has been panic in the Dallas and Dynasty camps over the past year as their ratings, and therefore the networks' advertising revenue, slumped. The mood over at Dynasty was compared, by Dallas executives, to the 'last days of Saigon'. At Dallas there was a bloody purge and the entire production and writing staff was fired. Dallas seems to have regained its market share, but Dynasty is still losing in the ratings war and the producers are revamping characters and plot.

What went wrong? According to the executives, both series began to get too confident and stray away from the magic ingredient – the family saga of the Ewings and the Carringtons. Last year Dynasty invented the principality of Moldavia in the erroneous belief that foreign royalty would add spice and class to the continuing story of the Carrington family. The

275

fans hated it. As Larry Hagman, who plays JR, astutely pointed out: 'People don't give a damn about foreign royalty.'

Moldavia was written out of the plot with a spectacular massacre. Moldavian terrorists mowed down almost the entire Dynasty cast, who were left in a bloody, moaning heap on the stone floor. The end of season cliff-hanger was: how many died?

In the event only two did, and the Dynasty fans felt cheated. Meanwhile, Blake Carrington was still burdened with his wife's evil, identical double. This was too much even for the Dynasty addicts. 'We strained their suspension of disbelief too far,' said a Dynasty executive. 'They could not believe that Blake would not know whether he was sleeping with his wife or not.' They began to turn off.

The plot took another twist when Joan Collins decided to renegotiate her contract immediately after the massacre. Collins, who was in a huff, did not appear for the first episode after the summer recess. The fans became distraught.

Dallas had its own problems. Patrick Duffy, who plays the hero, Bobby Ewing, decided to leave the show at the end of the 1985 season. He was killed with great drama and detail in a car accident. Millions of viewers watched as his heart monitor gave a final blip in the hospital and sobbed as Bobby's body was lowered into the grave. Even Duffy and Katzman were moved to tears.

Six months later the network executives were wailing as Dallas ratings slumped. Bobby, a plump, rather dull character who existed only as a straightman to Larry Hagman, was deeply missed by the Dallas fans. Katzman had left the series and the plot was in danger of moving in a Moldavian direction, away from the Ewing dining table towards foreign adventures. The fans grew restless, as the real drama of Dallas began to take place not on the screen but in the boardroom.

Hagman persuaded Duffy to rejoin the cast with a million dollar bonus as an incentive, and Katzman to come back as senior producer. Katzman sat at his typewriter and pondered the delicate task off resurrecting Bobby Ewing. He says that he played with a few ideas. Bobby had not really died and had spent a year in hospital having plastic surgery, or he could have been in hiding for a year, or a Bobby impersonator could take his place.

Katzman's problem was that Bobby's return meant tying up loose ends in the plot: he no longer owned Ewing Oil, his wife had remarried. So Katzman thought: 'The hell with it,' and came up with a solution that made the Moldavian massacre seem commonplace.

'We'll just say that the whole last year was a bad dream by his wife, Pam. We just do it. We say it once. Bobby never died and we just carry on with the plot from a year ago. Katzman admits that some Dallas fans found this twist outrageous. 'But a lot of people said, "Hey, that's terrific." And look at the ratings – we're doing fine. We created a Dallas reality, which is quite different from the reality outside.'

When Christopher Cazenove entered the Dynasty reality a year ago he found it surreal and disquieting. As Blake Carrington's long-lost brother, Ben, his first scene was in the Australian outback. It was filmed in the desert just outside Los Angeles and the props department brought along a kangaroo to add authenticity. He has never been quite sure where he came from – Britain, Australia or America – and has had to adapt his accent accordingly. It is now a strange melange of all three.

He distinctly remembers telling Alexis in his first episode that he had never been married. Earlier last month Cazenove was sent his script and discovered that not only had he been married but he had a daughter. 'I was surprised,' he said. 'I suppose I might have been lying a year ago.'

He also discovered that his character, who for the past year had been an unmitigated rotter, has turned, between episodes, into quite a kind, decent sort of chap. Unbeknown to Cazenove, the script writers have decided to change Dynasty. Alexis and Ben will be nicer, the clothes less gaudy and the plots more realistic. 'I think America has changed in the last five years,' said the senior producer, Elaine Rich. 'People are more worried about the economy, and we are going to tone down the opulence of Dynasty.'

These changes are disquieting for many of the actors, who earn magnificent salaries but live in constant and real fear of being axed from the series. They see the scripts only a week in

277

advance and never quite know if they have suddenly contracted an incurable illness or are about to be burnt to death.

It is perhaps the strain of working from dawn to dusk, six days a week, on the soap operas, combined with the knowledge that their livelihood depends on the whim of the ratings, that makes some of the actors more strange than the people they portray. Larry Hagman lives opulently in some of the most expensive real estate in the world, on the beach in Malibu, disturbed only by the roar of the surf and whirr of his neighbours' satellite dishes.

Hagman, who used to dabble in Zen and Tao, refuses to speak for one day a week. He will, however, whistle, one for yes and two for no. He carries prayer beads wrapped around one wrist, and spends much of his free time sitting in a huge wicker basket so that only the top of his head protrudes through the top. He calls it 'the box' and he meditates in it. He hopes one day to be buried in it. He is a passionate anti-smoker and carries a small, electric fan which he directs at anyone smoking in the vicinity.

His co-star, Patrick Duffy, is a Buddhist and has built a Buddhist altar in his home. He gets up each morning at four to chant for half an hour before going to the studio. He told the magazine *TV Guide* that his chanting helped him to renegotiate his contract last year. During love scenes with Victoria Principal in Dallas 'he always brings something into the bed with us,' said Principal. 'A mannequin, an arm, a leg, a frog, a chain. It's great to have him back.'

There is nothing wrong with any of this of course; it is just a little odd. Not as odd, however, as Candy Spelling, the wife of the televison mogul and the boss of Dynasty, Aaron Spelling. With Candy, fantasy and reality merge, and she makes even Blake and Alexis Colby seem down at heel. She and her husband bought, for $10 million in cash, a mansion that used to be owned by Bing Crosby. They then had it demolished and began to build another. It is said that Candy wears $4 million-worth of jewels to lunch and that she sends her nanny ahead on the beach to hide pretty seashells so that her daughter can find them.

Candy's lifestyle, along with that of Collins and Cazenove,

may be diminished shortly if Dynasty continues to slide in the ratings. The future of Hagman and Duffy and the rest of the Dallas cast lies in the agile fingers of Katzman as they zip across his typewriter. He will soon have to come up with another end-of-season cliffhanger, to ensure that the Dallas fans return for another year.

The joke on the Dynasty set is that Katzman will be summoned shortly by the White House and asked to come up with a plot to extract President Reagan from his present difficulties. For Katzman it would be simple: 'Just tell them that the Iran/Contra scandal was a bad dream, Mr President. That everything is all right now. They'll believe it.'

A town divided by the devil of dance

Anson's moral quandary – to dance or not to dance – may seem trivial against the social problems that plague America. But not to the people of Anson, and certainly not to the fiery Baptist preacher, the Rev. Robert Evans. The Rev. Evans, who is known as Brother Bob, is the preacher at the Northside Baptist Church and a passionate and committed anti-dancer.

'Be not deceived. God is not mocked. For whatsoever a man soweth that shall he also reap. For he that soweth to his flesh shall of the flesh reap corruption. Do I make myself clear?' said Brother Bob, jabbing a finger at his Bible.

The pro-dancing faction has been condemned from the pulpits of many of Anson's 14 churches. The issue has set congregations against their preachers, divided friends and even families. Anti-dancers, like Brother Bob, talk of the evils that will descend upon Anson if people dance in public: adultery, promiscuity, divorce, abandoned children, wife-swapping, liquor, drugs, fighting, even murder.

'Dancing is a ploy of the Devil,' said Leon Sharp, a preacher from the Church of Christ. 'It promotes promiscuity.' A Baptist preacher spoke darkly of the motives of the pro-dancers. 'They want to dance with each other's wives. And that is not all they want to do,' he said.

The news has spread. First to the city of Abilene, 20 miles away across the Texas plains. Locals were amazed when a newspaper from Florida came to report the story, and then appalled when the East Coast liberals, in the form of the *Washington Post*, came to town followed by TV teams from Los Angeles, Canada and Hawaii.

Anson's dilemma was featured by the US Army radio in Germany. 'It has exposed the town to ridicule,' said the Anson town secretary Mrs Dotty Spraberry, a fervent anti-dancer. 'If people don't want to dance in Anson what's it got to do with folks in Abilene or Hawaii? People think we are hicks.'

It will soon become a national issue. The pro-dancers, mostly middle-aged mothers with teenage children who have formed a group called 'Footloose', have appealed to the American Civil Liberties Union in Austin, Texas. They have engaged an Austin law firm and are preparing to sue the town council.

'These people have been repressed for long enough. There will be dancing in Anson,' said Dan Junell, one of the pro-dancers' lawyers.

'The anti-dancing ordinance violates the First Amendment of the Constitution of the United States,' said Gara La Marche from the ACLU. 'Dancing is a form of expressive activity. Why, even topless dancing is protected under the law.'

Anson's problem now seems likely to go to the Supreme Court in Texas and then perhaps to the US Supreme Court, highest court in the land. This interference by outsiders has outraged the anti-dancing faction. 'The ACLU are communists,' said one preacher. 'They are anti-Christian,' said Brother Bob Evans. 'Our ordinance was not written by a lot of cotton-pickers, but by attorneys,' said Leon Sharp.

Nothing has divided the town so deeply since a row over public *v* private utilities in 1949, according to Gerry Wallace, publisher of the local paper, the *Western Observer* (circulation 1,900). Even his paper is split. He, as a member of the Church of Christ (which opposes music during services, drinking, and even mixed bathing as well as dancing), is anti-dancing; both his editor and reporter (who is also a member of the Church of Christ) are pro-dancing. The *Western Observer* has taken a strictly neutral view.

'I don't get involved in anything this controversial,' said Mr Wallace. 'It could ruin the paper.' His daughter, however, is passionately pro-dancing.

Anson lies in the vast, flat plains of Texas in what is called the 'Big Country'. It is rich in wheat, cotton and oil, but since the prices of all these commodities, especially oil, collapsed in the early Eighties life has been hard. The town, dominated by its 14 churches, looks seedy. Shops have closed and are boarded-up, salaries have fallen and many of the oil workers have been thrown out of work.

Anson was named after the president of the Texas Republic, Anson Jones, who committed suicide in 1858. In the 19th century it fought off attacks by marauding Red Indians. Its only claim to fame is a poem about Anson written by Larry Chittendon in the late 1800s. He conjured up a romantic vision of this frontier town:

Where the coyotes come a-howlin' round the ranches after dark

And the mocking-birds are singin' to the lonely medder lark,

Where the 'possum and the badger and the rattlesnake abound

And the monstrous stars are winkin' o'er the wilderness profound.

Anson represents the myth of small-town, rural America eulogized by poets, painters and politicians. Ironically, most Americans would hate to live where social and spiritual life revolves round the churches and there is no drinking, dancing, restaurants of note, cinema, bowling alley or shopping mall. An Iranian mullah would, however, feel very much at home.

A ban on liquor is normal and uncontroversial in a town in the Texas Bible Belt. But why dancing? And why such a fierce ordinance which states 'that it shall be unlawful . . . for any person or persons, firm or association of persons, to carry on, foster or operate any public dance-hall.'

Nobody is quite sure. Paul Davidson from the *Western Observer* thinks it is because a particularly wild public dance in 1932 led to a murder. He has looked through the newspaper library and found that in the same year the paper condemned the gambling, drinking and prostitution that accompanied the dances. The ordinance was passed in 1933 and banned all dances with the single exception of the traditional Christmas cowboys' ball, a staid, annual affair for the older Ansonites.

Anson High School must be the only school in the USA where an annual 'Prom' is forbidden.

The revolution began in January this year when Mrs Jane Sandoval, a nurse from Anson, thought that, in a town where there is nothing for teenagers to do, a weekly public dance, with no liquor and under strict supervision, might be fun. 'Young people in Anson are bored,' said Mrs Sandoval. 'We didn't want our young people sitting in the backs of cars on the highways or in the parking lot of the Church of Christ.' The teenage pregnancy rate is disturbingly high. The parking lot, set just off the main street behind the church, is Anson's Sodom and Gomorrah. 'The kids go there to smoke pot, drink beer and get pregnant,' said Jalyn Johnson, a senior at Anson High School.

'Footloose' has 50 members and they laugh at the notion that they are trying to change Anson into the Las Vegas of Texas. They held an experimental dance for teenagers, off city property and outside the city limits, last month. There was no drinking, the teenagers were not allowed to leave the dance unless they were escorted, there was one chaperone to five dancers and the parking lot was patrolled regularly. 'We had that place secured tighter than a police SWAT squad,' said one of the chaperones.

Mrs Sandoval thought her pro-dancing coup would be simple and that the ordinance would be thrown out. She was wrong. She, and the other members of 'Footloose', faced the wrath of the Church, the elders and the town council.

'Dancing is wrong,' said Earl McCaleb, a businessman and deacon at the Church of Christ. 'The Bible teaches that the dances lead to drinking and other things that are immoral.'

The most outspoken critic is Brother Bob, a fiery fundamentalist who did not lose the opportunity of attempting to save the blemished soul of even a British reporter. 'If you die tonight do you want to go to Heaven or to Hell? I want you to think about that,' he said.

'If you find the Lord then ring Brother Bob, collect.'

Brother Bob used to work in the oilfields before he became a preacher, and he knows the world. 'I sinned,' he said. 'I drank. I went to honky-tonks. Ninety per cent of the men went to dance-halls to pick up loose women. Young girls who are pregnant have come to me for counselling and I have asked them "Where do you attribute the beginning of your downward road?" Nine out of ten times they had said "The dance-hall."'

He also counselled a square-dance team and found the group were riven by divorce and men deserting their children. 'The father of several children was murdered as a result of an incident on the dance floor. I had to preach at his funeral.'

He does not think much of the argument that local teenagers are bored. 'They can go to Bible study group – what better atmosphere could they have?' he said. 'And if they want to dance they can dance at home. My wife and I often dance up a storm in our own living room. If you misquote me I will sue you for libel and I will come to your front door.'

Mrs Sandoval and the members of her group, who claim to represent a majority in the town, have won a sort of victory. In response to her campaign and the unwelcome publicity it has attracted, the council produced a new ordinance on dancing which the Mayor, Gene Rogers, and town secretary Mrs Spraberry say allows dancing under certain tight regulations. The ordinance, called 'Dance and Dance Halls' has 22 closely argued legal clauses and is remarkable for its restrictions, requiring a permit or licence, prohibiting alcoholic beverages, requiring a dancing supervisor, regulating dancing hours, prohibiting dancing in or on city property, requiring insurance . . . and so on for five pages.

The pro-dancing faction and its lawyers say the ordinance is nonsense, unconstitutional and allows dancing in theory but not in practice. Anyone holding a dance will have to have their moral character approved by Mrs Spraberry. Many think that even a saint would fail to pass through the eye of that particular needle.

The battle lines are now drawn and the pro-dancers are preparing for the courtroom. One of the ACLU's arguments is that in Anson a religious minority is trying to impose its will on the majority. The ACLU's problem in this constitutional argument is that the majority in Anson is religious. The pro-dancing *Western Observer* editor, Don Jones, believes that 70 per cent of the town is against it. His reporter Paul Davidson

has written a Country-and-Western song on the town's dilemma. The truth of his plaintive lyric will probably remain for
years to come: *'There ain't no dancin' in Anson.'*

Sunday Telegraph
21 June 1987

Yawning gap between Bible and Scorsese

The Last Temptation of Christ opened across America on Friday with a good deal more drama outside the cinemas than in them. At the Avalon cinema in Washington Evangelical protesters, who believe the film by Martin Scorsese is blasphemous, wore plastic crowns of thorns and pushed a life size model of Christ up and down behind the police barriers. A rival group carried banners saying 'Freedom of Speech' and 'No Censorship'. We were frisked by police as we went in.

Inside, there was, after an hour or so, the sound of yawning, shifting in the seats and an unmistakable snore as we watched this long, ponderous and occasionally silly film for a numbing two hours and 40 minutes. It is an uncomfortable mixture of *Jesus Christ Superstar* without the music and a dash of Monty Python's *Life of Brian*.

Sight unseen it has aroused an unprecedented fury among religious fundamentalists who rallied on Friday from New York to Washington and Los Angeles. The American Family Association has sent 2·5 million letters attacking the film, and the Campus Crusade for Christ offered to buy it from Universal Films for $6·5 million and burn it. The end result has been to generate massive publicity and guarantee long queues at cinemas. It will probably make Universal a lot of money.

If the protesters believe the Scorsese film, based on a novel by Nikos Kazantzakis who wrote *Zorba the Greek*, is an attempt at an accurate portrayal of the life of Christ then it is indeed

286

blasphemous. But it isn't. *Temptation* is a personal interpretation which deviates wildly from the Gospels and from the accepted historical facts. 'It is fiction,' as Scorsese keeps repeating in his television interviews.

The lady behind me at the Avalon cinema kept muttering during the film: 'That ain't in the Bible.' She is right and these are just a few examples: Scorsese's Christ is a carpenter who generates a lifetime's guilt by making crosses to crucify his fellow Jews. In a film where blood flows frequently and freely, Christ tears out his own heart and shows it to his disciples.

Christ's oratorical skills are about as riveting as those of Vice-President George Bush. He mumbles the Sermon on the Mount and, like Mr Bush, is often surprised by the conflicting messages that emerge from his mouth. Like President Reagan's White House aides, the Disciples correct Christ when he makes his frequent mis-statements. At one point, when Christ seems to lose direction entirely, they bundle him out of the Temple.

Scorsese's Christ is, in his early years at least, a collaborator and an indecisive, tortured individual preoccupied by doubt and lust. His miracles are as inspirational as the late Tommy Cooper's magic tricks. He changes water into wine 'just like that', with a smug smile. An apple tree sprouts from a discarded apple pip.

The Devil appears in strange forms as a Bunsen burner, a snake with a seductive female voice and a lion which seems to have wandered from the set of *The Wizard of Oz*. The film teeters into farce with the Raising of Lazarus. As an ashen Lazarus is recovering from his resurrection, he is approached by three Zealots who ask him: 'How do you feel?' 'All right,' says Lazarus, to guffaws from the audience. 'What's the difference between being dead and alive?' they ask him. 'There isn't much difference,' says Lazarus, and the Zealots promptly stab him to death. 'That isn't in the Bible,' remarked the lady behind me.

A strange and more serious deviation is Scorsese's rehabilitation of Judas Iscariot, who becomes the sincere revolutionary and the conscience of a wavering Christ. Before the Last Supper, Scorsese's Christ asks Judas to betray him and, during the film's final fantasy, Christ reneges on being the Messiah while Judas stays true to his belief.

The audience had to wait two hours for the moment which caused the national outcry. In a long and complicated conceit, Scorsese has Christ fantasizing on the cross about being a man rather than the Son of God. A guardian angel, with a Roedean accent, appears and leads him off to marry the heavily tattooed reformed prostitute Mary Magdalene. They make love briefly and unexplicitly. Magdalene becomes pregnant and dies. Christ then lives in a *ménage à trois* with Mary and Martha before he is persuaded by Judas to resume his Crucifixion and become the Messiah.

This is understandably shocking for the Fundamentalists. To the wider audience it is merely confusing. Mr Scorsese may be making the point that the myth of Christianity is more powerful than the reality, and that the martyr is more powerful than the living saint. This is not an original thought, however, and surely it should not take two hours and 40 minutes to say it.

Sunday Telegraph
14 August 1988

Frightening world
of North the hero

Black, elongated limousines with darkened windows stood outside the Radisson Hotel and a private jet waited under heavy
security at Indianapolis airport. Motorcycle police guarded the
entrance to the hotel; deputies from the local sheriff's department guarded the lobby; inside the hotel a group of huge men
with pot bellies and walkie-talkie radios guarded a tiny and
familiar figure with a gap-tooth smile.

The hoop-la normally reserved for presidents and Frank
Sinatra had been laid on in Indianapolis last week for Colonel
Oliver North, a man who is treading a delicate line between
public appearances as an American hero and appearances in
court to face 16 indictments and a possible 80-odd years in the
federal penitentiary.

'It is a dangerous world,' Colonel North said during the
Congressional hearings into the Iran/Contra affair, and the
Colonel should know. Not only does jail loom, but a number of
international terrorist groups want to take the law into their
own hands. He has been threatened by the Abu Nidal organization, and two years ago Libyan hit-teams put him near the top
of their lengthy death list for his role in bombing their capital
city. He now travels in a cocoon of security.

Colonel North, the former US Marines officer and National
Security Council aide, virtually ran America's secret, and
possibly illegal, foreign policy, and for a time commanded more
power than the Secretary of State. He rescued American hostages, sold arms to Iran, sent funds and arms to the Nicaraguan

Contras, hijacked terrorists in mid-air, bombed Libya, invaded Grenada and sold secret communications systems to the Jamaicans.

He is now a star of the lucrative American lecture circuit, making fleeting appearances before groups of conservatives and fans across 'the length and breadth of this great, God-given country of ours,' as Colonel North describes it. Along with Arianna Stassinopoulos Huffington and General Al Haig he is one of the most popular speakers in America.

For a marine officer who has spent a lifetime serving, or some would say abusing, his country, it is a pleasant immersion in the private sector. He earns $25,000 a go, and over the past year he has earned more than he did during his entire military service.

Colonel North has no doubt that he is a hero, and last week in Indianapolis few denied it. There were shouts of 'Ollie, Ollie' as he entered the hotel. A few protesters paraded outside, but inside local Republicans, politicians, lawyers, police chiefs, businessmen and religious leaders had paid $250 each for the privilege of standing in line and shaking his hand. They paid $125 to hear him speak and seemed not to regret a cent of it.

The head of the local police burglary squad sat at my table and his voice trembled with emotion as he talked about Colonel North, who faces more serious charges than any burglar in Indianapolis. 'He is a great man. He believes in law and order. If there were more men like that our job would be easier,' said the police chief.

But hasn't he possibly broken the law? Isn't he accused of conspiring to defraud the country he professes to love, stealing government property, obstructing a presidential inquiry, and tax evasion, among many other things? 'Bullshit,' said the police chief. Other paying guests described Colonel North as 'sincere', 'moving', 'wonderful' and 'a man who isn't scared to tell the truth'.

The Colonel needs the money. He presents himself as a martyr whose only offence was to speak the truth and defend 'this great country of ours'. He is now confronted with millions of dollars in legal bills.

'Without your contributions it would be much more difficult for my family and me to make it. We are confronted by the largest investigation in the history of the Republic,' said Colonel North. 'There are more people in Washington trying to put Ollie North behind bars than in any other inquisition in the history of our land.'

In an odd historical comparison he says he is like the men who signed the Declaration of Independence. 'Fifty-six Americans who signed the declaration ended it with these words: "We mutually pledge our lives, our fortunes and our sacred honour." Five of them were captured by the British and tortured before they died. Twelve of the signers had their homes pillaged and burned to the ground . . . There are risks worth taking.'

Is Colonel North only doing it for the money? There is a suspicion, a fear among many Americans, that the Colonel is running for something else – perhaps a Congressional seat once his trials and tribulations are over. Colonel North says coyly that he is 'campaigning hard for one of the most difficult posts of all, the job of husband and father'. He also says he is campaigning for a more conservative Congress, and appeared in Indianapolis at a benefit for the ultra-conservative local Congressman Dan Burton.

For the true-blue conservatives of Indiana, one of the most right-wing states of the Union, there is little doubt that Colonel North would be a better presidential candidate than Vice-President George Bush. At my table at the hotel last week mention of Mr Bush caused a sharp intake of breath. Colonel North was viewed as little less than a saint.

The fears are fanned by the North speech itself, which is peppered with political clichés culled from the less-inspired speeches of Ronald Reagan. The Colonel sounds just like a Republican candidate for the Presidency. His audience is smaller than the millions of television viewers who watched him during the Congressional hearings, but he can still put on a good show.

He praises free enterprise and strong defence. 'I believe that government is best when it governs least,' he said. 'America's vision and will takes root and survives in the strength and solidarity of America's families.' He attacks the two demons of the right wing: the US Congress, which he says lacks will, patriotism and faith, and Communism. He describes himself as an 'unrepentant anti-communist'. 'Communism can only work in two places, in Heaven where they don't need it and in Hell where they've already got it.'

The police chief waved a chicken leg and the whole room applauded. North praises President Reagan and 'the leadership of a great President I am proud to have served'.

It is a curious performance. The majority of Americans, and certainly the US Congress, believe that Colonel North has severely damaged the very things he says he would lay down his life for: not only his country's foreign policy but also President Reagan, who was embroiled in the Iran/Contra scandal, the Republican Party, and Colonel North's beloved Constitution which set up checks and balances to stop people like Colonel North.

These ironies escaped both the Colonel and his audience. So did a new batch of revelations about him contained in *Guts and Glory*, a biography of North by Ben Bradlee Jnr. It is disturbing that Colonel North had a nervous breakdown in the 1970s and ran around his house naked waving a ·45 revolver at his wife, whom he always describes as his 'best friend'. He then changed his medical record to erase the incident.

He is also a liar. He lied when he boasted about his frequent meetings with the President, he lied about flying a mission into El Salvador and rescuing two soldiers in 1983 (there was no such mission), about serving in Angola (he didn't), about a mission to the Middle East with Philip Habib (Habib says he went alone), and about his dog being poisoned by terrorists (it died of old age). He even lied about his military record. He was not, as he told the National Security Council, a company commander in Vietnam. He was never involved in 'unconventional warfare'.

Colonel North's heroism is widely tarnished, but not among the true believers. There may be enough of them to help Colonel North get a seat in the Congress he despises so much.

Sunday Telegraph
14 August 1988

TV's unquenchable thirst for sleaze

The assistant producer of an American television chat show, weary of the daily diet of social misfits and sexual freaks, recently resigned. 'I am sick of trying to track down one-legged lesbian nuns,' she told her boss, and went to take up a job as a Congressional aide in the dubious moral atmosphere of Capitol Hill.

The thirst for sleaze and trivia on American television is seemingly unquenchable. Every day chat-show producers and their bookers search for those victims and perpetrators of violence and sexual abuse willing to be humiliated and further abused before a national audience.

Wife-beaters and beaten wives, rapists and rape victims, transsexuals, cross-dressers, racists, lesbians and homosexual priests parade across the screen from early morning to late at night.

There is no shortage of guests. Their names and addresses are often found in the 'yellow pages' of the bible of the chat-show business: the *Directory of Experts, Authorities and Spokespersons*.

On page 430 a brothel called the Chicken Ranch advertises its owner, Russell Reade, as an experienced chat-show guest. 'Mr Reade is a former high-school biology and sex-education teacher, an articulate speaker and expert information source,' says the directory. There are experts on rape, rape treatment and rape legislation, on pregnancy in politics, pregnant career women, suicide in rural America, teen suicide, suicide among the elderly, assisted suicide and survivors of suicide.

One host who has won a vast national audience is Morton Downey, a chain-smoking foul-mouthed braggart who harangues his guests, jabbing them with a nicotine-stained forefinger and shouting 'Bullshit!' and 'Scumbag!' He had his own brother, who suffers from Aids, on the show and accused him of being a homosexual. 'Do you have sex with men?' he screamed at his brother.

His studio audience, composed, it often seems, of fat-bellied, beer-swilling men with tattooed biceps, cheers him on with shouts of 'Mort! Mort! Mort!' The programme teeters on the edge of physical violence.

A programme by the acknowledged king of sleaze, Geraldo Rivera, went over the edge. A white racist guest was assaulted by a black guest and threw a chair at Mr Rivera, breaking his nose. The audience loved it and the programme broke records in the ratings. With blood dripping from one nostril, the unstoppable Mr Rivera went on to tape another show on sexual scandals in Washington.

Real-life crime programmes proliferate, especially on Mr Rupert Murdoch's American television network, Fox. Scenes of violence and sexual abuse are gorily re-created as victims eagerly describe their experiences. His programme *The Reporters* recently re-enacted the sexual assault and murder of a woman in Tampa, Florida. It showed a picture of the corpse.

The programmes have one thing in common: money for the companies that broadcast them. They are cheap to make and regularly command vast audiences and advertising revenue. Oprah Winfrey, a black chat-show hostess, deals with such subjects as subservient women, infidelity, threesomes and wife-beaters. Her formula is so successful that she earns several million dollars a year.

Americans have watched bad television for years, but some are now complaining about the avalanche of trash that has cascaded over them since the deregulation of television programming by the Federal Communications Commission in 1984 and the vast array of cable television channels that have reached most American households.

The Radio Television News Directors' Association met in Nevada recently to rail against 'trash TV'. 'What has happened now is that there is no sanction, no external pressure or internal sense of shame that prevents the new electronic barbarians from selling their wares to the most debased tastes and then boasting about it,' said Jeff Greenfield, a media analyst.

The British have little reason to be smug. Two American chat shows, hosted by Phil Donahue and Oprah Winfrey, have formed a beachhead of trash on British television. Mr Murdoch has a satellite in geocentric orbit over Europe poised to beam down an electronic torrent of US programmes.

Mr Howard Stringer, president of CBS, gave Britain a stern warning about the possible effects of sweeping television de-regulation: 'You've no doubt heard about all the space junk orbiting the earth. Well, you haven't seen anything until your new satellites begin beaming multiple channels back to Britain.'

Mr Rivera has already exhausted the *Directory of Experts* and moved into his own social twilight zone. Recent programmes have dealt with transsexuals and their families, teen prostitutes, swinging sexual suicide, mud-wrestling women, mass murderer Charles Manson, serial killers, kids who kill, battered women who kill, male strippers, white racists, kids abused by priests, patients abused by doctors, animals abused by scientists.

He compares himself with Edward R. Murrow, the distinguished radio correspondent who covered the Second World War for CBS. This boast proved too much for the Washington magazine the *New Republic*, which wrote a pastiche of Geraldo broadcasting his show from war-torn London. 'Now let's meet our first guests, parents of kids killed in the Blitz . . . Cecilia, let's start with you. How does it feel to see the light of your life, your own daughter, blown to bits right in front of you?' Cecilia (sobbing): 'It's awful' . . . 'It's time for a break, but stay with us because when we come back you'll get to talk with a genuine Nazi.'

Mr Donahue, dean of the chat show, is worried about the competition. He fears he is becoming the 'intellectual' of the chat-show circuit, which could mean a sudden death in the ratings. He says he would rather be 'sensational' or 'sleazy' like Geraldo than intellectual. He needn't worry. Mr Donahue recently wore a skirt for a programme about cross-dressing.

The chat-show hosts and sleaze merchants are preparing for their European debut on one of the new cable or satellite networks, and it might not be all bad. The cloistered reverence of the Clive James late-night chat show might be shattered, perhaps, by the stabbing, yellow finger of Mr Downey.

'OK baldy, shove off, haul ass,' he would no doubt say to Mr James. 'Let's cut the crapola, Clive baby.' His cigarette ash would spill over the desk as the audience screamed, 'Mort! Mort! Mort!'

Sunday Telegraph
1 January 1989

Not much glasnost at Pioneer Point

Every weekend a small convoy of black limousines and buses drives east out of Washington DC towards the Maryland shore. It turns right near the little town of Centreville, then winds, at high speed, through forests and fields, full of cows and horses, to the gates of the Pioneer Point estate. A large sign says that unauthorized people are banned, and that anyone who tries to get in will be prosecuted. The driver of the first car puts a plastic card into a slot by the gate, which swings open automatically. Under the fixed gaze of a remote control camera, the convoy moves slowly up the drive.

It was just possible, peering through a chink in a seven-foot chain-link fence and the foliage of a thick hedge, to see into the estate, which is about the best view any uninvited, casual visitor will ever get. It was a small vista of the American dream.

The estate covers 42 acres of mowed lawns, trees and a mile of golden beach. The chimneys of two neo-Georgian mansions jut above the tree-line. A man sat fishing on a rocky point, his line dipping into the tranquil waters at the confluence of the Chester and Corsica rivers. Just behind him some children played on swings and their parents sat in deckchairs in the sun and the cool breezes blowing off the river. A group of women walked along an avenue of trees.

There was a tang of barbecue in the air. To the casual observer, with his eye to the chain-link fence, Pioneer Point

297

looks like a secure, private compound for a very rich family from Washington. But there is a whiff of something more sinister. Down by the river a group of Pioneer Pointers, inside the chain-link fence, were walking out of the boat-house. I waved to them from the road. There was no response. I shouted 'Hello' and waved. One of the men turned his back, another made an angry gesture and they all walked away. The security seems a bit too tight, even by the standards of the very rich. When, recently, there was a fire in the big house, the local fire brigade was stopped at the gate and turned away. The local police from Centreville have never been allowed inside. The house and its occupants are watched, carefully, by three agents from the Federal Bureau of Investigations who are based in Centreville.

The clue lies in a small flag which sometimes flutters discreetly from the largest of the two mansions. It is red. Pioneer Point is owned by the government of the Soviet Union and its 42 acres are as inviolably Soviet as the grounds of the embassy in Washington. It is an exclusive resort where the 225 diplomats and their families from the Russian embassy in Washington can relax at the weekend. And they do so in distinctly capitalist splendour. They do not welcome Western visitors. My request to visit the estate was turned down with a sharp 'no' by Boris, the press spokesman at the Russian embassy in Washington. There isn't much Glasnost at Pioneer Point.

The largest mansion, called Hartefeld House, is the summer residence for the Soviet ambassador, who is now Yuriy Dubinin. He shares it with the secretary of the Communist Party from the Washington embassy and the Russian security chief, the KGB resident. They live in grand style. The mansion has 35 rooms, a chapel which has been converted by its new owners into a sitting room, 13 fireplaces, a walnut panelled gun room and a dining room where the ambassador and the KGB resident can bask in the reflected glory of the 2,000 crystal prisms in the chandelier. If they grow bored with the sun and the river they can go into the basement and watch films in the special movie theatre. They can get exquisitely drunk on 3,000 bottles of vintage wine which were sold with the house. The ultimate touch of decadent luxury is a storage room for fur coats. It is specially refrigerated.

The grounds have a mile of beach and a swimming pool for the exclusive use of the senior diplomats, although the Soviet masses in the form of more junior diplomats can use the tennis courts and look at the goldfish pond. The Russians have built a dozen chalets in the grounds and the second mansion, Mostley Hall, is a pioneer camp for embassy children.

Dubinin's predecessor, Anatole Dobrynin, loved Pioneer Point. He is now a senior member of the Politburo in Moscow, but he must have carried back warm memories of his country weekends. He liked cycling around the country lanes near the estate and would wobble along with his Russian security guard pedalling close behind him. He used to say hello to the local residents, but that was as far as he ever went.

Alexandra Costa, a Soviet defector who used to be married to a Russian diplomat in Washington until she defected from him as well, went to Pioneer Point every weekend in the summer. Her former husband was a first secretary at the embassy so the Costas were allowed to share a bungalow with one other family. The further down the diplomatic scale, says Costa, the more cramped the quarters were. Her short vacations were pleasant, and very cheap. The embassy charged staff a token two dollars a night for use of the accommodation. There was no food available so the families used to bring their own or go into the Acme supermarket in Centreville. They were lazy weekends. Alexandra's husband liked fishing off the rocky point or the pier. Alexandra swam and played tennis. 'In the evenings we drank vodka and talked. The Russians love gossip,' said Alexandra. She says that they were not allowed to have more than fleeting contact with the Americans in Centreville: 'You could have a casual contact but you always had to report it to the security people at Pioneer Point. If you had two contacts with the same person then the KGB would interview you. We all kept to ourselves.'

The Russians bought the estate in 1972 for a snip, a mere one million two hundred thousand dollars. It is now worth at least five times as much. They probably didn't realize that they were taking over a chunk of capitalist history. It was first owned by

John Jacob Raskob who conceived of and funded what was then the world's tallest sky-scraper, the Empire State Building in New York City. Raskob built the two mansions in the late 20s and decorated Hartefeld House with small gargoyles of his 12 children. The children lived in the other house, Mostley Hall, which Raskob named after the children correctly pointed out that it was mostly hall.

When the Russians moved in there was an outcry from the small and conservative town of Centreville which is not, even today, a great supporter of Soviet–US relations. Locals had wild fears of what would happen when the Godless Commies came to live in their midst. One of them wrote to a local paper saying that Soviet submarines would probably come creeping to the Chester river after dark and drop secret agents. Fears were only partially abated when the local council explained that the river was not deep enough even for a surfaced submarine. One outraged resident wrote a letter to the *Queen Anne's Record Observer*: 'In the name of God and our God-given country how could you sell any property to the Soviet Union, our enemy.' Bob Norris of Centreville wrote furiously: 'I have always been concerned about the doses of communist cancer being injected around the world and it is equally disturbing to me to be sitting in my front porch swing and see them coming and going at will.' 'The Hell with them. Let them go somewhere else,' wrote a member of the American Legion Hall.

But after a few months the fuss died down and the Russians established a kind of detente with Centreville. At first they invited some local big-wigs for cocktails at Hartefeld Hall. They threw a lavish banquet with boiled sturgeon and caviar, old wines from the cellar and vodka. The hospitality quickly ran out, although they still send the local police a bottle of vodka at Christmas.

The local businessmen began to see that they had a Soviet boom on their hands. The Russians spent 100,000 dollars putting up the chalets, 10,000 dollars at Herbert Goldstein's furniture shop and 500 dollars on fluorescent lighting.

Only Sam Fluharty, owner of Centreville's music and hobby shop, was disappointed. The Russians rented a piano from him and returned it with the keyboard cover wrenched from its hinges, half the action jammed and a foot pedal missing. The Russians offered no compensation. Then Fluharty waged his one man war against the Soviet Union which ended in a threat to go down to the Soviet embassy in Washington and chuck rocks through the window. The Soviets blinked and Fluharty got a check for 200 dollars. It was not enough, he said, but he had won a moral victory.

The Russians spend less money these days, but they still go to the Acme supermarket for basic provisions where they are polite, untalkative and pay cash. They drop in for the odd cold beer at Bob's bar. Their only local offence is driving too fast in their official cars. The police can do nothing about it. All the Soviet drivers do is smile and shove their diplomatic immunity cards through the window.

They are good, if quiet, neighbours. Mrs William Connor, who is in her seventies, has been their closest neighbour for 15 years. She says she never hears them and sees very little of them. The new ambassdor doesn't even cycle around the lanes. Her only brush with the former ambassador was a brief but dramatic one. He came roaring round the corner in his limousine and forced Mrs Connor's car off the road. After that he always waved and said hello.

David Sheaffer, who owns the duck hunting preserve next to the Soviet estate, says his personal relations have been cordial, but he is still suspicious and frankly wishes they would go away. 'I hear they've got enough arms in there to start a war,' said Sheaffer. 'Those Rusky bastards. You can't trust them to make a deal, you've got to keep your eye on them.' It is Sheaffer's opinion that their territorial ambition does not stop at 42 acres in Maryland: 'They want to take over the world.'

Shaeffer might be wrong about the Soviet arsenal at Pioneer Point (the local police and the FBI have never heard of it), but is it really as innocent as it all looks?

A new report suggests it is not – that the Russians not only fish and swim, they also bug. According to this report, 'Soviet Signals Intelligence: The Use of Diplomatic Establishments' by Desmond Ball from the University of Canberra, Pioneer

301

Point is a major centre for Soviet intelligence gathering in the US.

Arkady Shevchenko, a former senior Soviet official at the United Nations until he defected, says the Soviets were 'ecstatic' when they were allowed to buy the estate and not just because of the fine fishing. He said that it is in the main microwave transmission corridor between Norfolk, Virginia, the hub of the US Atlantic fleet operations and the Air Force's major base at Langley Field. Shevchenko believes it is a major intelligence centre.

The only visible sign of the secret activities at Pioneer Point is the array of aerials on the roof of the mansion. According to Ball they include a large 'HF long-periodic directional array' similar to the one on the embassy in Washington, a large mesh-type microwave dish antenna and several VHF antennas. VHF and UHF microwave antennas are fixed to the roofs of some of the holiday chalets.

Ball has researched the various US military and intelligence facilities which lie within a 50 mile radios and easy monitoring range. They are: the top secret headquarters of the US National Security Agency which is only 35 miles away; the Naval Intelligence Support Center at Suitland, the headquarters of the Air Force Systems Command at Andrews Airforce Base, the Naval Research Laboratory at Pomonkey, the Naval Security Group's Northwest Station at North Beach, the Naval Air Test Center and Electronic Warfare Integrated Systems Test Laboratory at Patuxent River and the Langley Air Force Base at Hampton.

The smiles of the Russians at Pioneer Point may not be due simply to the soft breezes and warm sun. Some of the most vital intelligence in the US may be flowing straight into the Russians' favourite resort.

Condé Nast *Traveler*
Unpublished, 1989

Bush telegraph
tells all

The news of the momentous events in Poland on Thursday came to the attention of the President of the United States in a curious and slightly disturbing way.

A reporter read about them on a news agency wire and told a White House aide, who told the President's press spokesman, who told the deputy National Security Adviser who tried to tell the President.

It wasn't easy. Mr Bush was buffeting around at 30 mph in a power boat in the Atlantic off the coast of Maine. It proved impossible to discuss the political affairs of Poland on a ship to shore radio, so Robert Gates, the deputy National Security Adviser, had to wait until the President roared back to port.

President Bush is on his three-week summer holiday and he is distinctly less interested in affairs of state than in getting his body in shape. Mr Bush takes 'fun stuff', as he calls it, very seriously indeed. He was asked about Poland as he played golf on Friday morning and said: 'No comment.' Asked about his holiday the President smiled and said: 'Now you're talking.'

US Presidential holidays are not simple affairs. Mr Bush flew to his holiday home in Kennebunkport, Maine, in Air Force One followed by US Air Force F16 fighters and a 727 jet full of accredited White House journalists.

He is accompanied by members of his staff, advisers and a small army of Secret Service agents who attempt to protect the

President in his highly visible and rather vulnerable house on a promontory in the Atlantic.

Mr Bush lives here like a Mafia Capo di Tutti Capi. Secret Service agents with their shirts hanging outside their trousers to hide their guns man checkpoints on the road outside the Bush house and lounge at the front of his driveway. Coastguard cutters protect the slice of sea around the house and Navy divers search the ocean bed. A US warship is rumoured to be lurking just over the horizon.

The President attempts to keep in touch with the world through an array of satellite dishes and secure communications. His press spokesman, Marlin Fitzwater, rosy-cheeked under a Panama hat, gives the White House reactions to great events every morning at 10.30. After fishing the President felt, according to Mr Fitzwater, that the US should react cautiously but hopefully to changes in Poland. After golf he was pleased at America's latest economic indicators.

The reporters will try to observe the tiniest 'Presidential movement', as the White House puts it, over the next three weeks. They will feed newspaper columns and television screens with a constant flow of junk news.

Friday morning's official report said, for example, that the President went out in his boat at 8.30 a.m. and added: 'We're going way out there.' Agency wires hummed with this latest revelation.

The late President Herbert Hoover said in the Fifties that in his opinion one of the major degenerations of the past 30 years was that Presidents no longer had privacy at prayer or fishing.

President Bush is fishing as I write, closely pursued by a press boat. The radio waves crackle with their descriptions: the President is sitting down, standing up, holding a rod, putting it down. Mr Hoover might have also included throwing horseshoes, tennis, playing golf, jogging and all the other things the energetic Mr Bush gets up to on his holidays in the Hoover list of major degenerations.

All the reporters have been issued with special White House bleepers which buzz to alert us to 'anticipated Presidential movements'. They went off on Thursday afternoon (golf), on

Friday morning at 7.30 a.m. (fishing), on Friday afternoon (golf) and at 6 a.m. yesterday (jogging).

The beepers have a more macabre purpose, however. The reporters are here, in 24-hour touch with the White House, in case the President falls off the back of his bucking power boat, jogs under the wheels of a truck, or a band of suicidal Shi'ites run their rubber boats into the Bush dock. It is a death watch, which is why these vacations have become such immense logistical events.

There was a private theory, expounded last week by Maureen Dowd, the White House correspondent for the New York Times, that these vacations are not just the relentless pursuit of the trivial but show US Presidents in their deeper, psychological colours.

Richard Nixon, for example, stayed with his sleazy friend Bebe Rebozo in Key Biscayne in Florida where he played cards. Dwight D. Eisenhower stayed with his mother-in-law in middle America. Jimmy Carter skulked, intensely and privately, on a small island off Georgia remote from the press.

So what does the Kennebunkport holiday say about Mr Bush? This little resort town, a bijou Bognor Regis on the Atlantic, is more form than substance, a tourist trap of gift shops and artisans' workshops. But the vast Bush complex is remote from the town, imperious on its stretch of high ground.

The general conclusion of the Bush-watchers is that the President is a man frightened of his own company. He has surrounded himself with 11 grandchildren, his daughter, his sons and daughters-in-law, his cousins and friends who teem through the complex. The President is always doing things at a frenetic pace from dawn until he slumps exhausted into his bed at about 9.30 p.m. 'Does he ever read?' asked Miss Dowd. 'I doubt it.' Is he ever alone? Almost certainly not.

The President, when he is on holiday, also begins talking in a private language with its roots somewhere in the Bush ancestry. When a sport is going well, whether it is jogging, golf, tennis, fishing or horseshoes – he will say: 'Nice, picture-smooth.' or 'Here comes Mr Smooth.' According to the White House doctor the 'Mr Smooth' expression infuriates his wife,

Barbara. 'She gets real mad,' said the doctor. When things are going badly the President mutters: 'Mulligan, Mulligan.' The doctor had no explanation for this.

Sunday Correspondent
Unpublished, 1989

EPILOGUE
BY
HAROLD EVANS

Is journalism
worth dying for?

One of David's friends and colleagues asked the question when the tragic news came through. One could put it grandly – are truth and justice worth dying for? And more bleakly. Is a newspaper paragraph worth dying for? It was, after all, a random bullet that took David's life when he was out in the *barrio* simply trying to top up a story he had already prepared for the *Correspondent*. He had done what he was paid to do. The last paragraph, we feel with poignancy, was not going to change a thing. No scoop or subtlety of history hung upon it. It was, it seems, a mortal redundancy.

And yet the unwritten paragraph is David's true obituary. It represents the central thread of his life. There was just a chance the material gathered for the last paragraph might affect the balance of his story, and to him that was all that mattered. He was one of those reporters who give what we call freedom of the press its moral energy.

That moral energy is renewed whenever journalism enables people to make free informed choices. It is destroyed when it does not. Journalism has many affectations, and some corruptions, but this one redeeming justification is the illumination – in the shifting mosaic of news – of fact and understanding that enables others to choose. 'To make a picture of reality,' as Walter Lippman put it, 'on which men can act.' The whole of ethics is based on the presumption of free will and the freedom to make choices.

David would mock the assertion that this is what he did, that he legitimised and honoured his profession. He would say: 'D'you think, do you think?' Yes, yes, because David Blundy was in the front line of truth. This is not so much because he exposed himself to danger as that he never ceased to expose himself to doubt.

This is a risk some of us go to great lengths to avoid. There is comfort in certainty. In journalism it is simpler to sound off than it is to find out. It is more elegant to pontificate than it is to sweat. It is prudent to follow the office line. It is more politic to take the handout. Official sources say this and that. Official sources most strongly deny . . .

David always travelled light. His shoulder-slung green rucksack, holding barely a blade and a change of shirt, was a metaphor for his approach to being a foreign correspondent. His gift for comedy has been well and rightly celebrated. It is as well to reflect that his ragged persona concealed a very serious man. His values were those of a humanitarian liberal, but they were as loose as his jacket. They had not ossified into convictions that he took with him wherever he went. If he did reach a conviction on an assignment, he would commonly bring it back like contraband, unwritten, undeclared, until he could put it to the test of a second and a third visit.

It is as well that he did not go abroad, as do so many, to discover what he knew at home, because the reality in all the places was either more subtle or more brutal than the confident commonplaces of our political rhetoric. He took risks; it was typical of him to take the risk of switching from the established *Sunday Telegraph* to a newborn newspaper. But his risk-taking on assignment was not bravado: it was his preoccupation with the story on hand that so often bore him into danger.

He used doubt, of course, as a tool of his craft. His nagging faux-naif perplexity acted like a truth serum on the resentments and suspicions of border guard, guerrilla and bureaucrat. His vulnerability was part of his appeal. But the vulnerability was real enough when he came to set down what he had seen and heard close up. As Robert Capa said of war photography: 'If your pictures aren't good enough, you aren't close enough.'

It is a testament to the integrity of David's endeavour that he hung his long frame over his portable for so long at such ungodly hours, scowling so gloomily at his notebook. 'Do you find a problem,' he said, 'of getting the words in the right order? What's it all about?' Of course! Writing may be hard for everyone, but it's easier to dazzle and shock and entertain than it is to get the words in the right order when you have set yourself, in the rough urgent compressions of journalism, to grapple with truth. Is the story accurate? Is it clear? Is it fair? Is it boring? David, naturally, doubted whether he met the tests he set himself; but he did.

Philip Larkin, in his poem 'Church Going', wrote:

> . . . someone will forever be surprising,
> A hunger in himself to be more serious

May we find that hunger in ourselves and in our dedication when we remember with affection and with gratitude David Blundy, a reporter who was forever valiant and restless for truth.